NO MORE HEROINES?

With the collapse of Soviet rule and the emergence of independent Russia, the image of Russian women in the western imagination has changed dramatically. The robust tractor drivers and athletes have been replaced by glamorous but vulnerable beauty queens or the dishevelled and downcast women trading goods on the streets.

The authors of this work take a closer look at what lies behind these images and examine how Russian women are coping with a very different sort of life. The main focus is on the effect of unemployment on Russian women and the strategies they are using to deal with it. The first part of the book looks at why women have been targeted for redundancy and the problems they face in the emerging Russian labour market. The second goes on to explore the response of the state, a range of women's organisations and of individual women themselves to the new situation.

This book is based on case-studies and personal interviews carried out in the Moscow region in 1993–4 and will provide both specialist and non-specialist alike with access to the thinking of women and their organisations in Russia today.

Sue Bridger, **Rebecca Kay** and **Kathryn Pinnick** are all at the Department of Modern Languages, University of Bradford.

WOMEN AND POLITICS
Edited by Haleh Afshar and Mary Maynard
University of York

Series advisers:
Kum-Kum Bhavnani, *University of California, Santa Barbara*
Haideh Moghissi, *Queen's University, Kingston, Canada*
Afsaneh Najmabadi, *Harvard University*
Pippa Norris, *Harvard University*

This new series will present exciting and accessible books covering both the formal and public domain of politics and the informal and practical strategies and organisations that women throughout the world use to obtain rights, to meet their needs and to improve their situation in life. The series will combine theoretical and empirical work, revealing how and why the political experience of women has been neglected, and contributing to the ongoing reconceptualisation of the political.

Also in the series:

WOMEN AND POLITICS IN THE THIRD WORLD
Edited by Haleh Afshar

NO MORE HEROINES?

Russia, women and the market

Sue Bridger, Rebecca Kay and Kathryn Pinnick

London and New York

First published 1996
by Routledge
11 New Fetter Lane, London EC4P 4EE

Simultaneously published in the USA and Canada
by Routledge
29 West 35th Street, New York, NY 10001

Typeset in Bembo by Michael Mepham, Frome, Somerset
Printed and bound in Great Britain by
Clays Ltd, St Ives PLC

British Library Cataloguing in Publication Data
A catalogue record for this book is available from the
British Library

Library of Congress Cataloguing in Publication Data
A catalogue record for this book has been requested

ISBN 0–415–12459–X (hbk)
ISBN 0–415–12460–3 (pbk)

CONTENTS

SERIES EDITORS' PREFACE

We are delighted to include *No More Heroines?* as part of the launch of our new series on women and politics. For the purposes of this series we have defined politics in its feminist context, to include the range of public and personal activities that women engage with to improve or maintain their position in life, meet their basic needs and obtain their personal and political rights. Both the formal and public domain of politics, and political theory and the informal and practical strategies, networks and organisations built and used by women are included.

The series will focus on struggles and activities that fuel the dynamics of change at both the macro and micro levels. In addition to political contexts, religions and ideologies and their impact and interaction with women will be included.

No More Heroines? is an excellent example of the kind of work that will be published as part of our new series. It is a timely, lucid analysis of the plight of Russian women in the post-Soviet era. Democratisation appears to have wiped women off the political map and the new political era has tended to emphasise women's domestic role and encourage the beauty myth. *No More Heroines?* analyses the factors that have contributed to this rapid erosion of emancipation and considers the alternative routes chosen by women. No longer the poster heroines of the revolution, but the unsung heroines of survival, they are carving slow onerous paths through a gamut of organisation towards a new form of liberation. The authors have spoken to a wide cross-section of women and looked at a range of women-centred organisations to produce this lively, informed volume which gives a voice to the many women who are seeking to regain lost ground in the post-communist era in Russia.

Haleh Afshar and Mary Maynard
Series editors

ACKNOWLEDGEMENTS

The research project on which this book is based was generously funded by the Leverhulme Trust through 1993–4. We are also grateful to the University of Bradford and the Department of Modern Languages for financial support for both research visits and conference attendance in 1992, notably in Helsinki, Moscow and at the Second Women's Forum in Dubna which prepared the ground for the project.

In Russia itself, the project could not have been undertaken without the continuing practical help, support and advice of Marina Malysheva of the Moscow Centre for Gender Studies. Her collaboration in research and, above all, her unstinting friendship have been an inspiration over the last five years. Many thanks are due also to members of her family for their warmth and hospitality during the summer of 1993.

The role of voluntary organisations which forms the focus of this study could not have been examined without the co-operation of those directly involved. We are indebted to Irina Razumnova, Elena Evseeva, Tatiana Luk'ianenko and Irina Savel'eva for their time and patience and for access to their records and customers which was so generously given. Similarly, we would like to thank Yuri Vetokhin and his staff at Dubna Employment Centre for their ready assistance and much-appreciated hospitality. The analysis we have put forward on the basis of this information, the conclusions we have reached and any errors or misinterpretations which may have crept into the text are, of course, entirely our own responsibility.

We would also like to thank friends and colleagues who have provided support along the way. Mary Buckley, Linda Edmondson, Hilary Pilkington and Frances Pine have all provided valuable inputs and much stimulating conversation while the project has been underway. Colleagues in the Department of Modern Languages at Bradford University have also been a regular source of moral support. In the case of Russian Section colleagues, Svetlana Carsten and John Russell, the support extends well beyond this into the kind of unsung, everyday practical help which makes a project like this possible. Heartfelt thanks must go to them both.

Finally, we would like to thank the women in Russia who agreed to be interviewed and showed us such hospitality, and all the friends and relatives who have made constructive comments, cups of tea or generally put up with us while all this was going on. We are indebted to you all.

INTRODUCTION:
NO MORE HEROINES?

Turn the clock back a decade or two and the images of Russian women which would spring most readily to the western mind would be very different from those which fill television screens today. Women on tractors and building sites, smiling and confident, the massive women shot-putters or the ethereal grace and strength of the Olympic gymnast, Ol'ga Korbut, the unique achievements in space of Tereshkova and Savitskaia: all these, however much the product of the Soviet propaganda machine, figured prominently in the popular imagination in the world beyond the USSR's borders. Whether officially 'Heroines of the Soviet Union', 'Heroines of Socialist Labour', 'Heroine Mothers' or the multitude of lesser heroines of the five-year plans, the image was overwhelmingly one of achievement. In production, in sport or at home with the family, the Soviet woman who graced political posters and monumental art was strong, progressive and capable of anything.

However far these particular images might have been removed from everyday reality in the former USSR, it is not difficult to argue that the country's traumatic history did indeed produce generations of genuine heroines. Behind the many bogus images of Communist Party myth-making lay the very real achievements of millions of women who survived repression and persecution, the appalling toll of the Second World War, the almost unimaginable rigours and privations of the Stalinist period and what, for many, were the far from comfortable years which followed. For the older generation of Russian women, writing or speaking of this period in their history, the stoicism and will to survive which they display remains an extraordinary and humbling testament to their courage and dignity.[1]

With the collapse of the USSR, the old hoardings proclaiming the unity of Party and people have been replaced by new ones extolling the virtues of Samsung, Phillips or McDonalds. The posters with their women

1

heroines have been consigned, if anywhere, to stalls for western souvenir-hunters and in their stead has come the image of the provocatively dressed or entirely undressed glamour model with a very different suggestion of what women are capable of. As the economic reforms have torn into the fabric of their society, the images of Russian women which now appear in the western media are far removed from the picture of sober achievement that characterised the past. Young prostitutes and strippers, middle-aged women forlornly offering items for sale on the streets, angry pensioners with their pictures of Lenin are the scenes that catch the eye of western reporters and are flashed around the world to create a new visual lexicon of life for the women of Russia.

The paper heroines may have vanished, but so too has the former visibility of women as key actors in their own society. Though the relative prominence of women in Soviet public life was no reflection of their actual political influence, they were at least there to be seen. The initial rounds of democratic elections in Russia have virtually wiped women off the political map and their re-emergence is now painfully slow and fraught with difficulty. Meanwhile, the developing labour market in independent Russia has already made plain its preference for men. Women are finding that their employment is in jeopardy at the same time as the Soviet-style welfare state is being dismantled, taking nursery provision and free health care with it. With a resurgent Russian nationalism calling for women to return to the home and foster the rebirth of the nation, the prospects for women to think in terms of personal achievement could scarcely be less auspicious.

The purpose of this book, therefore, is to shed some light on the complex nature of women's lives in Russia today and on the multiplicity of factors that are affecting their choices and behaviour. In particular, it seeks to examine the Soviet legacy for women as Russia embarked on its economic reforms, to analyse the impact these reforms have had on women and, most of all, to explore the options which remain open to them and their responses, both as individuals and in new voluntary organisations. As we shall see, in the conditions of the new Russia the slogans and images of the Soviet version of emancipation have entirely disappeared, but heroism for women, these days unsung and unregarded, is arguably as essential as ever.

THE PROBLEMS OF TRANSITION: WOMEN AND MARKET REFORMS

In the period preceding the demise of the USSR, economists and politicians contemplating the fledgling democracies of Eastern Europe were well aware that the future would be far from easy for the crowds who had cheered the collapse of their communist regimes. Transition from a planned, command-type system to a market-oriented economy had simply never been attempted before; as a result, the economic literature offered few clues as to how such a complex process of change might be managed. What was clear, however, was that the market would demand the dismantling of the certainties and safety nets of the old system. In the short term, the shock this would inevitably entail for the populations of the former communist states carried with it its own political risk.

In the midst of the euphoria which greeted the early days of transition, there was no shortage of western comment warning of its potential social costs. Whatever the arguments over long-term benefits, the impact of structural adjustment programmes in developing countries already offered salutary lessons in the price populations might be expected to pay, in the short term at least, for economic restructuring. In Eastern Europe transition could be expected to throw up major social and labour market problems which, if they were ignored, might bring in their wake both economic and political dangers. Effective policies to tackle the social costs of the reform process could not, in the view of observers in some of the major international institutions, be left out of the equation without the risk of social unrest or of a slowing down, or even reversal, of elements of the reform itself.[2]

For the USSR in 1990, with its rash of alternative plans for transition and debates over the pace of change, the dangers were all too apparent. Drastically falling industrial output, a spiralling trade deficit and rising inflation formed the backdrop for plans for marketisation. Yet, not only were the necessary legal framework and financial infrastructure not in place, but the position of a substantial proportion of the population on whom this experiment was about to be conducted was far from secure. Until the policy of glasnost (openness) began to relax the USSR's draconian censorship from the mid-1980s, poverty was a term which it was only permissible to apply to the citizens of capitalist countries. As the realities of life in the Soviet Union began to be revealed in print for the first time, it was at last acknowledged that poverty not only existed but affected millions. Just how many millions, however, remained a matter for debate, with some estimates ranging as high as eighty million, or over a quarter of the population. Even on far more conservative official figures, as a prelude to market reforms the scale of poverty and the evident inadequacy of the existing safety net were seen by international agencies such as the ILO as 'alarming' and by the Soviet government itself as potentially destabilising

(Standing 1991: 1). As V.A. Pokrovski, deputy chair of the State Commission of Economic Reform observed, 'a specific trait of the USSR economy is that its internal safety margins are too small' (Pokrovski 1991: 78).

By the time Russia was prepared to embark on its new course as an independent nation, the warnings of the likely social costs of transition could already be based on experience much nearer home than developing countries coping with structural adjustment. ILO observers, commenting in 1991 on the prospects for the then USSR were already able to conclude that, in all probability,

> moving to a market-based economy will create mass unemployment and worsening poverty for a substantial minority of the population, as has been the case in the former German Democratic Republic, Hungary, Poland and elsewhere in Eastern Europe. Such a prospect gives a very real urgency to debates over labour and social policy reform.
>
> (Standing 1991: 394)

Unhappily for the Russian population, the policy of 'shock therapy' embarked upon in late 1991 was applied to an economy which was already in a catastrophic state of decline. The success of the reforms, designed to be acceptable to the IMF, would depend on the support of the West in the form both of economic assistance and debt rescheduling. While there was no shortage of economic advice and promises of western assistance in the emergence of a democratic Russia, there was continuing reluctance on the part of the Group of Seven actually to deliver substantial sums unless Russia adhered to IMF demands on restructuring. This was not, however, something Russia was able to do. In the political battles over the future of reform that came to a head in October 1993 one of the central issues was the acute social and political danger posed by subjecting the Russian population to further privations at what was increasingly seen as the West's behest.

It was not, however, until the shock of the nationalist Zhirinovsky's success in the December 1993 elections and the subsequent rout of the leading reformers in government that the West seriously began to count the cost of its own myopia. With the people of Russia finally expressing through the ballot box their dismay at the price of reform, western observers and advisers were quick to point the finger at the major financial institutions. Jeffrey Sachs, in particular, in resigning from his position as economic adviser to Boris Yeltsin, was swingeing in his criticisms, firstly of the IMF for its lack of understanding of the Russian situation and its failure to support restructuring and, secondly, of the World Bank for failing 'in its most important task: to help to finance a viable social support system' (Sachs 1994). By this stage, however, the damage had been done.

Among the warnings on the potential social fallout of transition in the former USSR and Eastern Europe, particular attention had been paid by a number of western observers to the likely impact on women. If the transition to a market economy appeared to promise immense new opportunities for individual enterprise denied by the command system, it should not be assumed that such a change would be an unmitigated blessing for women. As a wealth of studies from both western and developing countries had demonstrated, the operation of market economies did not necessarily work to women's advantage. In particular, as the experience of western countries had amply shown, the labour market was far from being gender neutral.[3] It could be expected, therefore, that, given the particular history of women in the former communist states, they would be hit especially hard by restructuring, at least in the short term.

One of the factors which immediately drew the attention of western commentators on this issue was the operation of existing social policies designed to enable women to combine work and motherhood. As many of the benefits to which women were entitled in the former communist states were provided directly by their employing enterprises, women would be readily perceived as 'expensive' rather than 'cheap' labour during a period of restructuring, despite their relatively low wages. In addition, the perception that women's domestic responsibilities were extensive and that women were, or should be, primarily home-oriented would lead managers to seek to retain what they perceived as more performance-oriented male workers. The ideological framework of the former communist states which had emphasised and supported women's continuing responsibility for the domestic sphere was, therefore, likely to be a major element in women's vulnerability in the new labour market.

Nor could it be assumed that the slimming down of heavy industry, especially in defence-related fields, and the expected growth of the underdeveloped service sector would automatically favour women, at least in the initial phase of transition. In the first place, women's high levels of education in the former socialist states had secured them a significant presence as engineers and technicians in the defence industries and, secondly, their continuing predominance in potential growth areas such as economics and accountancy could not be taken for granted. Furthermore, evidence was already emerging from the initial period of restructuring in Eastern Europe to show that, where the conditions of the market were creating new and more prestigious employment opportunities, for example in the financial services sector, men were immediately beginning to move into previously highly feminised professions (Bialecki and Heyns 1993: 128–30). Western observers considering the prospects for women during the market reforms took the view, therefore, that men and women were unlikely to be treated equally in the process of transition unless positive action were taken, primarily to protect women's employment position:

> Deregulation of labour market institutions, social security systems and employment protection hits women harder than men. Since women's status in the labour market is already weaker than men's, the general crisis in employment will, if not faced up to politically, be solved at the expense of women's employment prospects.
>
> (Hubner *et al.* 1993: 236)

Yet, if some western observers considered government intervention essential to safeguard women's position, it was by no means certain that the political will or, indeed, insight existed in the former communist states to take the necessary steps. In countries where increasing emphasis had been placed on the value of motherhood and where the communist model of women's emancipation was now being roundly rejected, politicians whose primary interests lay with the broader economic objectives of restructuring were likely to have little time for arguments for equal opportunities or social justice. In Russia, certainly, political leaders and opinion formers were overwhelmingly concerned to present for popular consumption a view of the market as a benign phenomenon that would ensure future prosperity. They were not disposed to offer a sober analysis of its realities or to discuss western experience of the market's negative features. The resulting pro-market propaganda, therefore, frequently flew in the face of the evidence, especially where women were concerned. As Elena Mezentseva of the Moscow Centre for Gender Studies, for example, pointed out: 'Our best-known economists and politicians are fond of repeating the assertion that "the market has no sex", since in the conditions of competition it is the strongest person who wins, regardless of whether it is a man or a woman' (Mezentseva 1994b: 75). Curiously, among all the rhetoric emphasising women's nurturant roles, this was one area in which the image of the strong 'Soviet' woman appeared still to predominate.

If equal opportunities arguments were likely to fall on deaf ears, there were, of course, questions of the national interest which might have been expected to hold more sway. As some western specialists were quick to point out, the high levels of education and extensive professional experience of women in Russia and Eastern Europe represented a national asset that it would be unwise to squander, 'even temporarily, since qualifications are perishable goods' (Hubner *et al.* 1993: 214). By the same token, because the female labour force was more highly educated than the male labour force, it could be assumed that retraining women to meet the needs of a market economy would be quicker and more cost-effective than retraining men (Fong 1993: 29). In addition, for the good of society at large, the link established in western studies between female income and family poverty needed to be considered: policies which, therefore, assisted women to remain in employment or to get back into the labour force could be seen as 'one of the most effective ways of alleviating poverty' (Standing 1993: 266).

Yet, as we consider in more detail in Chapter one, the 'back to the home' lobby which had gained momentum during perestroika had become so powerful by the time Russia embarked on its market reforms that few in positions of influence were likely to be receptive even to arguments such as these. In the climate of the time it proved over-optimistic to hope that their position might be challenged by western politicians. Given the triumphalist atmosphere which prevailed in the wake of the fall of the Berlin Wall and the ideological preoccupations of western political leaders on their home territory, there was little prospect that any of the anxieties about the potential impact of change on women would be taken seriously; still less that they would 'acknowledge that some aspects of earlier [socialist] regulations and institutions worked to women's advantage', as contributors to an OECD/ILO conference in 1991 had recommended (Hubner *et al.* 1993: 236). Nor would key western economic advisers and financial institutions necessarily take these issues on board. Western economists considering the prospects for restructuring frequently managed to do so without a passing reference to the issue of gender.[4] Moreover, economic programmes featuring cut-backs in public spending of the type habitually demanded by the IMF had a track record of disadvantaging women.

Above all, given the extreme reluctance of western governments and institutions to commit substantial sums to Russian restructuring, much of the counsel of western specialists on the question of women's position remained just that: a series of 'good practice' recommendations from a West which not only had different traditions on issues of sex equality but whose overall credibility was rapidly diminishing in Russian eyes. As a result, researchers in western institutions might well draw up exhaustive action plans to secure the future of women in the Russian labour market, but, in practice, the political influence and, more importantly, the financial commitment which might see them translated into action were lacking.[5] In consequence, where direct western input has been specifically aimed at women it has tended to focus on just one principal issue: the creation of small businesses. In the conspicuous absence of significant economic assistance, the proliferation of small business advice and projects is one area, at least, where western institutions have been highly visible.

While it would be unrealistic to suggest that women in the transitional economies do not require advice and encouragement to engage in entrepreneurial activities, it is impossible not to be struck by the similarities between western programmes of involvement in Eastern Europe and job creation strategies in the West itself. In Britain, in particular, the formation of small businesses was explicitly promoted through the 1980s as the officially approved method of reducing unemployment. Where employment in the formal economy had been lost, self-employment and the development of small businesses were presented as the ways forward, both for the individual and for whole regions where traditional industries had collapsed. Whether or not these initiatives had any real chance of success, the wholesale promotion of an 'enterprise culture' ensured that the responsibility for safeguarding one's own future was placed firmly on the individual. As Teresa Rees has summed up this policy's inexorable logic, 'to be unemployed then becomes inexcusable' (Rees 1992: 161). Whether in Britain or in Russia, it is a strategy which is plainly inadequate for combating mass unemployment. Yet, in Russia as in Britain, the promotion of self-employment is very effective in pushing home the message that it is entirely in the individual's own hands whether she or he sinks or swims. In the absence of serious money from the West, this is, of course, little more than the simple truth.

In the chapters that follow we hope both to outline the complexities of the situation in which women in Russia currently find themselves and to explore their responses to the loss of job security and falling living standards. The book draws on recent studies by Russian sociologists and looks at the coverage of women's responses to unemployment in the mainstream Russian press. In addition, the major themes of the book are further illustrated by case-studies of three recently founded non-governmental organisations.

The degree of control that the Communist Party of the Soviet Union exercised over the country's citizens ensured that, until the late 1980s, voluntary organisations of all types were actively discouraged. From the initial founding of western-style charities and pressure groups under Gorbachev, a vast range of associations and organisations now exists in the former USSR, though there is still virtually no concept of partnership between the state and the voluntary sector. In order to explore how women were tackling the unfamiliar problems of unemployment and loss of security, we decided to focus on three Moscow-based organisations and their customers.

As the focus of this book is on the impact on women of the initial phase of restructuring, Moscow-based organisations were chosen, partly for their relative experience and diversity and partly because women in the capital had been immediately affected by the first wave of unemployment. Cut-backs in administration, particularly with the closure of the USSR ministries, in the many research institutes which had blossomed in the former USSR and in the defence industries of the capital and its surrounding satellite towns had had a disproportionate impact on women engineers, scientists, technicians and economists. In a city the size of Moscow, it would not be unreasonable to expect that new opportunities would be opened to them far more readily than in the provinces and that voluntary agencies would be better equipped to help them.

The three organisations chosen, Missiya, Guildia and Image, though Moscow-based, had all extended their activities in some way into the provinces.[6] They were all founded and run by women and served primarily women, yet only one, Missiya, saw itself as a feminist organisation. In each case, the women who were the driving force behind the organisation were using their particular skills to assist women to adapt to the new conditions, yet all three were, to western eyes, using unorthodox methods to achieve their ends. Finally, all three, while endeavouring to help individual women, had run into practical difficulties of their own which they were resolving with varying degrees of success. In focusing on these three organisations, then, we hoped to be able to shed some light both on the prospects and choices which individuals might face and on the problems of relatively new voluntary bodies themselves.

The research was undertaken over a period of a year between May 1993 and April 1994. The founders and organisers of the three agencies each gave multiple interviews throughout this period which allowed us to build up a picture of the development of each organisation. In addition, semi-structured interviews were conducted with thirty-six of their customers in the summer of 1993 and the spring of 1994. To protect anonymity, interviewees are referred to by a number within square brackets throughout the text. Further details of the research are given in the Appendix, and Table 3 (p. 202) gives details of the interviewees' ages, educational status and professions. This small study has no pretensions to be representative of the experiences of Russian women during transition, nor indeed of the customers of voluntary agencies. In a rapidly changing situation it does, however, in our view, shed some light on an area about which very little is known: the attitudes and behaviour of grass-roots organisations in Russia today. The histories and observations of the women we interviewed are, at the very least, illustrative of the situation faced by women in the first major wave of unemployment and of the strategies they decide to adopt. With the exception of seven women who were still in higher education, all but two had experienced unemployment, been temporarily laid off and obliged to find other work or were expecting imminent redundancy. All had higher or specialised secondary education, the overwhelming majority being qualified engineers, scientists and economists. Their experiences raise questions and identify areas of concern which need to be tackled both in future, more extensive, studies and by those engaged in practical action.

In addition to the three voluntary organisations, the work of one state organisation, the Employment Centre in Dubna, is examined. Dubna is a town on the northern edge of Moscow Region well known for its scientific research institutes and, more recently in the West, as the venue for the first two Independent Women's Forums. Cut-backs in the town's institutes and highly specialised enterprises create a potentially very difficult employment situation in this locality. After the Second Forum, the Employment Centre teamed up with Guildia to provide a day seminar for unemployed women in the town: spin-offs from this link provide both an unusual example of state and voluntary organisations in partnership and also of what can be achieved by good practice in a state-funded agency.

In presenting the information gathered in the course of this research project, our major aim is to offer an analysis of the situation confronting women in Russia in a way which will be digestible to non-specialists. In the light of the shortcomings of western institutional involvement in Russia's transition, there is ample scope for positive action at grass-roots level on the part of western voluntary organisations. Examples already exist where direct partnership between western and Russian charities and non-governmental organisations has been remarkably fruitful. In writing what we intend to be an accessible book, we hope that western voluntary bodies will be both informed and encouraged to take up links with Russian partners. As we have found in the organisations with which we have had most contact, there is certainly no lack of interest, not in charity and hand-outs, but in active two-way partnership and participation with like-minded bodies in the West. We hope that this book may have a part to play, however small, in fostering links of this type.

As always in a jointly authored book, acknowledgement needs to be given to the efforts of individual contributors. All three authors were involved in the research, both in Britain and Russia, in the analysis of its results and in the writing of Chapters two and four.

Rebecca Kay wrote Chapter three and co-authored Chapter eight with Sue Bridger. The remaining chapters were written by Sue Bridger with the final draft of the book being revised jointly with Rebecca Kay.

Part I

THE IMPACT OF CHANGE

1

THE LEGACY OF PERESTROIKA

In the mid–1980s the period of change ushered in by Mikhail Gorbachev's accession to power gave rise to an unprecedented upsurge of interest in the West in events in the USSR. As terms such as glasnost and perestroika became common currency in the English language, a wave of international optimism greeted the dawning of a new era in East–West relations. The former 'evil empire' was setting free its political prisoners, ending censorship and facing up to its Stalinist past. Alongside greater political freedom at home, the period heralded dramatic changes in foreign policy which brought the troops home from Afghanistan and ultimately redrew the map of Europe. The Soviet Union's new generation of leaders were fêted in world capitals, Gorbachev himself receiving the Nobel Prize for Peace even as the forces he had unleashed were spiralling out of control and bringing about the collapse of both communism and the empire it had created.

In the midst of the radical reforms which characterised the final years of Soviet power, government policies on issues of concern to women frequently appeared curiously conservative. While previous administrations, most notably that of Leonid Brezhnev, were being heavily criticised and characterised as a time of 'stagnation', Brezhnev-period policies on women and the family were not merely condoned but effectively extended. On the issue of sexual equality, perhaps more than any other, the Gorbachev administration embraced a different perspective from that of other advanced industrial countries and from the thinking of its many admirers in the West. Its approach to the issues of women's employment and domestic responsibilities was in part a legacy of the past and in part a preparation for the future. Soviet women were to find themselves squeezed between these twin constraints in a way which continues to be all too visible in the market-oriented Russia of today.

WOMEN AND EMPLOYMENT

The mass involvement of women in waged work outside the home was a central plank in Marxist–Leninist ideology on the emancipation of women. With the introduction of a planned programme of rapid industrialisation from the late 1920s and the enormous loss of male lives in the Second World War, women were drawn into Soviet enterprises in their millions. As late as the 1970s, the sex imbalance in the Soviet population was reflected in the fact that women formed over half the workforce, with around 90 per cent of working-age women in either full-time employment or education. The concept of the 'career break' was effectively unknown in the USSR as women on average were out of full-time employment for only 3.6 years to have their families (Kotliar and Turchaninova 1975: 106–7). By 1989, women still made up no less than 48 per cent of the Soviet workforce (*Vestnik statistiki* 1991: 39). Until the advent of glasnost, this high level of participation of women in the workforce was almost invariably presented as an indicator of emancipation, one of the prime achievements of the Soviet brand of socialism. As the Brezhnev years progressed, however, the statistics presented became ever more selective. While the numbers of women with higher degrees or employment in science and education were published as indicators of social progress, statistics on the armies of women manual workers became notoriously elusive.

Once the policy of glasnost had been instituted as the motor of economic and political reform, however, this situation was to change dramatically. From a position of state-enforced silence on the less palatable realities of women's working lives, the Soviet media moved rapidly and radically into a wholesale investigation of working conditions, health and safety provisions and discrimination against women at work. The signal for the relaxation of censorship on discussion of female employment came in July 1987 at the National Women's Conference in Moscow when the outgoing chair of the Soviet Women's Committee, former cosmonaut Valentina Tereshkova, spoke critically and at length on the subject. For the head of what had previously been one of the most docile Soviet institutions to break so abruptly with virtually all her past pronouncements on the position of women was the clearest possible signal of the Communist Party's policy shift ('Vsesoiuznaia konferentsiia zhenshchin . . .' 1987: 3). For the next two years press and television presented regular features on the nature of women's work and canvassed women's responses through studio discussions and letters to the editor.

What emerged from all of this, as with so many social issues explored through glasnost, was a picture of almost unmitigated gloom. On questions of low pay, night shifts, heavy and dangerous conditions or overt and systematic discrimination in promotion, the reality made a mockery of the much-vaunted emancipation of the Soviet woman worker. Inevitably, the investigation of women's working conditions led very rapidly into a discussion of how these multiple problems might be solved. Yet, as we shall see in the next section, given the Soviet record on sex equality, the social policies pursued by previous administrations and the economic agenda of perestroika itself, the solutions put forward would not necessarily be in women's best interests.

In launching the discussion of the issue of working conditions, Valentina Tereshkova quoted the latest national figures showing women's wide-spread involvement in heavy physical work in a range of industries. Subsequent press articles and readers' letters in response put flesh on the statistical bones. In textile factories and timber mills, on building sites and on the railways women were to be found lifting weights well in excess of the limits laid down by legislation. If the law allowed women to lift no more than a 10 kilo weight and a total of 7 tonnes per shift, women construction workers could be lifting 30 tonnes a shift, while dairy women and even shop assistants might be required to handle sacks weighing over 50 kilos (Redkollegiia zhurnala *Rabotnitsa* 1989: 11). Moreover, this excessive lifting might well take place in difficult climatic conditions:

> The work women do on the railways is exceptionally heavy. It's physical work and practically all done by hand. It's not every man who could cope with it. Our women have to work in the open air, in the heat and the cold, in rain and mud. They get paid the same as men and are on the same grades and they're expected to do the same work. We've got complete 'equality' here.
>
> (Baryshev 1988: 17)

As this example suggests, other factors came into play making women's work difficult. In textile factories, in particular, surveys had found women working in uncomfortable postures for as much as 80 per cent of their working day. In addition, high humidity and noise levels affected their health. As one journalist observed, 'The first time you come to Ivanovo it strikes you even in the tram from the station that you have to talk more loudly here than you would normally' (Telen 1988: 2). For women in the textile industry all this was crowned by compulsory night work. Here again, reality ran counter to legislation. Women, by law, could not be compelled to work night shifts except as a 'temporary measure', yet, in

17

practice, almost four million women worked nights and the number was expected to rise. Considerably more women than men were working nights not only in the highly feminised textile industry but also in chemicals and in other light industries. For women who continued to bear the brunt of housework and child care, night shifts resulted in extreme fatigue, for, as one textile worker put it, 'you don't get to sleep enough during the day because you've got to do your shift at the cooker and the washing machine' (Telen 1988: 2). In other industries, where women were not subject to conditions such as these, complaints came in about continual compulsory and, again, illegal overtime (Cherepakhova 1987: 15–17).

Night shifts and work in hazardous conditions remained, however, one way in which women could compensate for a further disadvantage they suffered, namely that of low pay. Women's wages, as women themselves were well aware, were consistently lower than those of men, around 70 per cent of male earnings, reflecting both their lower skill gradings and their concentration in sectors of the economy which had become relatively low-paid. Average wages in trade and catering, for example, where 83 per cent of the workforce was female, stood at only 64 per cent of average earnings in the construction industry, where 72 per cent of employees were male (*Zhenshchina i deti* 1985: 51; *Narodnoe khoziaistvo v SSSR . . .* 1985: 417–18). Employees in the highly feminised spheres of health, culture and education received between 53 and 78 per cent of average industrial earnings, while, within industry itself, the general rule was the greater the proportion of women workers, the lower the average rates of pay (*Narodnoe khoziaistvo v SSSR . . .* 1989: 77–8; Klopov *et al.* 1987: 30). In every branch of industry women's average skill grades were lower than those of men and, although women's gradings had been steadily rising since 1970, men's gradings had risen more sharply still, increasing the discrepancy between the sexes (Klopov *et al.* 1987: 59).

If much of this information was available prior to the advent of glasnost, what was new was both its extensive discussion in the mass media and the course that the discussion was to take. In the past, low skill grades and low pay were habitually presented as the effect of women's involvement in housework and child care. While women's energies were taken up in the domestic sphere, spending more than double the time spent by men on unpaid domestic work and leaving employment, however briefly, to have children, men's skill grades continued to rise with age and experience. In practice, women experienced great difficulty raising their grading once they had had children, and the more children they had, the further they lagged behind (Khotkina 1987: 60; Lukina and Nekhoroshkov 1982: 125–6). Moreover, the need to find adequate child care and to fit in with domestic routines often led women to look for work nearer home or offering better facilities, irrespective of whether it corresponded to their levels of education and skill. While these factors undeniably continued to exert a significant influence on women's gradings and, hence, wage levels, a further, previously unacknowledged factor now entered the discussion. Readers writing in from all over the USSR to the major Soviet women's magazines offered a catalogue of blatantly discriminatory behaviour by management in allocating skill grades. Where women and men had the same level of skills, only the men would be placed on a higher grading. After additional training, some women complained that they still failed to receive the appropriate grade, while the men they had trained with were automatically promoted. Others described being continually subordinate to men, despite their skills and experience:

> I'm a refrigeration plant operator in a dairy produce factory. . . . Two of us work together per shift – a senior operator (grade 5) and a junior operator (grade 4). My workmate (the senior operator) has usually gone harvesting for the whole summer. During that time I've acted as senior operator and been paid on grade 5. . . . But whenever he came back they put me back on grade 4. My workmate recently retired and who do you think was appointed senior operator? The young man who had been my assistant in the summer and had only just been put on grade 4. . . . That's sexual equality for you! What's more, in May I'd once more passed the test on knowledge of the plant. I passed with distinction and put in for a higher grade, but all in vain! It looks like there's a grade 5 for men but there isn't one for women, doesn't it?
>
> ('Prodolzhaem operatsiiu "Stupeni masterstva "' 1987: 20)

Zoia Pukhova, replacing Tereshkova as head of the Soviet Women's Committee, noted that, far from being atypical, these complaints reflected a well-established practice 'whereby managements keep down the wage bill' (Gavriushenko 1988: 21). Nevertheless, the fact that such actions could now be roundly condemned as the discrimination they undoubtedly were, in the short term brought women no closer to a solution.

Given the sheer scale of the problems thrown up by this exploration of women's working lives, the question of whether genuine improvements could have been quickly made appears highly problematical. In the light of the political and economic priorities of the time it seems doubtful whether they were ever on the agenda. Nevertheless, there were calls by journalists writing in both women's magazines and national newspapers to tackle what they regarded as the exploitation of women in the workplace.

Describing the extremely arduous and primitive conditions endured by so many women in Soviet factories and farms inevitably raised the question of what could be done. For some, the answer lay in increased and improved mechanisation, the effective enforcement of the USSR's extensive health and safety legislation and a more aggressive role for what they saw as the country's supine trade unions.

The question of automation remained, however, a very tricky one not only for factory managements and industrial ministries but also for women workers themselves. As long as there appeared to be sufficient numbers of women prepared to work in poor conditions the economic rationale for not mechanising production tasks could appear overwhelming. Because of wage discrimination, women represented a cheap and relatively docile labour force, readily accepting the status quo in return for wage levels and benefits they could not otherwise attain. Locked into economic dependence on the extra payments for heavy and dangerous work or for night shifts, women have often resisted mechanisation, both in industry and in branches of agriculture such as dairying, or been strongly opposed to redeployment onto lighter work (Zybtsev 1987: 110; Khotkina 1987: 69). When these factors were added to the massive cost of investment in new plant and machinery, the continual postponement of modernisation appeared virtually inevitable.

If mechanisation was problematical, transforming the role of the courts and the trade unions within the confines of the one-party state was an impossible goal, as subsequent events were to demonstrate. With the growing debate from 1987 on how the USSR might become a 'law-governed state', lawyers were frequently quoted in the press bemoaning the levels of legal illiteracy of the population at large. Yet a far more fundamental problem remained the difficulty of obtaining redress through the courts even where there was a case to answer. Derisory levels of fines and compensation in cases involving labour legislation together with political interference in the legal process led many workers to regard media publicity and press intervention as more fruitful avenues to explore. As journalists on national newspapers and magazines began to question why their role in this area remained so crucial, the issue of the function of trade unions in Soviet society was raised for the first time in decades.

In the former USSR, trade unions had a dual function of both defending workers and helping to ensure enterprises met their production targets. In practice, the latter function came to take precedence over the former and the trade unions' involvement in employee welfare was largely reduced to the allocation of benefits. With a more frank appraisal of working conditions the common perspective of management and trade union committees began, albeit cautiously at first, to be challenged. 'For decades, trade union organisers have in practice given unconditional support to management. They have viewed everything, including disputes with ordinary workers, through management's eyes', noted one journalist condemning the treatment of women workers, after carefully citing Gorbachev himself in her defence (Ronina 1987: 11).

Perhaps predictably, the heart of the official trade union structure, the AUCCTU (All-Union Central Council of Trade Unions), chose to counter developing criticism of its role by blaming 'the shortcomings of the local trade unions'. As the head of the AUCCTU's department for women's employment protection went on, 'The law provides every possibility for organising proper working conditions. They only have to make use of it' (Korina 1987: 18). Yet, as this speaker would have known only too well, neither the trade unions' habitual support of management, nor the ineffectiveness of the courts in civil matters arose because officials did not try hard enough. Both resulted from policy decisions made by the Communist Party in its assertion of control over Soviet society and its promotion of rapid industrialisation. The cautiousness with which journalists and social scientists initially tackled these issues in print reflected their appreciation that calling for improvements in women's working conditions might imply a major potential threat to the political status quo. By the end of the 1980s, when the miners at least had begun developing workers' organisations of their own, commentators could afford to be far more contemptuous of the official trade unions' efforts. Bitterly criticising the AUCCTU for its failure to take effective action over dairy women's working conditions, for example, the journalist, Nikolai Tereshchenko, could feel free to dismiss the official unions as part of a system which had outlived its usefulness:

> Special mention must be made of trade unions. The AUCCTU announced that it had turned to the ministries and government departments with a request that they start solving problems as soon as possible. That's the gist of the matter: the AUCCTU requests. . . . It ought to have demanded, as dairy women should also demand. But they don't know how to. They don't feel like the masters of production. They will feel like this only when the producer genuinely owns the means of production and the end result of his or her work.
>
> (Tereshchenko 1989: 10)

By the time this kind of statement was finding its way into the Soviet press, however, a rather different solution to the problems faced by women at work was gaining common currency.

BACK TO THE HOME?

If, as women's working conditions suggested, much of the detailed Soviet legislation on health and safety at work was effectively a dead letter, this had not prevented periodic extensions of its provisions. In addition, formal bans on women's involvement in work deemed to be injurious to their health had been introduced, most recently in 1981 when a new list was announced of 460 occupations that were to be closed to women. Whether these measures of 'protection' were actually enforced is, from the point of view of the debates which took place in the late 1980s, of rather less importance than the fact that this tradition was habitually presented as being of unequivocal benefit to women. Where the exclusion of women from certain occupations was officially viewed as evidence of the state's concern, it was but a small step to advocate the removal of women from large areas of the workforce where working conditions were poor. By the end of the decade, this had become the dominant theme throughout the Soviet media in any discussion of women's employment.

The alacrity with which so many policy-makers, media commentators and, ultimately, the mass of public opinion took up this theme appears at first glance somewhat puzzling in the light of the highly developed segregation of the Soviet labour force. It was not immediately apparent, for example, how production was to continue if women were to be encouraged to leave such highly feminised spheres as textiles or dairying. Yet, as the debate progressed, it became clear how far the assumptions on which it was based reflected the legacy of the Brezhnev years, the social policy preoccupations of the Gorbachev administration and the potential economic realities of perestroika itself.

From the mid-1970s, the falling birth rate in European areas of the USSR and the burgeoning population of Soviet Central Asia had given rise to much talk of a 'demographic crisis'. The ensuing pronatalist programme, instituted primarily in non-Asian areas, was described as 'strengthening the Soviet family', although its concern for the future of European areas and, especially, of the Russian nation was evident from the beginning. Thus it can be seen as the precursor of the draft family legislation which was to be introduced in the newly independent Russian state from 1992. The 1981 decree which extended maternity benefits also explicitly paved the way for an increase in literature, propaganda and direct instruction about family life. What followed was a sustained media campaign aimed at encouraging women in non-Asian areas to see themselves first and foremost as mothers. Crude propaganda eulogising heroine mothers, bearers of ten or more children and a medal instituted at the acme of Stalinism, was overtaken by a more subtle preoccupation with the theme of femininity. Women whose paid work was indispensable to the Soviet economy were exhorted to be equally industrious in the home. The existing gross inequality within marriage and the resulting overburdening of women, so well documented by Soviet social scientists, were cheerfully ignored as the media promoted self-sacrifice as the highest expression of femininity.[1] Women were warned that genuine happiness could only be found in producing the ideal family of three children and creating for them and, most importantly, for their father a 'strong home front', a refuge from life's storms in the comfort of the family hearth.

Much of this writing drew its inspiration from the work of Soviet educational theorists who, since the mid-1960s, had been propounding the view that only a form of upbringing sharply differentiated by gender was capable of producing stable families. The work of such writers as Khripkova and Kolesov, Levshin and Timoshchenko urged both parents and teachers to recognise that 'the formation of ideas about the necessary type of behaviour of a boy or a girl, a young man or woman, is an aim of upbringing' (Khripkova and Kolesov 1981: 84). Their work identified a range of characteristics which were deemed to be 'natural' to the two sexes: strength, activity, bravery, inventive and investigative behaviour, for example, were masculine traits, while weakness, emotionalism, intuition and nurturant qualities were feminine. From this basis, these writers went on to urge that the upbringing of girls and boys should deliberately seek to emphasise these 'natural' differences. It was then assumed that the 'real men' and 'real women' who would be produced in this way would be more capable of sustaining stable and fertile marriages.[2]

In 1984, a course entitled 'The Ethics and Psychology of Family Life', based firmly on work of this type, was introduced into the final years of the Soviet secondary school curriculum and effectively marked the culmination of the demographic policy instigated under Leonid Brezhnev. By the time glasnost began to reveal the uncomfortable realities of female employment, it had become utterly commonplace in the USSR to regard women's natural destiny and true vocation to be motherhood and the creation of domestic bliss. Sentiments which would, at the very least, produce raised eyebrows in much of Western Europe could be presented unchallenged in the Soviet media as the simple expression of natural law.

Against this background, the position of women as workers was further threatened by the beginnings of something of a moral panic. The relaxation of censorship both revealed the existence of an entire panoply of largely concealed social problems and allowed the beginnings of a process of liberalisation in society at large. The resulting revelations of drug abuse, crime, juvenile delinquency and sexual promiscuity, together with the appearance of a highly diverse and apparently anarchic youth culture, proved to be a profound shock to those who had grown up with the moral certainties of the Soviet state. While not attempting to put the genie back into the bottle, the Gorbachev administration was broadly in sympathy with the notion that the enhancement of women's mothering role could be an effective means of combating social ills. In particular, where women's working conditions themselves could be shown to have a deleterious effect on the family – the disruption caused by shift work, the work-related stress leading to marital conflict, for example – then the attitude of the state to female labour should be modified. Rather than attempt the Herculean task of changing conditions for the better, with all that this would imply in both political and economic terms, it would be easier to resolve problems here and now by changing women's behaviour, a task ostensibly made easier by the legacy of the Brezhnev years. As one group of sociologists expressed the equation, it was precisely because women suffered wage discrimination and bad conditions and because child care, health care and public services were all inadequate that

> it is obvious that in these conditions we must rethink the stereotypes which have developed and realise that, for the future of the country and of socialism, the most important form of creative work for women is the work of motherhood.
>
> (Driakhlov *et al.* 1987: 113)

Finally, and still on the theme of the good of society rather than of women, came the probable economic effects of perestroika itself. The restructuring of the economy on which the Gorbachev administration was embarking was predicated on the assumption that the achievement of greater efficiency and productivity would entail a slimming down of the workforce. If, as it was often assumed, there would not ultimately be enough jobs in the new economy to redeploy everyone, then shunting at least some women out of the workforce into what could be presented as simply a different and no less valuable 'form of creative work' might solve a range of problems at a stroke. The possibility of raising the birth rate, strengthening home and family to counter social problems and cushioning unemployment through this one expedient of challenging the nature of female employment makes clear the obvious attraction of this characteristically conservative policy for otherwise radical policy-makers in the late 1980s.

Nevertheless, on the issue of the role of women, as in other major policy areas, the Gorbachev administration was anxious to distance itself from the authoritarian nature of previous Communist Party programmes. More-over, in relaxing control of the mass media, the Party leadership was no longer in a position to mount the kind of orchestrated propaganda campaign that had characterised the pronatalist policies of their predeces-sors. The result was a series of diverse and contradictory pronouncements on what women might expect from the new administration, sometimes issuing from one and the same speaker. Gorbachev himself was particularly guilty of this, writing in his book, *Perestroika*, of the need to allow women to 'return to their purely womanly mission' within the family, yet at the 19th Party Conference in 1988 speaking of the importance of opening up a 'wide road' for women into government posts (Gorbachev 1988: 117).

This apparent flexibility on the question of women's roles largely reflected the uncomfortable results of Marxist–Leninist ideology which advocated women's emancipation through involvement in paid labour when combined with Brezhnevite pronatalism which laid its stress on home and family. The consequences of this very mixed legacy could be extremely jarring, particularly to western observers eagerly on the lookout for signs of cracks in the Communist façade, even if their implications were blithely ignored by those excited by the prospects for change. In 1986, for example, when the western press got its hands on a call for political reform emanating from the highest levels within the new administration, the uniformly radical tone of the document was lost only in its authors' statements on women. 'Low salaries lead to the feminisation of men who are unable to be the financial head of the family . . . men's inability to support their families results in the masculinisation of women', they declared in language straight out of a Brezhnev-era textbook which even the *Guardian*'s commentators chose to overlook (Walker 1986: 19). Yet the statements made by leading Party members in the mid-1980s were not without their appeal to women themselves. The propagandists of the Brezhnev era had attempted to square the circle of grafting pronatalism onto Marxism–Leninism by promoting the figure of the Soviet super-woman as a model for emulation. Now, the politicians of the new administration did at least appear to appreciate that exhorting women to be exemplary workers and at the same time self-sacrificing wives and mothers was a recipe for mass exhaustion. It was this new realism, the recognition that any human being can only do so much, especially in Soviet conditions, which was in such stark contrast to the heroic-style campaigning of the past and came as such a relief to women who felt hard-pressed in both their working and domestic lives.

It was on these foundations that the debate on women's roles, spurred on by media revelations of working conditions, ultimately arrived at the ideological synthesis which came to characterise the perestroika period. Rather than exhort women to be both worker and mother with equal devotion, women were to be encouraged to opt for either one or the other. In this way there would no longer be any contradiction between talk of 'wide roads' and 'womanly missions' when both options were made available to women: all they had to do was choose. As the decade progressed, this concept of 'choice' was energetically taken up by writer after writer in the Soviet press and earnestly discussed by the new generation of TV journalists on what, at the time, were the most politically ground-breaking shows. On the flagships of glasnost, men in comfortable studios shook their heads ruefully at footage of women manual workers and offered women 'choice' as the new form of chivalry. By 1990, women themselves had been so seduced by this notion that a female studio audience on International Women's Day was able to spend one and a half hours obsessively discussing how much, if at all, women with children should be involved in paid work.

Behind all of this lay the assumption that, while some women might 'choose' to have a career, the vast majority would seize with gratitude the opportunity to lead less pressured lives and 'choose' to spend more time at home, at least when their children were young. To this end, legislation on working conditions and leave entitlements for mothers was modified with a view to encouraging women to relinquish full-time jobs. Increasing maternity leave was continually discussed through the late 1980s, and a decision was taken in 1989 to phase in eighteen months part-paid leave with a further eighteen months unpaid leave thereafter. But the most widely canvassed change came in the sphere of part-time working. Though previously permitted 'by agreement with management', in practice man-agements would have little to do with it. From 1987, managements were obliged to provide part-time work, paid *pro rata*, at the request of women employees who were pregnant or had a child under the age of eight, although, as subsequently became clear, legislation made part-time work no more popular in Soviet enterprises. By the end of the decade no more than 1 per cent of Soviet women worked part time (Vasilets 1988: 20; *Zhenshchiny v SSSR* 1990: 7).

To western feminists unfamiliar with Soviet conditions the readiness of Soviet women to see themselves as housewives could appear perverse in the extreme. They had, after all, achievements to be proud of: ready access to higher education, social acceptance of full-time work, employment in non-traditional spheres and the support of a network of child-care institutions. Yet they also had the constant problem of shortages, the ill-stocked shops, the shoddy goods, the queueing and the bureaucracy for the simplest transactions, the virtual absence of labour-saving devices and, above all, almost sole responsibility for running the home and caring for the family. In a society which had been saturated with pronatalist imagery the redefinition of gender roles was on scarcely anyone's agenda. For women who could see little evidence that men were contemplating sharing domestic responsibilities the possibility of opting out of part of the burden they bore was very attractive. The Communist Party, whose leaders had spoken for so long of the need to tackle the 'double shift' worked by Soviet women, was at long last doing something positive to address the problem.

Women who wrote in to women's magazines describing their experience of extended leave or part-time working expressed very clearly the sense of having a weight removed from their shoulders, as in these observations by a mother of two on maternity leave:

> Nearly every day my elder daughter says, 'It's so good you're at home!' I can do her plaits properly and give her a meal before school. When she comes home I'm in a good mood (because I haven't been doing my hellish job and haven't got tired). After all, what was it like before? You fly out of work round the shops, buy as much food as you can so you won't have to go again tomorrow, get home from the shops as fast as you can. At home you've got to cook supper and prepare tomorrow's lunch, your daughter's coming out with all kinds of questions which you haven't got time to answer. . . . You go on putting up with it all and taking your 'patience' out on your husband or your child. Whereas now. . . ! I'm amazed myself at how calm I've become.

> (Kuznetsova 1990: 14)

For women with young children time was perhaps the most important potential gain. If their mothers and grandmothers had slaved their lives away in exhausting jobs and homes that were not designed for busy people, younger women had no wish to tread the same path. Yet they were not only expressing the desire to cut down their workload, but also to change the quality of their lives, to have time not only for tasks but also for their relationships and for themselves. In this final element of the new deal women were seeking lay a further compelling aspect of change in the USSR. As the country became ever more open to western influence, women wanted their share of what they saw as the good life that western women could take for granted: glamour, fashion, frivolity and all the trappings of consumerism. Time for themselves, for younger Soviet women of the late 1980s, meant very firmly time to indulge in all the paraphernalia of the growing beauty industry as the ultimate antidote to the image and reality of manual labour.

FASHION, GLAMOUR AND THE SEX INDUSTRY

The new preoccupation with glamour and sexuality was the final element of the equation which was to determine the nature of change in women's lives as the planned economy moved towards its ultimate breakdown. With the relaxation of censorship from the mid-1980s, the Soviet media began with ever increasing boldness to discuss sex, display nudity and dabble with erotic imagery. This process of liberalisation began very much as an attempt to sweep away the hypocrisy and prudishness of the post-Stalin years and, in particular, to combat the widespread ignorance that was producing alarming levels of teenage abortion, sexually-transmitted disease and hasty, ill-starred marriages. Yet, perhaps inevitably, it almost immediately produced an entirely new iconography for Soviet women. In place of the woman worker in overalls and hard hat came the scantily-clad glamour model draped over a gleaming, and usually foreign, car bonnet, inviting the onlooker not to produce but to consume.

The flirtation with western-style consumerism implied in images such as these became ever more explicit with the penetration of the Soviet market by western firms. International Women's Day 1987 was marked by the launch of a Russian edition of *Burda* magazine and followed by a range of other fashion imports which women crowded three deep round state newspaper kiosks to see. Slimming, skin care and advice on personal hygiene found a place in home-grown Soviet magazines and even village girls felt the need to spurn the time-honoured advice of their regular columnists on appropriate attire for young women:

> Let's just imagine a modern girl, armed with your advice, getting ready for a disco. She's so clean and healthy that she doesn't need to look in the mirror as she puts on her modest dress. . . . Her healthy, shining hair needs no attention – after all, if it's so healthy and shining it can just hang somehow or other and shine away. And as for make-up – saints preserve us! – girls have happy smiles instead. So, clean and healthy, with shining hair she goes to the disco in her modest dress with no make up and starts smiling happily at the young

men. And they, of course, immediately queue up to ask her to dance. Or do they?

(Elenikova 1987: 36)

The continued attempts by journalists, and even fashion designers invited to comment on letters such as these, to suggest that self-confidence, self-respect and self-esteem were the essence of femininity on which fashion was merely the froth were beginning to fall on deaf ears.

If young women swiftly fell prey to the lure of fashion, eagerly sending in their photographs and vital statistics for a chance to join the stars of *Burda* on the catwalks, the entire nation rapidly became entranced by the sheer novelty of a further western import, the beauty contest. At the very point at which western interest in such proceedings was flagging alarmingly for their organisers, Soviet schoolgirls, factory workers, nurses and sociologists were to be found parading in bikinis, while whole families settled down for an evening's unsophisticated talent-spotting in front of the television, much in the manner of so many families in the West some two or three decades earlier. The first of these events to gain major media coverage, the Miss Moscow contest of 1988, was rapidly followed by similar performances in provincial towns right across the USSR. Youth programmes and newspapers were especially enthralled: the TV programme *Vzgliad*, a major proponent of political reform, delightedly featured a row of aspiring Miss Lvovs disco-dancing in bikinis, while the Komsomol (Communist Youth League) paper, *Sobesednik*, championed a young contestant and her family in Tiumen against her scandalised school. 'We are in favour of girls dreaming dreams and wanting to be beautiful', they boomed ('Shkol'nitsy . . . v kupal'nike?' 1989: 4).

For most commentators, as the beauty contest became an ever more profitable venture, the successive rounds of Miss Photo, Miss Charm and, ultimately, Miss USSR which followed simply allowed Soviet women to take their rightful place in the international glamour line-up. What criticism there was of the new phenomenon was mostly directed at poor organisation or the distinctly unglamorous behind-the-scenes conditions contestants were expected to endure. The overwhelming mass of comment about these events evidently took for granted that beauty contests were a normal aspect of any modern society and that it was entirely natural for young women to flock to take part. All that was required was a little more commercial slickness to bring them up to western standards. Virtually the only voices raised in protest at the entire concept were, interestingly enough, those of one or two male journalists who had worked in the United States and who now expressed their distaste at seeing women treated as sex objects: 'The men sit there and ogle beautiful women. . . . And women don't shout about it but regard it as perfectly acceptable. They should be boycotting these contests, going out with placards and protesting' (Skliar 1989: 23; Guseinov 1988: 14–15).

Women's silence over the beauty contests was little short of deafening, and the volume did not increase as glamour began to turn to sleaze. By the end of the decade, scarcely a play was staged without female nudity, scarcely a pop video could be made without ample displays of naked breasts. Women appeared nude in photo features promoting rock bands, commercial outfits and advertising agencies or simply to sell more newspapers. Meanwhile, the waters were muddied by artists and intellectuals welcoming the opportunity to work uncensored with erotic and explicitly sexual imagery. Young women, working for some ageing would-be impresario of the nearest thing to strip shows then available, could thus be found mouthing lines about 'beauty' and 'artistic expression' to cover their disquiet at taking off their clothes in public.

As the sex industry developed apace, with prostitution becoming an increasingly visible aspect of big city life and both imported and home-produced pornography becoming widely available, the protests which came were inevitably on moral grounds. Larisa Kuznetsova, a regular writer on women's issues, complained in 1990 that of all the many letters received by the press in response to articles about pornography, not one had come from a woman condemning the way that women were portrayed (Kuznetsova 1990: 14). Why were women so uncritical of these new trends in a country which had promoted such powerful images of women for seventy years?

A piece of photo-journalism that appeared in *Rabotnitsa* magazine in 1989 provided arguably the neatest encapsulation of the paradox. On the top half of the page sat the country's three top beauty queens decked in silk and surrounded by flowers, at the bottom were three other heroines of Soviet reality, toiling, queueing or slumped exhausted with the heading 'Miss Work, Miss Shortage and Miss Queue' ('Stop-Kadr' 1989 7: 8). If these pictures portrayed the constant daily struggles of millions of Soviet women, then those of the beauty queens represented, however frivolously, a lifestyle where fighting for the basic necessities would be over. Though pornographic representations of women might, for some, be taking things too far, they merely represented an extreme version of something women actually wanted. Beauty contests and glamour modelling, though providing money, travel and a genuine escape only for the few, served as symbols to the many of a different way of life. For so many women it was a breath of fresh air, a relief from the moralising and hypocrisy of the past and, at a time of general reassessment of the country's history, a rejection of the Stalinist legacy with its heroine mothers and its 'Glory to Soviet Women Workers' slogans. Women were simply sick of exhortations and the stock images of female emancipation. As the head of the Soviet Children's Fund observed in *Rabotnitsa* in 1988:

> We have found so many fine words to extol the work of the woman tractor driver or worker in construction and heavy industry. Like the discoverers of a new world, we placed into women's hands the controls of tractors and combines, pickaxes and drills, hammers and sickles, if you'll pardon the metaphor. Isn't it time we stopped? Isn't it time we understood that, slowly but surely, we are killing all that is female in women?
>
> (Skliar 1988: 4)

By the end of the decade, the concept of femininity had come to embrace something much broader than merely looking pretty. At its roots lay both a rejection of the past and the embracing of an as yet uncertain future. However, as the shortages got worse and the queues got longer, the tantalising glimpses of capitalism offered by the few western firms which had moved into the USSR had convinced most women that the future had to be better. The market economy, when it finally came, would turn Moscow into Paris or Copenhagen with the lifestyle they fondly imagined all western women shared. Few foresaw that the lifestyle which would be presented to the majority in Russia would be very far removed from these glittering images.

DISSENT AND ORTHODOXY

There were, nevertheless, some women ready from the early years of perestroika to express their unease that the promotion of 'choice' might leave some women with no choice at all. At the historic 19th Party Conference in 1988, where delegates applauded unprecedentedly hard-hitting criticism of the results of past policies, Zoia Pukhova, head of the Soviet Women's Committee, was received in virtual silence as she spelled out the dangers of perestroika itself. With the introduction of economic reforms which encouraged enterprises to look more closely at costs, increasing the range of benefits and leave entitlements to mothers was already emerging as a mixed blessing:

> In attempting to make use of their entitlements to work part-time or flexitime and to additional leave, women unwittingly come into

conflict with management, with the work collective of the shop or the brigade and become an undesirable labour force. Women are the first to be dismissed when redundancies occur.

(Redaktsionnaia kollegiia 1988: 11)

As she went on to explain in a series of interviews that year, the Committee was receiving letters from women from all over the country complaining at suddenly finding themselves out of a job. Over the next twelve months letters published in the national women's magazines underlined the fact that women with young children had become a particularly vulnerable group whenever enterprises were laying off staff. More particularly, women who had 'chosen' to leave the workforce to spend time at home with their baby were already experiencing some difficulty getting back in again (Gavriushenko 1988: 10–12; Menitskaia 1989: 12; Ivanova 1989: 31).

Aiming benefits legislation exclusively at women, in underpinning this state of affairs, also came in for criticism in Pukhova's speech. Raising the unpopular question of the father's responsibility within the family she advocated the extension of leave entitlements to the family as a whole. Largely as a response to this kind of pressure the final round of benefit and leave increases to come into effect before the USSR's demise brought in an element of parental leave. From January 1991 any family member would have the right to take leave to look after a child to the age of three. Yet, at the same time, the right to request part-time work was restricted to the mother and extended until the child reached fourteen years of age ('Postanovlenie Verkhovnogo Soveta SSSR . . .' 1990: 1–2). As this latter provision suggests, the government was not seriously expecting any dramatic change in attitudes towards parental responsibilities. Previous experience of the use of leave to care for sick children provided few grounds for optimism. Although theoretically available to both partners such leave was taken almost exclusively by women and commentators on the new leave provisions did not anticipate that the situation would change. Given both women's lower earnings and prevailing public attitudes, only the emergence of 'a new type of man, capable of seeing sexual equality not as something which prejudices a man's rights but as the dialectical development of them', as Larisa Kuznetsova put it, would make a significant difference (Tolokina 1989: 4; Kuznetsova 1988: 23).

As this statement suggests, not all commentators in the Soviet media in the late 1980s were equally enamoured of the 'back to the home' drive. In response to the conservative orthodoxy of the perestroika years a new and more challenging voice began to emerge, in some cases allying itself closely to western feminism. If, in the past, western 'bourgeois' feminism had been derided in the USSR as a movement aiming to make women the same as men, a small number of Soviet women were now becoming increasingly confident in borrowing terms such as sexism and talking freely about discrimination. 'Emancipation has got to be two-sided, it must be the emancipation of both women and men from patriarchal culture and outdated stereotypes', stated the philosopher, Ol'ga Voronina, in an interview with the CPSU Central Committee newspaper, *Sotsialisticheskaia industriia* (Kharchev 1982; Voronina 1988: 4). In 1989 a group of women academics who were later to found in Moscow the USSR's first Centre for Gender Studies produced a lengthy and thoughtful article describing the stress women were experiencing in their working and domestic lives and advocating not the shunting of women back to the home but what they saw as genuine equality, the ending of all forms of discrimination and a redefinition of men's responsibilities towards their families (Zakharova *et al.* 1989: 56). In much of this writing there appeared a sense of exasperation with the prevailing tendency to lay the newly revealed problems of society at women's door. As Zoia Pukhova had put it in her 19th Party Conference speech, 'Women should not be blamed as the source of all evil' (Redaktsionnaia kollegiia 1988: 11).

Yet as the decade progressed the overwhelming majority of the writing on women which appeared in the Soviet press was indeed doing just that. Writers, artists and academics produced pieces and gave interviews which were little more than thinly veiled misogyny. Advocating an end to the virtually automatic granting of child custody to the mother as a means of making women think twice about divorce, one psychologist, for example, wrote with evident distaste of what he saw as women's unreasonable demands on their husbands in the early years of marriage. Time, however, was on the husband's side: 'when she's 30–35, he's 35–37. He has become an interesting young Candidate of Sciences while she's become a middle-aged woman' (Egides 1986: 13). Pieces such as this, written, incidentally, by a Candidate of Sciences, in which women were portrayed as manipulative, sullen, aggressive, hysterical and in need of receiving their come-uppance littered the pages of the press through the late 1980s. With the new emphasis on women's lot at work some of these writers expressed sympathy for the many trials women were obliged to suffer yet, at the end of the day, would hammer home a message that had not changed one iota from the heyday of the pronatalist campaign. The playwright, Edward Radzinskii, for example, in just such a piece, announced that his ideal woman was one 'who is happy not because of the happiness she experiences but because of the happiness she brings' (Ershova 1987: 32). Small wonder, then, that according to public opinion polls at the end of the decade, most men believed women were paying less attention to their family responsibilities than they should (Sazonov 1991: 4).

Indeed, if members of the intelligentsia managed to produce some kind of veneer for their misogyny, many readers who wrote into the national press during this period felt no such scruples:

> In our free society women have been cherished and put on pedestals for seventy years, while men have been brought down lower and lower every year. Aren't the things Soviet power brought you enough for you women today?

> Women today are too free, independent and self-sufficient. No obstacles exist for them.

> What's it like for us men? We come home from work tired and hungry and there's no-one at home – the wife is at work or queueing for food. . . . Everything's empty – both your home and your heart. I think that only a family where there's a strong man supported by the angelic generosity of a woman, his wife, the mother of his children, can form the foundation of our country's power.
>
> (Vasil'eva 1987: 3; 'Zhenshchina ishchet sebia' 1988: 5)

Though by no means all the men who wrote in expressed themselves so uncompromisingly, the message was almost always the same. As one man, anxious to distance himself from the more rabid writers on the subject and offer his credentials as a cook and helper around the home, summed the matter up, 'Give men the chance to feel like men. Bring back the joy of finding your wife waiting to meet you at the threshold' ('Semeinyi klimat: vchera i segodnia' 1988: 10).

In this, at last, lay the heart of the matter. Amid all the talk of caring for children, of women's natural destiny, the special nature of the female psyche and other such 'semi-literate psychological twaddle', as Larisa Kuznetsova summed it up, lay the simple fact that the 'back to the home' lobby was profoundly attractive to men. For the entire debate was founded on the premise that women's participation in paid work could now be rationally questioned, and indeed was questioned constantly. At the same time, to question their responsibility for unpaid work was to be a voice crying in the wilderness. For most people with a view to express on this subject it went without saying that there was one half of the 'double shift' that women would work, come what may. The only issue was how far they needed to be let off the paid work in order to have enough time for the unpaid.

While surveys consistently found women putting in almost as many hours at home as in the workplace and the majority of men doing little or no domestic work, a tidal wave of exhortations and admonishments to women to put the family first continued to pour out of the Soviet media. The clichés of pronatalism, endlessly repeated, had been elevated to the status of eternal truths. 'Woman is destined by nature to be a mother, a wife, the custodian of the family hearth', intoned male journalists introducing documentaries on women's employment. Taking it as axiomatic that a capacity to give birth implied a contract to care for the male sex for the duration of their lives produced the awesome logic that not caring sufficiently was 'unnatural'. Any doubt that the care of men, rather than children, was the central issue on the agenda can be dispelled by a brief glance at the group of women singled out for the most venomous treatment during the perestroika years: not, as one might imagine, the heartless divorcees with their semi-orphaned children, but women who, for whatever reason, had never been married. If commentators expressed sympathy for men who had been unable to 'fulfil the function of creator and protector instilled in men by nature herself', there was nothing but censure for single women from psychologists, doctors and, most curiously, a collection of women writers and poets. The cause, apparently, was 'their own stupidity, egotism and an underestimation of the role of the family in a person's life'. 'In my opinion', announced the writer, Viktoria Tokareva, 'the greatest damage done to society comes from single women and men who are layabouts' (Tokareva 1987: 8–12, 53; Minasian 1988: 10).

If single women were left in little doubt that their behaviour was deviant, women with successful careers were increasingly to be found stressing the importance of their family life. Those who did not were often apologetic or defensive about their position or evidently felt unable to declare their love for their work without at least some small preamble. Zoia Novozhilova, Soviet ambassador to Switzerland, for example, when asked which was more important to her, work or family, replied, 'I can tell you without the slightest embarrassment and without even having to think about it that the main thing, the greatest joy in my life is work, work and once again work', clearly betraying in this response a recognition that this had now become a daring thing to say (Mekhontsev 1988: 12). For the older generation of Soviet heroines the 'back to the home' drive might well feel like the world turned upside down: women cosmonauts, for example, who had trained alongside Tereshkova in the 1960s expressed bewilderment at the new orthodoxy, while Tereshkova herself criticised the prevalence of reactionary views on women 'reminiscent of the *domostroi*' ('Vsesoiuznaia konferentsiia zhenshchin . . .' 1987: 3).[3]

35

Yet, for the advocates of perestroika in the family, women such as these were precisely the symbols of a former age that they were intent on sweeping away. If women had been artificially drawn away from their traditional place in society then blame for this had to be apportioned and the culprit, of course, was not hard to find. 'Emancipation', as it was understood in Soviet society, was clearly to blame. In a country where women were better educated than men, initiated most of the divorces, made up almost half the workforce yet still did the vast majority of unpaid domestic work, the obvious question to ask was, 'hasn't emancipation gone too far?' In the discussion which ensued, the prescription for emancipation which came under scrutiny was the classic Marxist–Leninist precept of drawing women into full-time waged labour. On top of this were added popular notions of women no longer knowing their place. As Svetlana Kaidish, writing in *Moscow News* in 1988, ironically noted, 'If she's saddled with a job, the children and the housekeeping, it's because she's emancipated, so let her pay for it' (Kaidash 1988: 13).

As the debates raged on in the Soviet press, words such as emancipation, egalitarianism and equality were more and more frequently preceded by the adjective 'accursed'. Words like these 'stick in everybody's throat', are 'a nightmare', readers said. From a position where the deeply flawed concept of emancipation of the old communist model could now be criticised, it was but a short step to throw the baby out with the bath-water. In the clamour to shout down the power of the old, the new could simply not be heard. It was not merely that those who sought new definitions and solutions to the problems women faced were in a tiny minority; it was, much more disturbingly, that their language had been hijacked. Emancipation, liberation, equality were dirty words from the Stalinist past, only to be employed with heavy irony. What hope, then, for a new discourse of empowerment for women when the very vocabulary of change was proving absolutely unusable?

The immediate answer was that the prospects were far from good. As the linguist, Galina Iakusheva, observed, the prevailing discourse was aiming at precisely the opposite. By 1990, the manifestos of parliamentary candidates tacitly or even quite openly embraced the following logic:

'Make women sit at home with their children for about three years. That will make them financially dependent on their husbands and it will make the husbands more responsible. That way women won't go rushing off to petition for divorce so easily.' . . . Centuries of human experience show us that materially dependent women don't leave their husbands, like serfs don't leave the village.

(Iakusheva 1990: 17)

More worrying still for the future of women was the way in which the language of nationalism was increasingly making its presence felt in the political arena. As centrifugal forces began to pull the USSR apart, some of the most outspoken reformers at the heart of Russian politics were already beginning to identify the family as central to the regeneration of the nation. In August 1990, for example, after the Congress of People's Deputies of the Russian Federation had voted in favour of Russian sovereignty, no less a figure than Boris Yeltsin gave an interview to the major Soviet women's magazine, *Rabotnitsa*, in which he assured its twenty-four million subscribers that, 'mother, child and family have always come first for the peoples of Russia' (Skliar 1990: 5). These attitudes, emanating as they did from the highest levels, underline once again an absence of radicalism in policies relating to women, even in an era when radical reform was the order of the day in all other areas. Behind Yeltsin's words lay an intention to strengthen social attitudes on women's roles, transforming them into a central plank of domestic policy.

As the new decade began, then, the overwhelming thrust of the discussion on women and the family was that women's primary responsibility lay in the home. If the media deluge had made it very plain that this was exactly what a substantial number of men wanted, little attention had been paid to what this might mean. The assumption was simply made, as was apparent from the manifestos of would-be politicians, that, when a man was supported by a stable and caring home life, he would automatically become industrious, faithful, sober and have an appropriate income to boot. When the focus had been so firmly placed on women's misdemeanours, men's righteousness was simply taken as read. Yet, in the light of the evidence available on the state of personal relationships in the 1980s, this was an extremely dangerous assumption to make. Even on the issue of income, the 'back to the home' lobby was on far from secure ground. Although the ability of some groups of workers to strike for higher pay began to change the situation by the late 1980s, most families still required two incomes in order to live with some degree of comfort. On the moral aspects of the case the evidence was shakier still. For two decades women's divorce petitions, surveys and the reports of women activists had catalogued or hinted at male alcohol abuse, violence and infidelity. The upright and loving husband who could genuinely support his wife's return to full-time motherhood had, as one observer put it, 'become an endangered species' (Kuznetsova 1988: 23).

Whether it was desirable in such a situation to encourage women out of the workforce was a matter for debate. At the very least it could be said that the USSR still had a system of benefits, however much they might be criticised as inadequate, and a range of public services to support women who left full-time employment. Yet how much longer this would last was becoming a matter for conjecture. Policies which might appear rational and attractive to women themselves within the confines of a planned economy would look very different when this was swept away. Where the triumph of the 'back to the home' campaign became particularly disturbing was in its timing. For women living through the final days of the Soviet state, its consequences could be serious enough. For those who were about to be hit by the waves of market forces, the results were likely to be little short of catastrophic.

2

WOMEN AND UNEMPLOYMENT

As the Russian Federation embarked on its independent existence in January 1992, the legacy of twenty years of Soviet pronatalism was imported lock, stock and barrel into policies concerning women in both the domestic and economic spheres. This heritage has, not surprisingly, placed women in an especially vulnerable position as the cold winds of job insecurity and unemployment have begun to blow. The rationale, first introduced in the Gorbachev era, that easing women out of the workforce would kill the two birds of social disintegration and growing unemployment with one stone, has been eagerly adopted by Russia's new rulers, so vehement in their condemnation of virtually all other aspects of late Soviet policy. This tunnel vision where these issues are concerned was not then unique to the Soviet radical reformists, as described in the previous chapter, but has continued on, even beyond the death of the Soviet Union itself.

Russia embarked on its course of fast-track, market-based reforms even before the demise of the Soviet empire in January 1992. It was assumed by both Russian and foreign economists that this would lead very quickly to widespread unemployment. This prediction was based on what had been observed in other East European societies making a similar transition from a centrally administered economy to one governed by market forces. It was therefore thought that structural change involving the conversion of the military–industrial complex to consumer-goods production, privatisation of state-run enterprises and the closure of obsolete and inefficient establishments would bring about a wave of mass redundancies. However, the policy implemented by the Russian government and Central Bank in an attempt to shore up the floundering economy has meant that official Russian unemployment statistics tell a quite different story to the one expected.

The Russian economy was already in a parlous condition prior to the introduction of price liberalisation in January 1992. Production had fallen to 81 per cent of its 1988 level by the time the Russian Federation began its independent existence and this, combined with the crisis of payment between enterprises, had created a vicious circle in which cash flow problems and debts had brought many companies to a standstill (Luk'ianchenko 1993b: 1). However, in order to bolster industry, the Russian government released billions of roubles in credits through the Central Bank, thus saving these enterprises from complete bankruptcy and staving off mass unemployment.

One year into marketisation, in December 1992, only 577,700 people were officially registered as unemployed and, although this number was predicted to grow to five million by the end of 1993, in September of that year official statistics still only gave a figure of 716,000 people out of work, 1 per cent of the active population (Khudiakova 1993a: 2). Even the bankruptcy law which had come into effect on 1 March 1993 had not by August 1994 caused the expected spate of liquidations and attendant mass redundancies. In part, this phenomenon was due to the input of government credit, which continued despite both its direct link to high inflation and regular government statements that this source of funding would soon dry up.

Behind this picture of a workforce apparently untroubled by the market reforms, two more worrying aspects of change had quickly emerged. Firstly, the officially recorded level of unemployment massively underestimated the numbers actually affected by lay-offs: the phenomenon of 'hidden unemployment', as we discuss on p. 53, had reached substantial proportions by 1993. Secondly, redundancies and lay-offs were not evenly spread across the workforce. From its very beginnings the new wave of unemployment was disproportionately affecting women. Since the first months of Russian independence, the frequently quoted 70:30 female:male ratio among the unemployed has been one of the few apparently stable factors in a picture which is otherwise often unclear and marred by conflicting reports and an ever-changing landscape.

The underlying reasons for women's vulnerability in the emerging Russian labour market form the focus of this chapter. The Soviet legacy of occupational segregation, discrimination at work and protective legislation are examined as a background to a discussion of current levels of unemployment, both official and hidden. If debates in the Soviet media had prepared the ideological ground for women to return to the home, the position of women within the workforce ensured that, when cut-backs occurred, they would be the first to go.

THE IMPACT OF OCCUPATIONAL SEGREGATION

Women's position in the Soviet labour force has made them particularly vulnerable to changing circumstances in the new Russia. Occupational segregation was a pronounced feature of the workforce, and was characterised by both exclusively female professions and by women's jobs within 'male' professions. Nearly 80 per cent of working women have been employed in 'female' sectors and jobs, where over 70 per cent of the personnel are women (Mezentseva 1994b: 111).[1] Table 1 illustrates the concentration of female workers in certain sectors of the national economy and the relative rates of pay in those sectors. This feminisation of specific sectors has had a particular effect on women's position as workers, both historically, in the Soviet Union, and today, as the new Russian labour market begins to experience the phenomenon of unemployment. Soviet women's pay levels were never on a par with those of their male colleagues. This wage differential has been linked to gender segregation in the labour force:

> Zakharova et al. (1989: 62) suggest, with particular reference to the low pay of Soviet doctors who are predominantly women, that the low pay in female-dominated sectors is a cause of the feminisation of such sectors. Alternatively, the sequence may be the reverse, and occupational crowding may be the cause of the low pay.
>
> (Chapman 1991: 185)

Whichever of these explanations is closer to the truth, and it seems likely that a combination of the two will have influenced the situation, women's concentration in low-level jobs and low-status professions has left them especially vulnerable in view of the change in course of the country's economy.

Women may be hit in various ways by economic change. As shown in Table 1, women in the caring professions have received some of the lowest levels of pay. These women are public sector employees and, although their jobs have not necessarily become redundant, they are greatly affected by the degeneration and underfunding of all areas of this sector. The lack of money available in these institutions has kept salaries depressed and has led to extensive delays in the payment of wages. These workers, who are paid directly from the state budget have been dubbed *biudzhetniki*, and are frequently cited in discussions of the growing problems of poverty and falling living standards. A characteristic story was told to a female reporter at a jumble sale, which she stumbled upon while visiting a Moscow computer centre:

Table 1 Feminisation of certain sectors of the labour force and relative levels of pay

Sector of the labour force	Women as percentage of workforce	Average wage as percentage of national average
National economy	48	100
Non-manual occupations:		
Medicine	86	69[a]
Education and science	73	78[b]
Planning and accounts	88	93[c]
Manual occupations:		
Trade and catering	89	75
Services	89	76
Communication	84	89
Textiles	83	94
Clothing	93	81

Sources: Vestnik statistiki 1991: 39–40; *Narodnoe khoziaistvo v SSSR v 1988g.* 1989: 77–8, 377–8

Notes: [a] This figure is for all workers in health and social security.

[b] This figure is for education alone, in science average wages were 113 per cent of the national average in 1988.

[c] This figure is for those employed in administration; in credit and insurance average earnings were 94 per cent of the national average.

'You see that woman over there, the tall one, who has already got a whole pile of things in her arms. That's our Anna Mikhailovna, the biudzhetnitskaia mother. . . . This woman, Anna Mikhailovna, . . . had three grown up daughters and six grandchildren already. All her daughters, as if to spite themselves, had ended up in state-paid professions – one was a teacher, one a librarian and one a nurse. . . . Yes, even their husbands were all on the same state-financed pay roll. All in all they get paid very little. . . . We call her the "*biudzhetnitskaia* mother" ' said my friend, 'Every third month she spends her entire salary here at these second-hand children's clothes sales.' This '*biudzhetnitskaia* mother', with her bundle of worn out little cardigans and kids trousers, appeared in my mind's eye when I heard an analysis of wage levels in the state-financed sector at the Russian Ministry for Labour. 'The wages of half the workers in the state-financed sector, continue to be below the level of subsistence. These wages are half the level of the industrial wage.'

(Levina 1994c: 11)

The low level of women's wages also plays a role in encouraging families to see the loss of a woman's job as preferable to and less traumatic than the loss of her husband's wage. The preponderance of this type of attitude is of obvious advantage to policy-makers, who have shown their clear preference for returning women to the home, rather than protecting their right to employment. The discrepancy between male and female wages further facilitates the argument that a correct policy would be one of simply increasing men's pay to a level where this would be sufficient to support a family without the extra income brought in by a working wife and mother. Regardless of this political agenda, however, the very nature of some of the fields of work which have become highly feminised puts women in danger of redundancy.

Women have predominated in white-collar professions such as book-keeping and government administration; according to the 1989 census, 98 per cent of bookkeepers and 93 per cent of economists, the vast majority of whom were employed by state enterprises, were women (Rzhanitsina 1993: 21). These professions were inextricably linked with the planning and administering of the Soviet economic system. Once this system was swept aside and replaced with market-based mechanisms, requiring far less government and bureaucratic input, these women found themselves in redundant posts.

This has also been true for women employed in certain jobs in industry. Women have been in the majority among workers in communications and trade and catering, both areas that worked in close conjunction with the relevant Soviet ministries and were as a result particularly guilty of hoarding labour and having to fulfil unnecessary bureaucratic functions. In the Soviet era, the hoarding of labour was a national phenomenon found in every enterprise and institution to compensate for the shortages and irregular deliveries and to guarantee that the plan would be fulfilled (Kuznetsov 1994: 964). One of the most pertinent illustrations of the extent of this practice can be seen in the Soviet tradition of 'patronage assistance'. This was an extremely widespread phenomenon which involved enterprises and institutions in sending their employees out into the countryside free of charge to work in agriculture, vegetable stores and other areas where there was a temporary demand for labour (Kostakov 1991: 89). Although 'patronage assistance' may have served a useful purpose in its time, it was a symptom of an ineffective use and distribution of the labour force. In addition, in white-collar work, there were thousands of unproductive clerical workers and underemployed specialists in the Soviet Union, most of whom were women. One of our interviewees who had been previously employed as an engineer in the defence industry characterised her old job in these scathing terms:

> When there wasn't any work to do the boss would make you look as if you were working and you just sat in this sort of post-box with armed guards all round, you couldn't go out. . . . I just had to sit there and pretend! The worst thing was that the work I did was completely unnecessary.
>
> [30]

Women such as this were not at all surprised to find themselves made redundant when an attempt was made to rationalise the system and cut down on overspending. Their understanding of the situation has done little, however, to sweeten the pill of redundancy and its attendant material hardships for them and their families.

Women engineers and technical personnel concentrated in science and research are in danger of unemployment, since they work in areas where there has been a problem of overemployment handed down from the Soviet era (Rzhanitsina 1993: 11). Fifty-nine per cent of engineers and 70 per cent of technicians were women at the time of the 1989 census (Rzhanitsina 1993: 21). When the question of thinning out the labour force in these sectors has arisen, it has been the women who have been the first to go, while men employed in these same professions have been more likely to be retained. The reasons for this discriminatory redundancy policy are manifold. It can in part be attributed to women's disadvantaged position in terms of professional training and skill levels, which has been described in the previous chapter (p. 19). It is also, however, a result of continuing support for protective legislation and pronatalist social policy which are considered in more detail on p. 46.

Another side to this many-faceted problem is seen in the case of industries such as textiles and clothing where the entire workforce has been overwhelmingly feminised. The Soviet planned economy caused certain regions to concentrate solely on one form of production: Ivanovo region, for example, was a principal centre for the textile industry. The vast majority of the local population was employed in the mills and, since this was seen as a women's profession, there was an outmigration of men and Ivanovo became known as a *zhenskii krai* or women's region. Beset by a plethora of obstacles and problems, not least of which have been competition from cheap imports and the loss of an internal supply network of raw materials from Uzbekistan and Turkmenistan, the mills have come to a standstill. Although official unemployment had still been restricted to only 5.7 per cent in July 1994, short-time working and unpaid leave were already rife and causing widespread hardship and unrest, especially given the lack of any alternative employment prospects in this highly specialised town (Hearst 1994: 7).

PROMOTION, TRAINING AND RESPONSIBILITY

Even within sectors employing both men and women there is a definite pattern to be seen in terms of the type of jobs which are done by male or by female workers. Office jobs and clerical work have been clearly marked out as a woman's sphere and, while many women have been promoted into middle-management positions, jobs with higher levels of responsibility tend to have been reserved for men. Although 49 per cent of management positions overall were held by women at the time of the 1989 census, feminist sociologist Elena Mezentseva points out that, while 50 per cent of men with higher or vocational secondary education are employed at the management level, only 7 per cent of women graduates can expect to end up in a managerial post (Mezentseva 1994a: 115). Instead, women with higher education often work in tedious and routine jobs where their knowledge and qualifications go unused and where their potential is unrecognised and undervalued. Once again this situation left women in the most vulnerable position when reorganisation of the management structure, changes in accounting procedures and the curtailment of certain types of activity in this sphere connected with the ending of the administrative–command system caused a first wave of redundancies in 1991–2.

In blue-collar jobs, the well-documented gap between men's and women's skill gradings and management reluctance to support on-the-job training for women has condemned many women to remain in monotonous routine jobs (McAuley 1981). Despite the suggestions of some psychologists promoting the idea of gender differences, this has not been caused by some female preference for simple work. Women have done these jobs because they have had no choice (Rzhanitsina 1993: 6). In the transition to a market economy, when cut-backs make job losses inevitable, these women face the threat of redundancy, since they are simply not able to compete with their better qualified male colleagues.

The concentration of women in poorly paid, low-skilled, low-prestige jobs has encouraged a view of them as easily disposable members of the labour force. However, the very fact that women have done the least rewarding and most badly paid jobs gives them a certain value in their employers' eyes. A survey of forty-three people in top management positions, carried out in 1990, found that 77 per cent were in agreement with the statement, 'It will be hard to find candidates for many of the jobs currently done by women, since they will not be attractive to men' (Rzhanitsina 1993: 98). Nonetheless, the prevailing view is that women are more troublesome as employees, the result being that although men might prefer not to do certain 'women's' jobs, employers would prefer that they did.

PROTECTIVE LEGISLATION: THE COST OF EMPLOYING WOMEN

As we have already seen, the pronatalist policies initiated in the Brezhnev period, carried over through the period of perestroika and on into the new Russian Federation encourage the view of women as being primarily family oriented and destined to be wives and mothers. This policy and its associated propaganda has, not surprisingly, had a considerable impact on women's role in the national economy and their position as employees.

When a new draft Russian employment law was published in 1993, those concerned about women's position in the labour market were eager to see how it would handle issues of discrimination and protective legislation. Point one of article 11 began well on the subject of equal opportunities, stating that,

> No one shall be limited in their labour rights, nor shall they have any advantage in the implementation of these rights on the grounds of sex, age, race, nationality . . . religious persuasion . . . or other circumstances not pertaining to their professional abilities as a worker or the results of their labour.

Point two of the same article, however, promptly undermined these words with the following proviso:

> Differences in the spheres of work, brought about by the particular demands of a given type of work or by the state's special concern for individuals in need of extra social protection (women, minors, people with disabilities) do not count as discrimination.
> ('Osnovy zakonodatel'stva . . .' 1993: 3)

As feminist economist, Zoia Khotkina, has pointed out, this does not provide women with equal opportunities, but instead labels them 'social invalids' who, as she foresees, may be forced into specialised workplaces or 'female ghettos' rather than integrated into the main workforce (Khotkina 1994: 98–9, 101). This prediction might be less likely to be dismissed as simply feminist rhetoric if placed alongside a statement made by Georgy Kanaev of the All-Union Central Council of Trade Unions of the USSR (AUCCTU) back in 1991. Writing on the prospect of unemployment as a result of perestroika's rationalisation of the Soviet economic system, Kanaev points out that, 'The national employment system is incapable of protecting people from unemployment and of finding new jobs for certain categories of people, notably the handicapped, youth and women' (Kanaev 1991: 267). Here again we see the Soviet roots of a contemporary Russian attitude to women and their place in employment.

This view of women as a group of social invalids continues to prevail. As a result, a great deal of Soviet protective legislation has been imported directly into the chapter of this draft Russian employment law which relates specifically to women and labour. For example, under article 140, employers are obliged to provide women who have infants up to the age of eighteen months with less strenuous jobs and, if no such work is available, to send them home on leave on full pay until it is. Article 142, on maternity leave, entitles all women to seventy days before and seventy days after the birth with full pay to be guaranteed by their employer. The same article also provides various options for extended leave, including the right to three years' unpaid leave with the woman's job held open for her to return ('Osnovy zakonodatel'stva . . .' 1993: 6). Such stipulations may have been feasible in the Soviet era, when women were in any case employed in state industries and it was an employer's responsibility to provide special work regimes or maternity pay. However, with the advent of private enterprise and a new profit-based rationale this is no longer the case.

As suggested by the wording of point two, article 11, the new law does in fact go on to provide for the explicit exclusion of women from certain areas of employment. Continuing the trends set in the Soviet period, the draft law forbids the employment of women in work in poor conditions, mining or other underground work and work involving the lifting of heavy weights. Pregnant women and women with children under the age of three are also banned from doing overtime, working the night shift or going on business trips, whatever their personal feelings on the matter. Just as before, however, where it suits the interests of the management, these stipulations are likely to be largely ignored. According to official figures quoted in *Rabotnitsa* magazine, in January 1994 'over 3.6 million women are working under poor working conditions, of whom 290,000 are working in particularly bad and health damaging spheres of production' (Levina 1994a: 11).

These same provisions are, however, taken very seriously by those aiming to justify women's exclusion from the workforce both in terms of improving production and of benefiting society as a whole, by increasing women's involvement in family life. The idea that women are a nuisance as employees is one which has been carefully cultivated in order to support their permanent removal from paid employment. As one female journalist writing for the loosely feminist newspaper *Delovaia zhenshchina* (*Business Woman*) caustically observed, 'it is obvious that an employer will strive, using every available means to be rid of such a capricious and frail worker' (Kononova 1992: 6). Over half of the interviewees involved in the managers' survey mentioned above expressed the opinion that female redundancies were a positive phenomenon which would, they believed, lead to production running more smoothly without women taking time off to have babies, look after sick children or due to their own ill health (Rzhanitsina 1993: 98). These arguments are given official weight by the stated aim of protective labour legislation, which has always been 'to ensure more favourable conditions for fulfilling women's motherhood functions' ('Rossiiskaia Federatsiia Doklad . . .' 1993: 35). Managers in favour of reducing women's involvement in the workforce also see as a benefit that 'liberating' women from paid employment would improve family relations. Eighty-six per cent of the sample of managers felt that this would be an automatic spin-off, since 'women will be able to give more time to their families, husbands and to bringing up their children' (Rzhanitsina 1993: 96).

This attitude to women was epitomised by the draft family law which was discussed in the Russian parliament throughout the second half of 1992, and which aimed to highlight women's role in bringing up children, not bringing in a wage. As a part of the continuing drive to return women to the home, this bill proposed to establish a norm of part-time work for women by requiring any woman with a child under the age of fourteen years to work no more than thirty-five hours per week.[2] It would be erroneous to imagine that such an outrageous proposal was spawned solely by parliamentarians pursuing a political agenda of pronatalism and strengthening the family. In fact such ideas had already taken so strong a hold on Russian society that a study carried out in 1990 at the huge truck manufacturing plant, Kamaz, based in Tataria, found that for no less than six years the management had been paying a sum of 100 roubles a month, no mean amount at the time, to numerous women with children just in order that they should stay at home. When questioned on the logic of this approach, the manager in charge of the enterprise's finances agreed that this programme cost millions of roubles. He went on to point out that the company's policy on this topic was 'a very simple one: our aim is that there should be no women in production' (Posadskaya 1994: 197).

Whatever the social, economic or political arguments which might be brought to bear for and against such a policy, one important factor which its proponents fail time and again to mention is what women themselves feel on the subject. From the mid-1970s onwards, numerous sociological surveys in the former Soviet Union posed the question, 'Would you be prepared to give up work if your husband earned an adequate wage?' The overwhelming response from women of all age groups and social backgrounds was consistently negative. The wording of this question reflects the prevailing presumption of those in favour of women's withdrawal from the labour force, that women only work as a result of financial need. Their proposed solution to this problem has therefore been either simply to raise male wages, or to introduce an alternative source of income. Vladimir Kostakov of the Scientific Institute for Economics under the USSR State Planning Committee, writing in 1991 on the desirability of reducing women's 'excessive employment levels', was convinced that 'It would be possible to reduce their demands for employment through a well-thought-out benefit policy' (Kostakov 1991: 97). Women's consistent responses to the survey question cited above, however, did not back up this theory. Our contact with Russian women in the 1990s would certainly suggest that, now, as then, Russian women want to work, and not only in order to earn a living:

> A woman who stays at home all day becomes spiritually drained. She needs some kind of stimulation, to get out to an exhibition, to have some contact with people. I think I would just get spiritually exhausted if I were at home all day stuck inside four walls. Monotony wears people out. It presses down on you.
>
> [24]

This speaker and her colleague were still in full-time employment, although they had both experienced short-term unemployment. Elaborating on this theme they suggested that younger women with less life-experience than themselves would probably be more attracted to the idea of a housewife's existence. This supposition was not born out by our interviews with women in the younger age group. Two nineteen-year-old fashion students expressed the following opinions on the importance of a woman's career and the choice between work and family:

> A career is important, of course, but there comes a point when a woman should give it up and go back to the family. Of course it depends on the woman, on her character. I couldn't be just a housewife, staying at home all day. If I had children to bring up then

maybe, but just like that no way. If you just had to stay at home all day, no it's unbearable.

[35]

I think work is very important. I don't know about *all* women, but speaking for myself I know I would just die of boredom. I'm not saying a family's a bad thing, of course you should have a family, but work is essential. And not just anything, but interesting work which you love.

[36]

Repeatedly the women we interviewed said that for a woman to stay at home was a fine thing, as long as it suited her particular personality and aspirations. However, most of our interviewees did not feel that this was a choice they wanted to make for themselves, and it was certainly not one which they appreciated having made for them or which they felt should be imposed on women *en masse*.

In an attempt to protect women from employers' eagerness to rid themselves of their female workforce, article 149 of the draft employment law stipulates that employers cannot make a woman redundant because she is pregnant or has young children under the age of three, unless the whole enterprise goes into liquidation ('Osnovy zakonodatel'stva . . .' 1993: 6). This article is also clearly being evaded. Employers may not officially sack these women, yet the fact that they are not wanted is made abundantly clear to them. In the words of one of our interviewees, who had had to resort to homeworking as a way of supporting herself and her young child:

I was on maternity leave. I am in the position of being a single mother and so of course I am in need. I would never have dreamed of leaving work. I worked as a construction engineer in the military–industrial complex. There were staff cut-backs at work, and although they couldn't sack me as a single mother, it was obvious that no one expected me back.

[4]

Even in cases such as this where the woman involved knows her rights, and many do not, this type of overt discrimination goes unchallenged (Oleinik 1993: 7). The draft law stipulates that a woman has the right to take to court an enterprise which does sack or refuse to employ her because she is pregnant or is due maternity benefits. However, this is clearly unlikely to occur. In any country, whatever the support system, it is a daunting proposition for an individual to take on a large organisation in the courts. In Russia, where social attitudes weight the system so heavily against the woman and where compensation, should it be awarded, is likely to be negligible, it is hardly surprising if women cannot see the point in initiating such a process. Indeed, official attitudes to a woman's right to employment, despite such paper legislation, were amply highlighted when the Minister for Labour, Gennady Melikian made the following remark at a press conference in February 1993:

> Why should we employ women when men are unemployed? It is better that men work and women take care of children and do the housework. I do not want women to be offended, but I seriously don't think that women should work while men are doing nothing.[3]
>
> (Martin 1993: 7)

Women's position in paid employment is, therefore, at best extremely tenuous. The Soviet legacy is one of segregation, undertraining and the concentration of women in expendable posts. To this has been added an ongoing policy aimed at returning women to the home and protecting their ability to reproduce as their main function. The result is a fatal combination which has a devastating effect when placed in the context not of a communist society boasting full employment, but of a country facing the prospect of widespread unemployment as it attempts to make the transition to a free market economy.

UNEMPLOYMENT: OFFICIAL AND HIDDEN LEVELS

At least 70 per cent of Russia's unemployed are women and this was already very much the case as early as 1992. Even while national and international commentators were remarking cheerily on the very limited levels of unemployment being recorded, reports were coming in from regions all across the Russian Federation, and from both industrial and agricultural centres, of a bias towards female redundancies of up to 80 per cent. Once made redundant, women experience greater difficulty than men in finding a new job. In 1993 the average length of a redundancy was four months for a man, but five months for a woman ('Rossiiskaia Federatsiia Doklad . . .' 1993: 34). Although it is becoming increasingly difficult for women school-leavers and graduates to find work, the majority of unemployed women are over thirty years old (Rzhanitsina 1993: 73). Some of these women are of pre-retirement age and may have been retired early on either a voluntary or a compulsory basis. Nevertheless, the largest group among the urban unemployed appears to be middle-aged mothers with fifteen–twenty years' work experience, usually in one place of work, where they have been employed since graduating with either secondary, secondary technical or higher education (Beliaev 1992: 2).[4]

One of the reasons for the high profile of this group is that the first waves of redundancies have occurred in heavily 'feminised' spheres where there is a large proportion of women with higher and specialised secondary education (Rzhanitsina 1993: 7). Specialists in white-collar professions, for example, engineers, economists, technicians, administrative and research staff, were all among the first to be affected. In Moscow, where there is an especially high concentration of research institutes employing women in these professions, they account for 66 per cent of all the capital's registered unemployed.[5]

In November 1993, an investigation carried out by the State Statistics Committee (Goskomstat) found that, although Russian official figures still placed unemployment at 1 per cent of the economically active population, according to international criteria 5 per cent of the potential working population was in fact jobless and a further 5.4 per cent, or some four million people, were no longer employed on a full-time basis (Deliagin 1994: 1). This combined figure of approximately 10 per cent was also in line with the figure then put forward by Guy Standing of the ILO (Khudiakova 1993a: 2). One year on in November 1994, a new ILO report described an exacerbation of this situation. This report pointed out that, although government statistics still placed the jobless rate in Russia at 1.6 per cent, open unemployment had, in reality, reached almost 10 per cent, while 'suppressed unemployment' – workers sent home on 'administrative leave' without pay – stood at more than one-third of the workforce (Luce 1994: 16). The reasons for this discrepancy stem from several sources.

The additional 8.4 per cent among what are described as the openly unemployed may to some extent be accounted for by a reluctance on the part of both enterprises and individuals to go through the official redundancy procedure. Employers may fail to inform the Federal Employment Service of redundancies in order to avoid having to pay severance monies. Even those enterprises which are following the letter of the law may not inform job centres immediately when they make workers redundant and these workers will not be able to register for unemployment benefit for three months while they receive redundancy pay. These factors obviously cause a delay in the updating of unemployment statistics. However, even once they are entitled to claim benefit, many of the unemployed do not bother to register with an employment centre because they see the system, which is very similar to the British model, as complicated and time-wasting for negligible levels of benefit. This attitude is especially prevalent in rural areas and small towns, where only very few employment centres have so far been set up. For people living in these areas, visiting their 'local' centre may well involve an entire day of travel, costing a disproportionate amount of their prospective benefit simply in order to get there and back (Khudia-kova 1993a: 2).

The other twenty-four million jobless or semi-employed people must be attributed to a more complicated factor: the phenomenon of hidden unemployment (*skrytaia bezrabotitsa*). As factories and enterprises found themselves increasingly unable to continue production throughout 1992–3, but were not necessarily required to go into final liquidation, many chose, rather than taking the step of making the entire workforce redundant, to fall back instead on Soviet practices of hoarding labour. This can take several forms. Employees may be transferred to working on a short-time basis, putting in a three-day week or a two-week month and receiving *pro rata* rates of pay. This option is obviously preferred by enterprises which are still able to function to a limited extent. In other cases where production has come to a complete standstill, employees will be sent on what has been termed 'administrative leave'. This signifies a long-term lay-off which is usually entirely unpaid. This practice had become so widespread by December 1993 that the government was finally forced to introduce a system of benefits for people in this position. For many employees a combination of these two forms of hidden unemployment may come into play. An entire workforce may be sent to 'rest' for a period of two or three months and then be called back into work on a short-time basis for a while before once again returning to their administrative leave. Despite the high levels that hidden unemployment has reached, the Russian government and its western economic advisers have continued to underestimate and understate the problem, in the view of ILO researchers, 'in order to show that free market "shock therapy" is working' (Luce 1994: 16). In March 1994, I. Zaslavskii, head of Moscow's Department for Labour and Employment, said that unemployment 'was not a catastrophic problem' in the city. He based this assertion on the official figure of 16,300 unemployed, which represented 0.5 per cent of Moscow's working population. However, an additional 600,000 Muscovites were at the time experiencing hidden unemployment (Boikova 1994: 2).

Moscow's unemployment situation is, however, far from the worst example to be found in Russia today. In Riazan, for example, half of the town's entire workforce, including all employees of several enterprises, were on compulsory leave for the whole of the summer in 1993. This was sarcastically referred to as a long summer holiday by some of those affected who found it ironic that, while those in work were forgoing holidays in favour of overtime pay, they were in this position of enforced inactivity:

Not long ago I bumped into Valentina, who works at the metalwork and ceramics factory. She was looking tanned and healthy, so I potted the 'high society' question, 'So, how's things, have you been on holiday?'

'We've been on so-called holiday for three months already', Valia replied, 'I've been helping the old folks out in the countryside. To tell the truth they've been sending me food parcels all through the winter: potatoes and meat. And now's the time we ought to be the ones to be feeding them.'

(Novikova 1993: 8)

By dealing with enforced stoppages in this way, the employer is saved the cost of redundancies, can continue to receive government subsidies and retains a ready-trained and experienced workforce on the company's books. These workers can then be called back into work whenever the enterprise receives a contract for manufacture or has the materials necessary to restart production. Guy Standing of the ILO has characterised hidden unemployment as 'a cost-effective, though unfortunate, way of dealing with the crisis affecting the Russian labour markets' (Luce 1994: 16). Russian sociologist Leonid Gordon also sees certain advantages in hiding unemployment to some degree, though his argument is based on controlling popular unrest and dissatisfaction, not on saving employers' profits:

In many cases, especially where one-horse towns and populations with a single labour profile are in question, it is better not to throw thousands and tens of thousands of people out onto the streets all at once. It is better to draw out this process over a period of time, maintaining a limited and even fictitious level of employment.

(Gordon 1994: 8)

However, if, as the ILO now suggests, all forms of unemployment are as high as 40 per cent, the continued success in avoiding unrest is little short of astounding. Whatever the actual level of hidden unemployment and its short-term attractions, be they cost efficiency or keeping the population quiet, in the long term hidden unemployment is having a devastating effect on the population at large in terms of family incomes and general living standards, as we shall see in the following chapter.

54

3

LIVING STANDARDS: THE NOT SO SMOOTH TRANSITION TO THE MARKET

When the Soviet Union finally ceased to exist in January 1992 there was a sense of optimism and eager expectation in the newly independent Russian Federation. At last, with the burden of the Soviet legacy thrown off and communist rule utterly discredited, there was nothing to prevent a speedy and smooth transition to a free market economy. This contention was not limited to Russian opinion, but was also prevalent in western policy-makers' attitudes and commentaries. Unfortunately for the Russian population, however, the reality of price liberalisation, creeping unemployment, growing poverty and falling living standards has been anything but painless. It is these problems and pitfalls, together with the loss of the Soviet-style welfare state and the shortcomings of the new social security system, which this chapter aims to address, with particular reference to the impact of these developments on women. Since the perpetual changes taking place in Russian society make it impossible for any published work to be entirely up to date even at the time of going to print, statistical data in this chapter will focus on the period after the demise of the USSR and leading up to the two major pieces of fieldwork undertaken for this project in the summer of 1993 and in March 1994. In looking at these figures it is hoped that the reader will be able to build up a picture of what the transition to a market economy meant to the women we interviewed at that particular stage of its development.

Only late in 1993, prompted by the shock success of Vladimir Zhirinovsky's extreme right-wing party in the December elections, did western politicians begin to admit that things were not going entirely as planned in the Russian economy. The problems faced were then summed up by the Clinton administration's catch-phrase of 'too much shock and not enough therapy'. Within Russia itself, however, although the government had, up until this point at least, been relying on western support to maintain faith in its programme of reforms, various 'unofficial' and 'independent' voices, many of them women's voices, were already protesting about the effects of new economic policies on the living standards of the general population.

In April 1993 a conference of over 300 women, organised by the movement, 'Mothers for social justice', declared that, 'the present policy of an enforced and accelerated transition to an uncontrollable market economy, has made it impossible for women to produce and bring up their children, and has deprived the rising generation of a dignified future' (Shuvalova 1993: 1). This statement was designed to turn the audience's attention to the effects of increasing poverty and material hardship on women's willingness to bear children: a pertinent subject in a land preoccupied with its own declining birth rate. It also pointed out the predicament of those who had already become mothers. As we shall see later in this chapter (pp. 61–2, 65), children place a great strain on minimal family budgets and the privileges and benefits which formerly compensated for the expense of raising a child were, in 1993, rapidly disappearing or becoming worthless.

If anyone had been inclined to write off this protest as simply the reaction of a few panicky mothers, they would perhaps have been more ready to accept the results of an opinion poll, which was conducted at the first congress of the association 'Entrepreneurs for New Russia', held in August of the same year:

> Not a single respondent . . . assessed the economic situation in Russia as normal. Only 7 per cent evaluated it as 'on the whole satisfactory'. Another 28 per cent described it as tense; 54 per cent called it a crisis; and 11 per cent said it is catastrophic. . . . A total of 72 per cent of entrepreneurs are discontented with the implementation of reform in Russia. The rest are only satisfied to a degree.
>
> (Savin 1993: 3)

Alongside these more organised and formal criticisms of the reforms, came a flood of individual letters to the press, written mainly by women, especially single mothers, mothers of large families and old-age pensioners, complaining of desperate poverty and often begging for help and financial support.

So how had it come to this? What had happened since January 1992 to turn euphoria into pessimism and despair and what, if any, responses did Russia's leaders have to offer to a population on whose support they and the success of reforms were ultimately dependent?

PRICE LIBERALISATION AND THE FALLING VALUE OF REAL WAGES

The first step in Russia's independent economic policy was the major price liberalisation which took place in January 1992. State control of retail and wholesale prices, which had once been universal, as well as state subsidies on all but a very few basic items such as bread and milk were removed virtually overnight. Predictably, the immediate result of this action was a huge leap in prices: inflation for that first month of 1992 was 252 per cent. Thereafter, however, the monthly rate declined, reaching a low point of 8 per cent in August, then bouncing back to 20 per cent in September 1992 and wavering at a level of between 20 and 30 per cent throughout 1993. Although this means that the economy has not, since January 1992, suffered from what is officially termed 'hyper inflation', since this is defined as a monthly rate of over 50 per cent, the effect on family budgets has been far from salutary. By the time the monthly inflation rate was brought back down to single figure levels in the second quarter of 1994, the damage, in terms of the living standards of the Russian population, had already been done.

The crux of the problem is that, although there has also been a considerable increase in wages, they have not in fact risen at the same rate as prices. From July to August 1993, for example, retail prices rose by 30 per cent while wages increased by only 20–2 per cent. A report published in the financial supplement to *Izvestiia* in December 1993 suggested that wage increases since the end of 1991 had only managed to compensate for 50 per cent of consumer price inflation (Nemova 1993: 2). The fall in annual inflation in 1993 did little to alleviate the strain on family budgets, since it was brought about largely by a reduced growth in prices for luxury goods, such as cars and televisions, while everyday essential items, like basic foods and medicines, were actually more seriously affected. A loaf of Russian black bread, for example, became nine times more expensive over the course of the year, and a litre of milk cost twelve times as much by the end of 1993 as it had in 1992 (Kolchin 1994: 8).

As a result of these trends the spending patterns of Russian workers has had to change. An ever increasing proportion of consumer spending has been taken up by the cost of buying food, while the amount spent on paid services and goods has fallen in order to compensate. Figure 1 illustrates the way in which family spending patterns changed with the advent of price liberalisation.

Because the figure represents average levels of spending, the actual situation will vary in individual families. By March 1994, however, 59 per

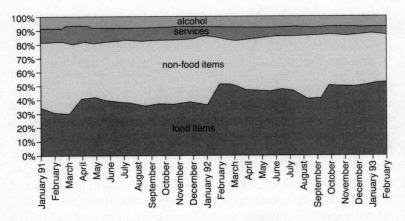

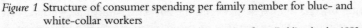

Figure 1 Structure of consumer spending per family member for blue- and white-collar workers
Source: Council of Ministers' working centre on economic reform (Luk'ianchenko 1993a: 4)

cent of respondents in a survey carried out by the All-Russia Centre for Public Opinion Research said that they spent almost their entire income on food; 19 per cent spent two-thirds; and 15 per cent approximately half. These responses suggest that the situation shown in Figure 1 had worsened substantially by this time. Moreover, 52 per cent of respondents felt that their families had begun recently to eat a poorer diet than previously (Arkhitektor 1994: 8). This reduction in the amount of money available for buying in services and consumer goods has hit the women in Russian families particularly hard. It is they who have to make up the deficit by doing for themselves the washing that they might previously have sent to the cleaners, repairing and altering old clothes and shoes and making do with ageing and often faulty household appliances. This added strain has in turn had an immediate effect on women's employment prospects. A young woman interviewed at a special women's job fair told reporters that although she was currently still employed she feared that she would soon be made redundant as a direct result of the increasing pressures of family life:

> Everything has become so expensive, you can't even dream of it. So it turns out that I have become the public caterer, the dry cleaner, the launderette and the repairs workshop. . . . By the time I get to work I'm exhausted. Before they used to praise me in the laboratory saying I was quick to catch on. But now the lab head says, 'Ania, I

don't recognise you. You've made five mistakes on one diagram. You want to watch out, you're first in line for the sack. I need workers who give their all.' Well and what can I say to him? He's right, how can I give my all now, when I get to work and I've already given all I have at home.

(Levina 1994a: 10)

These comments are made all the more salient when offset against the predominent rhetoric on the market's ability to release women from their double burden through improving the availability of consumer services. In actual fact, prices for services have risen more sharply than in any other sector, prohibiting rather than encouraging access.

Women are also likely to suffer the most individually, as a family collectively has to tighten its belt. As L. Rzhanitsina, a professor at the Institute of Economics, has pointed out, despite being the person who controls the majority of family spending, a wife and mother is most likely to economise on herself first and foremost while protecting her husband and children from the worst effects of a diminishing budget (Rzhanitsina 1993: 211–13).

THE GROWTH OF POVERTY AND FALLING LIVING STANDARDS

During the first two years of Russia's independent existence, the number of people struggling to survive on incomes that placed them and their dependants below the official poverty line was a source of constant concern to Russian sociologists. Although there was some contention about where the poverty line actually lay, the generally accepted version of what had been termed the subsistence minimum was based on a basket of nineteen basic food items which was initially devised in 1989 for the Shatalin 500 day programme.[1] The allocated quantities were designed to allow a daily intake of 1,600 kilocalories, which is approximately 20 per cent above the minimum needed to sustain a constant body weight. The foodstuffs included were still based on what was available in the shops in 1989, not a very exciting range of goods, as one might imagine, and one which consists mainly of cheap but filling foods such as pasta, bread and potatoes. Indeed this is precisely the staple diet on which some families were still having to survive in the early 1990s, despite the appearance of a far wider range of goods in the shops, a predicament which one mother described with obvious distress:

My friends at work try to feed me up at dinner time, but that just

59

makes it feel even worse. I think how I have just eaten some hot soup or sandwiches, while my poor children sit at home, hungry, with only potatoes or pasta and no butter or meat. These anxieties have sapped all my strength, I simply can't find it in me to talk about clothes.

(Shuvalova 1993: 1)

Unfortunately, the failure of wages to keep up with price rises has put many families in a similar, if not quite so extreme situation. Table 2 shows the relationship between wages and the subsistence minimum during the first nine months of 1993. It was during this period that debates in the press were particularly concerned with the concept of a subsistence minimum and its relative value; after the autumn of 1993 similar articles were more likely to focus on poverty in general, the non-payment of wages and the buying power of the rouble. The figures relating to the minimum wage are of special interest when comparing Soviet and post-Soviet concepts of poverty. Although the problem of poverty certainly existed in the USSR, poor people were then deemed to be those existing on less than the minimum wage. By 1993, however, as illustrated in Table 2, the minimum

Table 2 Incomes and the subsistence minimum for January–September 1993

	January	*March*	*May*	*July*	*August*	*September*
Average monthly wage in roubles	15,140	23,559	37,505	56,000	65,400	80,000
Minimum monthly wage in roubles	2,250	2,250	4,275	7,740	7,740	7,740
Minimum wage as percentage of average wage	14.9	9.6	11.4	13.8	11.8	9.6
Subsistence minimum in roubles	5,000	8,000	11,860	21,000	27,000	30,000
Minimum wage as percentage of sub-sistence minimum	41.7	28.1	36.2	36.9	28.7	25.8
Subsistence minimum as percentage of average wage	35.6	34.0	31.5	37.5	38.5	37.5

Source: Nemova 1993: 2

wage was well below one-fifth of average monthly earnings and was only worth approximately one-third of the subsistence minimum for a single person.

It should be remembered that the subsistence minimum indicated in Table 2 is for one person only and covers solely food costs without incorporating any extra money for expenditure on clothing, heating, lighting, rent or other household bills. If such expenditure was virtually negligible in 1989, this was rapidly ceasing to be the case by 1993, and growing numbers of Russian citizens were finding that even the then still relatively low charges were already beyond their overstrained purses. As Table 2 shows, during the first nine months of 1993, the subsistence minimum for each individual consistently swallowed up over 30 per cent of the average monthly wage. If other basic living costs are included it has been estimated that a family of four would be unable to survive unless both parents earned 1.5–1.7 times the average wage (Gontmakher 1993: 4).

For this reason there exists what might be described as an equation of poverty in Russia today, whereby the greater the number of dependants per wage-earner in a given family or social unit, the greater the degree of poverty. As a result, single parent and large families are the worst hit by the current situation. Throughout 1993 it was generally agreed that 30–5 per cent of the entire population was living below the poverty line. That is to say that for one in three families, their joint income when divided between all family members was not enough even to cover the subsistence minimum per person. Of families with children under the age of six, almost half were in this situation, while three out of four large families, with three or more children, could not afford even the basics for survival (Gontmakher 1993: 4).

Even those families which were not in such dire straights inevitably came to feel the effects of an almost universal fall in national living standards. The increasingly large proportion of income being taken up by expenditure on food and other absolute essentials, as illustrated above, left less and less money to spare for 'luxuries' such as new clothes, visits to the hairdresser, leisure and cultural activities and holidays. Many of the women we interviewed when researching the material for this book expressed their regret at no longer being able to go to plays or exhibitions, which, as they pointed out, used to be quite a regular pastime. In August 1993 there was some discussion in the press of the fact that it was not uncommon for workers to find themselves too badly off to be able to countenance the idea of a summer holiday – hardly surprising since even a subsidised two week camping holiday for a family of three, organised by an institute of higher education, cost 18,000 roubles, or half of a lecturer's pay for the whole of August (Novikova 1993: 8).

When we consider that women's wages in the Soviet Union never reached a level that was equal to men's wages and that women in the Russian Federation continue to be primarily employed in those sectors of the economy with the lowest pay, such as health care, education and the state sector in general, it is not hard to understand why women are the most affected by Russia's growing poverty problem. It is important to note here that 20 per cent of women are the sole wage-earners for their families; single-parent families in Russia consist overwhelmingly of a mother and her children. Among pensioners, another social group where poverty is a serious problem, 75 per cent were women at the time of the last census in 1989.

As life has become more and more difficult to sustain even on an average wage, those people who are not able to earn that much have been forced to rely on state benefits. As we saw in the previous chapter (pp. 51–4), although official unemployment is still fairly low its unofficial forms are depriving many more workers of a regular and reliable wage. These people and their dependants also depend on financial help from the state for their survival. Certain segments of the population such as old-age pensioners and women on maternity leave have always relied on cash benefits as their main source of income. In the following section we will consider how these various groups have been affected by inflation and changing social policies, and the measures that are being taken to protect their living standards.

CASH BENEFITS

As illustrated in Table 2, the level of the official minimum wage is nothing short of derisory. Since 1992, it has never been of a level high enough to provide even half of the subsistence minimum for a single person. It was raised on 1 December 1993 to 14,620 roubles. However, in March 1994, when the subsistence minimum had reached 60,000 roubles, a proposal from the Ministry for Labour to raise the minimum wage again was refused on the grounds that there was simply no spare money in the budget to finance such an increase. Although the Minister for Labour, Gennady Melikian, shrugged off this set-back, arguing that only 0.4 per cent of the population actually receive the minimum wage and that these people 'as a rule have several jobs, or else receive a pension in addition. So that in reality they receive more' (Valiuzhenich 1994: 5), he failed to address the fact that the minimum wage is used as a point of reference in calculating and allocating many of the cash benefits currently available to Russian citizens: the level of basic unemployment benefit, for example, is equal to the minimum wage. At the time of writing, in December 1994, the minimum wage had been increased slightly to a level of 20,500 roubles, which still would not even have been enough to cover a single person's minimum subsistence requirements eighteen months earlier. On 24 November 1994 the Russian Duma voted to more than double this amount, and to introduce a new minimum wage of 54,100 roubles on 1 January 1995. This measure was met with immediate disapproval by Mr Melikian, who accused the People's Deputies of electioneering and labelled the move 'a purely populist decision'. Prime Minister Viktor Chernomyrdin also voiced his disapproval, telling an economic conference, held on 26 November, that this would aggravate inflation and cause increased unemployment (RFE/RL 1994).

Be that as it may, the minimum wage continues to be well below the level of subsistence. As increasing numbers of people have become reliant on benefits that are still calculated on this basis, therefore, new measures have obviously had to be introduced in order to cope with the developing situation. In December 1993 several new benefits were announced. One, a so-called 'bread benefit', was designed to provide aid for the most disadvantaged members of society. It is available to all citizens with an income of less than the minimum wage and was fixed at a level of 1,400 roubles per month. Since at the time of its introduction, this would have bought approximately seven loaves of bread it may truly be said to be purely a bread benefit and nothing more.

At the same time, a benefit was also introduced to help ease the financial position of the victims of 'hidden unemployment'. A temporary scheme was devised by the Federal Employment Service to allow all workers who have already been on enforced unpaid leave for at least one month and who have a family income of less than twice the minimum wage per family member, to be paid a benefit equal to the current minimum wage. If the enterprise involved wishes, it may also receive further funds on a returnable basis in order to pay its idle workers a monthly benefit of up to four times the minimum wage. However, even in this case, a worker would still be receiving less than the subsistence minimum for one person ('Vyplaty rabotnikam, nakhodiashchimsia . . .' 1993: 7).

These benefits are clearly inadequate for survival; they are also not available to all those who might be in need of them. There is, for example, no benefit available to the workers at over 40,000 enterprises which have fallen behind in the payment of their wages. Since delayed wages are paid several months late, without any compensation for the intervening price inflation, they are of greatly reduced real value when they are finally received. Another startlingly common practice is the payment of wages in kind. Whether this system is introduced by enterprises as a way of 'selling' products while avoiding taxation on cash revenue, as Minister for Labour, Gennady Melikian, has suggested (Valiuzhenich 1994: 5), is of little relevance to workers who are presented with saucepans, teacups, nails, lead piping or dried peaches instead of a wage packet. If they are lucky they will have been given something which they are able to sell themselves for cash, as is the case for workers at a crystal factory in Bryansk, but for those employed in plants manufacturing plumbing materials, for example, the outlook is far less promising: 'What am I going to do if they give me my salary in pipes?' is not a question to which there is any straightforward answer (Graff and Gracheva 1994: 5).

For the officially unemployed the benefit system is also not without loopholes and ambiguities. Although the minimum level of unemployment benefit is equal to the minimum wage, a maximum level also exists and is recalculated each month to be equal to the local average monthly wage. Thus in March 1994, although the basic level of unemployment benefit was a near worthless 14,700 roubles per month, some people were receiving 140,000 roubles. The decision about who receives which amount appeared to be fairly arbitrary and based on the local employment centre's estimation of the degree of a person's need and their family situation. Whatever the monthly sum allocated to an unemployed person, however, benefit will only be paid for twelve months after redundancy, followed by a six-month break in benefit after which, if the person is still out of work, the cycle is renewed with a further twelve months of benefit. This pattern of payment can officially continue ad infinitem. However, the obvious logic behind it is that in the six months when no money is forthcoming people will be forced into finding a job in order to feed themselves. If this theory is reminiscent of Soviet punitive measures aimed at forcing all citizens to work, it breaks down in a situation where there simply may be no jobs available for a person to find. Trapped in this predicament, families where one or more wage-earner has been made redundant have to rely on the minimal income from other social security benefits for which they may be eligible – the bread benefit, child benefit, pensions – or else find an alternative source of income outside the formal sector. This issue of survival is considered in more detail in Chapter seven.

While newly introduced benefits fail to cure all the new ills of the present situation, long established benefits such as the old-age pension and child benefit have not been index linked to inflation and therefore do not represent a constant level of income for their recipients. In December 1993, increases in child benefits and old-age pensions helped to bring the proportion of the population living below the poverty line down from around one in three, or 52,600,000 people, to roughly one in six, or 24,800,000 people. However, since these increases were, once again, made on an ad hoc basis it would be over-optimistic to assume that this improvement will necessarily be of a lasting nature.

The December 1993 decree rationalised the various subsidies and benefits available for children into a single monthly payment. For women on extended maternity leave, a benefit equal to the minimum wage was to be paid until the child is eighteen months old. The rate for children under the age of six was set at 70 per cent of the minimum wage and for children aged between six and sixteen, 60 per cent. Single mothers are eligible to claim one and a half times the ordinary benefit. Commenting on this new level of benefit one of our interviewees expressed the following opinion: 'Apparently Boris Nikolaevich has put it up now to 8,000 or so [60 per cent of the minimum wage] – you can get a kilogram of bananas for that! For a whole month! It's OK – you'll be getting your vitamins! [30]. As this statement makes amply clear, child benefit is far from sufficient to provide for the needs of a child. Moreover, the subsistence minimum increases as the child grows older, yet the level of benefit decreases when the child reaches age six, precisely at the point when they have to go to school with all the additional expenses which this entails. In September 1993, the newspaper *Moskovskii komsomolets*, calculated the cost of equipping a first former for the start of the school year at between 14,364 and 87,406 roubles, depending on the quality and origin of the goods bought (Semkiv 1993: 2). Either figure represents quite a hefty sum at a time when the average wage was 80,000 a month, and not one which would be greatly compensated for by child benefit. According to E. Gontmakher, section head of the government's Centre for Information and Social Technology, in the autumn of 1993 child benefit compensated only 21 per cent of minimum expenditure for children under six and only 10 per cent for older children (Gontmakher 1993: 4).

The need to keep pensions at a level high enough to have some meaningful value for those who have to live on them has also proved problematical. In the Soviet Union, pensioners were on the whole seen as a disadvantaged group, although of course some were always better off than others. Large numbers of retired people had to supplement their monthly pension by continuing to work, as caretakers, ushers and cloakroom attendants in museums and theatres, for example. Since pensions have always been calculated in relation to the person's previous wage it follows that women, who as a unit in the labour force never achieved more than

70 per cent of male workers' average wage, receive the lowest pensions. It is also clear that, as contemporary wages increased elevenfold over the course of 1993 and still failed to keep up with inflation, pensions could not continue to be calculated solely on the basis of wages earned in the Soviet era. Since April 1992, various attempts have been made to find a satisfactory method of updating pensions, but as yet none have met with any great approval from pensioners themselves. The word *indeksatsiia* which is used when referring to the regular reappraisals of benefit levels has led to some confusion where it has been translated as 'indexation'. This term does not, in fact, imply an automatic increase in line with consumer inflation as might be expected, but a much more ad hoc system of arbitrary compensation. Simply index linking the level of pensions and other benefits to the consumer price index, although this would solve the problem of keeping the real value of benefits constant, has not been introduced, because it is felt that the effect on inflation would be too great.

The first law on increasing state pensions, which was passed in April 1992, involved updating all previous wages for the calculation of pensions, by raising them by a fixed coefficient. Pensioners were particularly unhappy with this method, because the coefficients, which depended on the previous sphere of work of the individual, appeared to benefit those who had been the least qualified and the lowest paid the most. As a result, 'many pensioners, who had been receiving the maximum pension before, ended up with a minimum pension or something close to it, after the "updating" of wages' (Khudiakova 1993b: 2).

In response to these complaints, the next method introduced was to increase all pensions to 1.8 times their previous value. However, this way of doing things was seen to disadvantage those pensioners who already had the lowest incomes.

> Each time [there is such an increase] the gap between the minimum and the maximum pension widens. Let's say for example, that you get the minimum pension of 10 thousand, and I get the maximum 30 thousand. This indexation takes place and more or less doubles our pensions. Now you will get 20 thousand, and I'll already be on 60 thousand. Next time the regular increases come around, doubling pensions again, yours will go up to 40 thousand and mine will have reached 120 thousand! Quite a difference, eh?
>
> (Vasil'kova 1993: 3)

In 1994, in addition to continuing across-the-board increases, additional compensation was awarded to the poorest pensioners. In March 1994 Yurii Liublin, deputy head of the State Pension Fund, told reporters that the new increased level of compensation had been set at 20,000 roubles. Since the basic minimum pension was then equal to the minimum wage, this meant that those eligible for the lowest pensions would, even after the payment of this compensation, receive no more than 34,620 roubles a month. When asked whether he thought that he would be able to survive on this amount, given that the subsistence minimum was then 50,000 roubles, Mr Liublin replied:

> I find it hard to imagine what my way of life would be on a pension. This amount of money would probably not be enough. But then, by the time I am 60, my needs will probably have changed somewhat. Perhaps I will not want to go to the cinema for example, or I will not drink beer. Most likely I will have different dietary needs. I will probably be happy to eat milk and dry bread for instance, whereas now I can't do without meat.
>
> (Sivkova 1994: 5)

Such a response was hardly likely to be of much comfort to those twelve million people, that is every third pensioner, who at that time actually did have to live on this amount.

When pressed on the inadequate level of cash benefits, ministers and officials reply simply that there is no money available to increase them further. 'What's to be done?' asks Mr Liublin: 'If it were possible we would pay pensioners an extra 18 rather than 8 thousand. But you tell me, where is the money to come from?' (Sivkova 1994: 5). Faced with an economic crisis, the Russian government is making savings by cutting back on public spending. Not only cash benefits, but social services as a whole are suffering from a lack of financial input. When speaking on what she termed 'the feminisation of poverty' to the General Conference of Trade Unions in May 1993, deputy chairperson N. Podshibiakina made particular reference to the fact that 'social guarantees and privileges are gradually disappearing' (Os'minina 1993: 11). This loss of what was once a highly developed welfare system is particularly damaging for women.

THE SOCIAL CONTRACT IS BROKEN

Under the Soviet system, workers were compensated for their low wages and poor working conditions through the provision of extensive social and welfare services, organised by the state-owned enterprise where they worked. These perks included housing arrangements, health care and child care and, in many cases, subsidised and queue-free purchasing opportunities for goods which were in short supply in the shops. Since enterprises have been privatised and have become market-oriented and profit-making concerns, the expense of offering these privileges has meant that they are rapidly disappearing. Having once been the primary beneficiaries of such services, women are now doubly disadvantaged: firstly, because they are perceived as unattractive and costly employees by the new labour market; and, secondly, because they are the most acutely affected by the loss of this social wage. For many women, the social benefits provided by a given enterprise may have been a factor of at least equal importance in choosing their job as the level of pay.

One of the first casualties of the new system has been the system of heavily subsidised child care. During the era of glasnost there was much open criticism of state enterprise-run kindergartens and crèches, which were frequently overcrowded, understaffed and with a long waiting list for places. Nonetheless, these establishments did then exist and most enterprises also helped to organise subsidised summer camps for their workers' children. In May 1993, Galina Tsigankova, deputy head of the municipal administration on social questions in the Siberian city of Kemerovo, announced, 'We are losing our greatest achievement, kindergartens' (Os'minina 1993: 11). She went on to explain that, although a presidential decree on the transfer of child care establishments from federal to municipal administration had been passed as early as 1990, the question of funding remained as yet unsolved.

The result is a huge leap in prices which parents are expected to make up. In February 1993 the Russian Supreme Soviet was working on the bill on 'Fundamental legislation for the protection of the family, motherhood, fatherhood and childhood' (see Chapter two, note 2). Two People's Deputies involved with this project, B. Almazov and V. Iushkevichus, expressed the following opinions in an article published by *Rossiskaia gazeta*:

> If, from the point of view of material provisions, the state previously took over the role of a child's father (free medical treatment, curative measures, education – the cost of all this was many times more than what a father's modest income could cover) then now, when it has decided to give up this mission, it falls to the parents themselves to pay for everything. . . . An entrepreneur will never be induced to take upon himself the protection of motherhood and childhood, will not become the state's heir in terms of caring for mothers, whatever legislative norms the state may attempt to compel him by.
>
> (Almazov and Iushkevichus 1993: 2)

Almazov and Iushkevichus' solution of a return to the home for women and an increase in men's wages which would allow them to be the sole breadwinners for their families was entirely in line with the tone of the drafted law. Although the latter has since been shelved, this sentiment is still prevalent among Russian politicians, and is supported by the principles of Russian nationalism to which a great many mainstream political figures adhere. However, even setting aside all ethical concerns about such an approach, and without addressing the issue of whether such a solution would be acceptable to women themselves, we have already seen that such a proposition is currently completely impracticable given the present buying power of the average wage.

Returning to the issue of the growing expense of child care, in May 1993 a place in a kindergarten or crèche cost 10,000 roubles per month, over one-quarter of the average wage, while a trip to a children's summer camp cost 22,400 roubles, almost two-thirds of the average wage. Consequently, a number of women are finding that it is no longer financially viable for them to continue to work; others are having to leave because as child care provisions disappear they are unable to make alternative arrangements. For those who simply cannot countenance the loss of their wage, however small, for single mothers, for the many rural women who are responsible for tending the family plot and for those women who are their family's sole provider, the only option may be to leave their babies in the care of other older children or of retired neighbours or relatives.

The prohibitive cost of holiday camps is also seen as a significant loss. In the summer of 1993 several doctors as well as anxious mothers wrote letters to the press warning that the lack of a month's break in the countryside, when their systems would be boosted by fresh air and extra vitamins from home-grown produce, would inevitably increase the incidence of illness in children over the long, harsh, Russian winter; a prospect which must have been made all the more distressing by the deterioration of the national health service.

In June 1993, Minister for Health, Eduard Nechaev, claimed:

> Our health service today is financed at a level of only 50–60 per cent of what is needed. How can you live when you are allotted only 50 per cent of what you need to survive? . . . In developed countries three–four times as much is allocated to the health budget.
>
> (Nechaev 1993: 3)

In September of the same year health workers threatened to strike in protest at the level of funding which they claimed covered no more than 35 per cent of necessities. Whatever the exact figures, there is a general consensus that hospitals and polyclinics are in a dire situation. They are on the whole in need of refurbishment, poorly equipped with outdated instruments and suffering from a severe shortage of vital medicines. Even emergency health services are not always fully stocked: 'It is hard to admit', says the Minister for Health, 'that these doctors sometimes have to tell the patient: we don't have this medicine, or that one. . . . Perhaps you might have some in the house?' (Nechaev 1993: 3).

The problem with medicines is currently the most extreme. The centralised administration which used to purchase imported drugs at a specially reduced exchange rate and controlled distribution to chemists shops has been replaced by several commercial structures which are failing to co-ordinate the various activities that they have taken over. Despite laws which limit the profit margins allowed on the sale of medicines to 50 per cent, Mr Nechaev claimed in September 1993 that he had found instances where chemists were charging prices which included a 2,000 per cent mark up (Nevel'skii 1993: 5). The loss of state control means that prices have become erratic, and that the same preparation may cost widely differing amounts depending on where it is bought. What is more, market forces now control the cost of a drug and there is no concept of a standard prescription charge. As a result some illnesses are simply more expensive than others: in April 1993 the total cost of a prescription for flu from an ordinary Moscow polyclinic came to a total of 3,146 roubles, the cost of antibiotics varied from 100 to 3,000 roubles and the price of a cure for stomach ulcers was 22,000 roubles. Many groups of people, including children under the age of three, or six where they are members of a large family, are legally eligible to receive free or subsidised prescriptions. However, this system is also failing. Chemists are reluctant to issue free medicines and may refuse altogether, or else limit allowances to a single packet, because the central administration is often slow in refunding these subsidies (Sivkova 1993: 5).

These various developments place Russian citizens in a position where falling ill is a luxury which they may not be able to afford. It is a common occurrence now for newspapers to publish letters from people who are unable to procure the medicines needed by themselves or their loved ones and who hope that some more wealthy reader might be able and willing to help them. The newspaper *Rabochaia tribuna*, for example, dedicated a regular column, entitled 'SOS!', to this organised form of charity, which is not really so far removed from the more traditional, but less socially acceptable forms of begging on the streets and in the underground.

THE CLASS DIVIDE

Despite this desperate situation which has become a reality for so many Russians today, there are of course some people who are enjoying a higher degree of affluence than previously. After all, as pointed out by a report for the World Bank in 1992, 'A widening earnings and income distribution is . . . an inherent part of the reform (indeed, a major purpose of the reform is to allow a wider distribution of earnings)' (Barr 1992: 1). However this broadening social stratification at a time when poverty is so widespread is causing a high level of resentment and is no longer seen as so desirable by those who are not among the lucky few. This bitterness is exacerbated by the feeling that commerce, which up until recently was outlawed and branded corrupt and dishonest, is one of the only routes to material well-being. 'What kind of a society are we building', one newspaper correspondent demands, 'where honest working people are reduced to eating soup made from old bones and the only ones who eat and drink well are kiosk owners and traders?' (Androsenko 1993: 1).

In 1994 the top 10 per cent of the population earned eleven times as much as the bottom 10 per cent, an income divide that would hardly appear shocking in the context of a country with a long-standing capitalist history. However, in the context of Russian society where, until recently, almost everybody had approximately the same, and where monetary wealth was of little consequence anyway, since there was not much available to spend it on, the speed with which this schism between rich and poor has appeared makes it an issue of public concern, especially since this uneven distribution of wealth is very visible in a social context. Despite a general reduction in surplus income, there has been a very marked increase in the number of expensive foreign cars to be seen on Russian streets and it is easy enough to pick out those individuals who can afford to buy expensive western clothes as opposed to those wearing the much cheaper and poorer quality imports from China and the Third World. Many women find these differences particularly hard to swallow where they relate to children. While some families can afford to kit their young ones out with colourful imported school bags, decorated with American cartoon figures and slogans written in English, other pupils have to make do with a plain brown satchel at a tenth of the price and continue to wear the Soviet-style school uniform because, although it is no longer mandatory, 'The high price and low quality of clothes, many of which are light cottons from China, Pakistan and Syria and unsuitable for cold Russian weather, is forcing some parents to stick with uniforms, which cost about 15,000 roubles' (Seward 1993: 8).

Imported advertisements and western culture are also no longer greeted with the same enthusiasm for anything from 'over there' as they once might have been. Advertisements promoting expensive pet food are met with an especially high degree of resentment in a country where many people are struggling even to feed themselves properly. War veterans queuing for food they could barely afford were overheard discussing such advertisements between calculating how best to spend this month's pension:

> 'No, but you just think about it! According to this one, "Chappy" dog food contains all the essential nutrients for your dog (calcium, protein, carbohydrates).'
> 'Your cat would buy "Whiskers".'
> 'If only someone would think so well of us, to calculate what we get fed so carefully: how much protein, carbohydrate or even calcium we get.'
> 'What do you reckon, they could invent "Widowhiskers" couldn't they, for us widows!'
>
> (Levina 1994c: 10)

As the lights go dim on dreams of universal affluence and western agencies are seen to be not entirely committed to saving Russia's floundering economy, there has been an increasing general rejection of what is perceived as a cultural invasion from the West. Several of the women we interviewed said that they had had more than enough of American films and Mexican soap operas, and that they longed only to see some of their own old films. Younger women too expressed their concern at the Americanisation of their culture, even to the point of declaring:

> I don't see why we need all this imported chocolate anyway, it's not as good as ours even. Everyone knows that Soviet chocolate was always the best you could get. We went on a school trip once to Poland and they were all on about how much they loved our chocolate.
>
> [34]

If such a statement smacks of Cold War, Soviet superiority in the eastern bloc, it is probably because these feelings are, in part, a result of the growing tendency towards Russian nationalism which targets women in particular as the preservers of Russian culture and the educators of new generations, responsible for the handing down of customs and traditions in the process of recreating a Great Russian state. However, such sentiments may also bear witness to the disappointment experienced by a nation which believed that it would come to prosper very quickly under a capitalist system and finds that this is not to be the case.

After two years of so-called transition, the women we interviewed were no longer optimistic about what the future would hold:

> You wonder when it is all going to end. There's no end in sight at present. No doubt our children will grow up and live out their lives during the period of market transition! We'll still be on our way, crawling there. It doesn't exist, this market transition.
>
> [30]

Some experts are just as pessimistic. L. Rzhanitsina characterised the Russian situation in this way:

> They say that we are currently experiencing a crisis. Well, let's see, what in fact is a crisis? Negative phenomena accumulate in the economy, production drops, unemployment, of women in the first instance, occurs. In order to get out of the crisis, production must be transformed, adapted to suit the demands of the market. When this happens, a turn for the better should take place, employers take on new workers, spend money on training, retraining, even leisure activities. They pay out bonuses because they need a workforce. But is Russia really in a crisis? No, we are in a different position. The entire economic system, a gigantic mechanism, has been destroyed and no new mechanisms of a new system have arisen to replace it. Therefore the present situation is what economists term a 'dead zone'. . . . Nobody knows how we will get out of this, all we know is that it will be a long hard climb.
>
> (Os'minina 1993: 11)

As 1994 draws to a close, prospects for 1995 appear to be no more comfortable. Indeed, with the crisis in Chechnya making massive inroads into the country's finances it appears increasingly likely that Rzhanitsina is right and that a return to normality for the people of Russia will take many years. In the meantime, life goes on, and women are being obliged to find ways of coping with the rigours of unemployment and plummeting living standards.

In these first three chapters we have seen the predicament which Russian women were facing in 1994. The legacy of perestroika, in particular the failure of Gorbachev and his reformists to introduce any radical thinking where women's roles were concerned, paved the way for a strengthening of gender divisions and an overt policy of returning women to the home.

In the context of post-Soviet Russia with its nascent free market and growing problem of unemployment, especially of the unofficial variety, these attitudes have allowed discriminatory redundancy practices to go virtually unchallenged. Leading figures in both politics and business have been able openly to propound their theories of the desirability of excluding women from the labour force entirely. Finally we have seen how the national economic crisis is reflected at the family level in terms of falling living standards. Poverty in the new Russia predominantly has a female face.

If this first part has painted a particularly gloomy picture of the realities of life for Russian women in the early 1990s, the second part of this book aims to investigate some of the various responses which are being made in an attempt to deal with this state of affairs. Chapter four will focus on the official responses to unemployment offered by the Russian government, through the Federal Employment Service, taking as an example the activities of the Dubna Employment Centre, which the authors were able to visit both in the summer of 1993 and in March 1994. Chapter five then turns to look at the responses of women's organisations and their role in helping women survive this difficult period through programmes of job creation. This chapter is largely based on a study of the positive and negative aspects of one such organisation's attempt to put this scheme into practice through the setting up of its own enterprise.

Chapters six, seven and eight deal with the responses women themselves have found or been presented with as solutions. Chapter six begins by investigating the option of setting up a small business. The case-study for this chapter is provided by an organisation run by women and organising business training courses used mainly by women. The experiences of the customers of this organisation whom we were able to interview illustrate some of the many drawbacks and obstacles to this particular response, which has been so often presented as the logical way forward.

Survival in material terms has become an issue of great importance to many women as a result of their family's impoverishment. In Chapter seven we will see how a substantial number of women have been able to supplement the family income through various forms of trading and the use of their plots of land for subsistence farming. Chapter eight describes how increased contact with the West, the attraction of a glamorous lifestyle and the prevalence of pornographic images of women in the popular press have led many women, especially the young, to become involved, in one form or another, in exploiting their sexuality for material gain. The case-study focuses on the range of original methods one women's organisation has come up with in trying to help young women maintain some control in negotiating the world of modelling and glamour and in dealing with sexual harassment. Our aim is to show that while the state of affairs for Russian women today may indeed be grim, they are not helpless and passive victims of this situation. Nonetheless, because of the depth of the crisis facing Russia today, each of the responses they or those working on their behalf have attempted is far more complicated and frequently turns out to be far less attractive and viable than it initially seemed.

Part II

RESPONDING TO CHANGE

4

TACKLING UNEMPLOYMENT: THE STATE'S RESPONSE TO A CHANGING LABOUR MARKET

In July 1991 the Decree on Employment was adopted in the Russian Federation and paved the way for the subsequent creation of the Federal Employment Service. The activities of the Service have been financed by local payroll taxes: enterprises in the area of a given employment centre are required to register with the centre and contribute to its operation at the rate of 2 per cent of their total wage bill. In this funding principle there inevitably lies a fundamental contradiction: the more workers made redundant, the greater the need for the employment centre, yet the less revenue there will be to pay for it. In this situation, increased direct state funding may become unavoidable.

Nevertheless, despite this inherent difficulty and criticisms both of FES policy and practice, setting up such a service from scratch in a country which had no official concept of unemployment has been no mean feat. Employment centres have been involved in processing job vacancies, setting up retraining schemes and developing initiatives such as assisted business start-ups and programmes of work in the community. For reasons which have been outlined in Chapter two, however, numbers officially registered with employment centres have remained extremely low. Nevertheless, the centres are used as a source of information on vacancies and training opportunities by people who are on administrative leave or are newly entering the workforce, even if they do not officially register as unemployed. In the course of this chapter, we will be looking at the experience of one employment centre, at Dubna in Moscow Region, in order to examine more closely the types of problems such centres may face and the strategies they may adopt.

RESPONSES TO THE NEW JOB MARKET: WOMEN NEED NOT APPLY

A casual glance at the 'situations vacant' columns and specialist jobs supplements confirms the proposition that there is a marked preference for men on the part of employers in the new Russian labour market. Nearly all the most prestigious professional jobs advertised baldly state that they are looking for male applicants only. In addition, many vacancies for skilled manual workers, such as joiners, lathe-operators, fitters and technicians have similar men-only specifications. Where women are designated as preferred applicants it is usually for secretarial jobs and other relatively low-level office staff. There is, moreover, frequently an age cut-off at thirty or, more rarely, thirty-five, precisely the age above which most unemployed women find themselves. The message of the job vacancies makes it frighteningly plain to women out of work that the future may be very bleak:

> I sometimes look through the advertising papers that they put through the door. . . . I've only once seen an advert for women up to the age of forty in all the time I've been reading them. Only once. Usually it's adverts for young girls to be secretaries, up to the age of thirty, that's the maximum. It's upsetting, and the main thing, the most unpleasant thing, is I worry about what will happen when I get to retirement age.
>
> [31]

On the rare occasions jobs for older women are advertised, they are not designed to offer many crumbs of comfort to redundant engineers: unskilled work of the most menial type, such as selling cigarettes outside metro stations, is virtually all that is available for the thirty to fifty age-group. Not that the future offered to the under-thirties may be much less problematic. If jobs are at least on offer to them, the advertisements may have blatantly sexual overtones and include a person specification far removed from an outline of essential office skills:

> Secretaries required: attractive girls with office experience, aged 18–22, at least 168 cms tall.
>
> (*Reklamnoe prilozhenie* 1993: 6)

> Secretary/personal assistant required with knowledge of English, pretty girl under 25.
>
> (*Priglashaem na rabotu* 1994: 2)

This emphasis on personal appearance inevitably exerts a discriminatory effect on women of the appropriate age with inappropriate figures, as one of our graduate interviewees remarked: 'It's a problem for me because I'm overweight. They take that into account and often they won't take you because of it' [12]. Being young and beautiful, however, may still not be enough in a climate in which employers can so blatantly pick and choose: in addition to the personal appearance qualifications, many adverts specify that women must be unmarried and/or without children. Clearly, if employers feel the need to take on women, they expect them to create as few problems as the men.

The discriminatory attitudes which underlie these job advertisements are clearly seen by employers as simply a fact of life which they have no need to keep quiet about. Because there is so little social pressure and legal guarantees are so inadequate, there is nothing to make them pay lip-service even to any notion of equal opportunities. These attitudes had already been well established before the demise of the USSR: the 1990 managers survey cited in Chapter two, for example, found that 79 per cent would only select a woman if the job 'was not suitable for a man' (Rzhanitsina 1993: 105). As a result, it comes as no surprise to learn that, when employers notify employment centres of vacancies, they usually state their preference for male or female applicants and, moreover, expect it to be acted upon. The employment centres, which rely on the co-operation of local enter-prises, are therefore placed in an extremely difficult position when dealing with their overwhelmingly female users. It is clear, however, that, in the present climate, no employment centre would be able to push an employer into taking staff they did not want.

There is, moreover, a further factor in recruitment which flies in the face of equal opportunities policies: the question of personal contacts. Far from being frowned upon, nepotism, the exploitation of personal networks and bribery are all well-established routes to employment in Russia. For employers, personal recommendations are extremely important and may be accompanied by a marked unwillingness to take people 'off the street'. For young women straight out of college with neither experience nor suitable references, contacts may be crucial, as one woman who had made numerous speculative applications explained:

My friends from my course all just went to work where their parents or people they knew worked. You've got to have contacts to get a job. . . . Let's say I go along to some institution and they ask me what I can do. Suppose I say I can do everything. Then they start asking

me who my parents are. . . . I should say that 90 per cent of my year
got nowhere without their parents' help.

[12]

As a system, the use of personal influence is considered by those who can
make it work to be more reliable and effective than anything the state is
likely to offer, as one woman whose spells of redundancy were extremely
short observed: 'I got work through friends twice. They wouldn't have
found me anything at the job centre' [25].

This lack of confidence in the usefulness of employment eentres reflects
less a distaste for bureaucratic procedures than it does the central problem
women such as this experience in the changing labour market: the
vacancies on offer are few in number and in no way compatible with the
skills they have. In 1994, after two years of operation, the Employment
Service was still not obliging people to accept work they considered to be
unsuitable, a policy which was doubtless influenced by the low official level
of unemployment. Job-seekers were entitled by law to turn down jobs that
would involve them in relocating, had poor health and safety standards or
offered lower wages than their previous employment (Khotkina 1994:
103). An individual was not obliged to accept any work outside their
profession and was also allowed to turn down two jobs in their profession
without losing benefit. It was, however, apparent by 1994 that Employment Service attitudes on this issue were soon likely to change. Women
questioned in some of the earliest surveys on unemployment showed little
inclination to change profession. A 1992 survey of 3,500 unemployed
women, for example, found that 81 per cent believed they should have
the right to turn down any job they considered unsuitable (Rzhanitsina
1993: 81).

In the light of the work on offer, attitudes such as these are scarcely
surprising: if the majority of the unemployed are women with higher
education, the majority of the vacancies are for manual jobs such as
sewing-machinists, cleaners and other unskilled service sector workers. It
would, however, be misleading to suggest that women cannot make
headway in moving into new professional jobs. One of the new areas in
which women are beginning to make a mark is financial services where a
number are now in prominent positions as directors of commercial banks.
There is some evidence that women such as these may well favour female
employees for what they perceive as their efficiency. The female director
of a commercial bank interviewed in 1994, for example, observed: 'Around
200 people work in our bank. Approximately 5 per cent are men, the rest
are women. I personally take the view that women are the best workers'

(Skliar 1994b: 17). While a development such as this gives some grounds for optimism for the future, it is by no means enough to counteract prevailing levels of discrimination or the mismatch between the unemployed and the vacancies available. On 1 March 1994, the Federal Employment Service had information on 270,000 vacancies, 83 per cent of which were for blue-collar jobs (Nemova 1993: 2). Even had they been the right kind of job, this very small number of vacancies was, by this time, in stark contrast to the millions who were effectively out of work. To see more closely what this situation might mean in practice in one locality, we will turn to the example of Dubna.

DUBNA: SOVIET DEVELOPMENT AND THE RUSSIAN MARKET

The town of Dubna is situated on the Volga, 110 kilometres from Moscow at the northern extremity of Moscow Region. It was constructed in the 1950s as a centre for secret defence establishments and remains an archetypal example of Soviet planning. The town is dominated by five major enterprises. These are either in the defence industry and have been hit by the abandonment of orders for the military, or are public-financed institutions affected by cut-backs in state funding. With the exception of these major employers, little else existed in the town, not even a bakery, everything being imported from Moscow. As a result, when mass redundancies began, there was literally no alternative employment for the population of physicists and computer programmers.

With an able-bodied population of 42,000, Dubna, like so many other Russian towns, has had an extraordinarily low level of officially registered unemployed. In the first six months after the Employment Centre opened in early 1992, there were just thirty-five. Within a year this figure had risen to between 800 and 900, yet this too failed to convey the increasing seriousness of the situation in the town. By mid-1993 two of the town's major enterprises each had around 1,000 people on administrative leave receiving 4–5,000 roubles per month at a time when the hopelessly inadequate minimum wage was set at 7,740. It was estimated that around 5,000 people were in redundant posts, yet were being deliberately artificially retained; the local authorities, for example, had taken over the financing of enterprise nurseries in order to cut their costs and help them avoid redundancies. Nevertheless, official notification of future redundancies was beginning to filter into the Employment Centre by the summer of 1993.

Occupational segregation in Dubna, with its highly educated population, had not been as pronounced as in many other towns, in the sense that there were no 'women's' factories. Nevertheless, women were still the first to go, being perceived as less effective specialists because of their frequent absences to care for sick children. Women therefore made up 60 per cent of newly redundant workers in the town. In addition, the advance notification of redundancies – 450 here, 200 there – were expected to be primarily women who had been working in aerodynamics or ballistics and who would be extremely difficult to place elsewhere. During the second half of 1993 official unemployment stabilised, but then began to rise significantly from January 1994 with much more expected in the near future. By March, the rate of officially registered unemployment in the town was around 2 per cent with approximately 150 new registrations per month. The real situation was, however, more closely reflected in the increased rate of enquiries about vacancies, with around 100 people a day coming in to the Centre to see what was on offer.

Unhappily, in this situation, vacancies registered with the Employment Centre were running at a mere 150 per month, most of them for skilled manual workers. Women were being offered work in shops and kiosks or in various forms of trading, although, given the lack of retail and service outlets in Dubna, placement even in jobs such as these was by no means straightforward. Not surprisingly, this had little appeal for the Centre's educated clientele. As a result, the Centre was taking an increasingly active role in seeking vacancies and developing employment. By mid-1993 the Centre had doubled its staff to sixteen, including employment and training specialists, legal advisers and a psychologist. They were now involved in tracking down vacancies by phone, visiting prospective employers and creating temporary employment. This led to a steady rise in the number of vacancies reported to the Employment Centre. Much of this had to do with changing attitudes on the part of local employers. In the new circumstances, employers could get rid of workers with poor performance, and especially with drink problems, far more easily than in the past, in the knowledge that the Employment Centre would provide them with staff who genuinely wanted to work. If this increased the number of vacancies, however, it did not decrease the number of unemployed, but merely altered their composition. In addition, links with new commercial firms were being developed: new firms which had managers who previously had been redundant themselves, would automatically return to the Employment Centre when their firms needed more staff. Finally, the town's major organisations were now turning to the Employment Centre for help with the recruitment and selection of top and middle managers, economists and chief accountants.

If vacancies were being actively sought by the Employment Centre, however, this did not necessarily improve women's chances of being recruited. During the first half of 1993 ninety-five people took part in the recruitment round for the professional posts listed above, yet only 18 per cent were women. In the same way, the realities of the new labour market were underlined by the use made of the Employment Centre's services during this same period. Careers and educational guidance was sought by three-quarters of women users but by only just over a third of the men. Sixty-two per cent of the men using the Centre were those involved in the recruitment round, compared with only 12 per cent of the women. The implication is plain: it was far easier for men to find alternative employment using the skills they already had, while women were much more likely to have to make a complete change of direction. For all the women who make use of the services of the Employment Centre, however, there are far more who prefer to remain as they are, even if their jobs have effectively disappeared. As Yuri Vetokhin, director of the Dubna Centre, observed, 'There are a lot of women who are on administrative leave but are still on the books at work and who don't come to us. It's because it's seen as such a loss of face, like being a second-class citizen' (Vetokhin 1993).

WOMEN'S RESPONSES TO THE NEW JOB MARKET

The situation which has developed in Dubna is, of course, mirrored in towns and cities across Russia. Women's skills and qualifications do not match the jobs on offer, or, if they do, they then face overt discrimination in recruitment. Small wonder that this is a situation that women are finding difficult to come to terms with. First and foremost, there is simply the question of shock at the unexpectedness of it all. Graduates are, for the first time, having to find jobs for themselves, perhaps in quite different areas from their degrees. Something which is an entirely normal phenomenon in the West has arrived quite suddenly in Russia and hit hard the young women who were coming to the end of their courses and expecting to be assigned a job.[1] In particular, prospects for new graduates in professions which are busy shedding workers may look very bleak indeed. For older women who now face both age and sex discrimination the situation is harder still. They may find it very difficult to talk about their reactions without becoming distressed, like the engineer who made the following comment:

My friends and I try and support each other, but it's really difficult. . . . Sometimes I feel as if I'm sleepwalking, especially the way things are now at the factory. You turn up and you don't know if they are going to make you redundant or not, if there'll be any work or not.

[19]

The stress women experience in this situation inevitably depends on their family circumstances, but it is also directly related to their view of their former job. Women who feel that they had simply been marking time in a Soviet enterprise on the road from graduation to retirement often appear to be dealing fairly well with redundancy. Those who had genuinely loved their jobs and felt deeply committed to their choice of profession exhibit distress, anxiety and bitterness in describing their situation. Some, particularly younger women, feel bitter primarily at what they see as a waste of the years spent on their education. Others, notably older women with many years' work behind them, are clearly experiencing a direct sense of loss:

I've worked in my profession for twenty-six years and now nobody wants it. It makes me feel really upset. I've got to go on a course but my heart's not really in it. What can you do? My profession, the one I loved, is useless now.

[21]

This reaction appears to be particularly characteristic of engineers and other former scientists. In the course of our interviews, women, not necessarily scientists themselves, frequently expressed the view that a particularly fine generation of women had been irrevocably damaged. This idea was perhaps put most eloquently by one former engineer:

I want to tell you what I'm always saying. We are nothing now, we are nobody. And women like us, all these women engineers, they were the cream, they were the flower of the nation. They'd been to the most prestigious institutes, worked in the defence industry – they called us engineers but we were specialists in electronics mostly. All these women, they were better than the men – not better scientists necessarily, but more intellectual, on a different level. They were interested in art and music and literature. Now they're all working as cleaners and traders. We don't exist any more, no one is interested in us.

[32]

The phrase, 'the flower of the nation', was used by several women to convey the notion of a particularly well-educated and cultured generation which had been thrown wholesale onto the scrap heap. In describing their plight, the concept of a loss to the cultural life of the country itself was an intrinsic part of the concern expressed.

In stark contrast to this, then, would come their assessment of what was available to women in the new job market. While many of the older women were expecting little in the way of formal employment, more recent graduates who had seen what was on offer were scathing in their views:

Men have taken over all the best-paid jobs and women get a pittance. The men have seized hold of everything, while the women are at their beck and call – 'get the tea, get the coffee'.

[13]

I think it's the most outrageous discrimination. The bosses are nearly all men and the subordinates are women. It's just a reign of terror, on the lines of 'I'm the boss, you're the idiot'.

[12]

In comments such as these, the offence which has been caused to educated women by the current state of play is palpable. The transition from potential 'flower of the nation' to 'bimbo with coffee tray' is a plunge in status and respect which is evidently fiercely resented and regarded as blatantly discriminatory, which indeed it is.

Russian studies of unemployment have observed that changes in attitude will be essential if women are to find a place for themselves in the new labour market. At present, it is felt that too many are unrealistic in simply expecting the state to find work for them in their chosen profession and fail to look for alternatives for themselves. Used to being protected in the labour market, women are unused to competition and have little idea of how to present themselves at interview (Rzhanitsina 1993: 79; Khotkina 1993: 18). The director of a training centre offering advice in the press on job search and interview skills, for example, felt obliged to advise women, 'It is quite possible that the manager you have to deal with will be twenty-three, while you are fifty. . . . Whatever you do, don't call him "sonny" ' (Meliksetova 1994: 12). While there is undoubtedly some truth in all of this, and, indeed, it would be surprising if there were not, blaming the individual cannot disguise the fundamental problem. Women made redundant face few vacancies and crude discrimination; a situation which is unlikely to be resolved by better job-search skills.

In the same way, the Federal Employment Service has been criticised as just another bureaucratic institution which offers little real help to the unemployed. There have been calls for major retraining schemes and programmes of job creation to be put into place by the Service (Rzhanitsina 1993: 89–90). Yet the fundamental question here is also one of scale. As increasing numbers effectively find themselves without work, substantial funds will be required to make any significant contribution. These, as the Minister for Labour indicated in early 1994, are unlikely to be forthcoming (Polovezhets 1994: 8). If the success of the Service appears to be in doubt, this has to be placed against the climate in which it is operating. To look more closely at the kinds of initiatives an employment eentre may be involved in, we will turn again to the case of Dubna and the issue of retraining. Whatever the limitations of work by a centre of this kind it is apparent that, for some women in Dubna, contact with the Employment Centre has been extremely important to them at a particularly difficult time.

RETRAINING – THE KEY TO A NEW FUTURE?

Since 1992, newspapers and job supplements have been full of advertisements for private training courses promising, on completion, a route into exciting new employment opportunities. The range of subjects they cover is, however, very limited: bookkeeping, foreign languages, computing, typing and office skills, hairdressing, child care, beauty consultancy, arts and crafts and even domestic service, another recent growth area. Many of these courses are clearly both aimed at women, as the major constituency requiring retraining, and reflect the restricted nature of where they are likely to find employment. The advertisements once again speak volumes about what women can expect: subordinate positions in offices, low-paid work in the service sector and home-based informal sector employment.[2]

The picture is not dissimilar in training courses offered by official and voluntary organisations. The Moscow city employment department, for example, has had an agreement with the Union of Russian Women, the successor organisation to the Soviet Women's Committee, to provide free training courses for women who are officially registered unemployed. In its first year, the scheme trained 603 women in hairdressing, dressmaking, hand- and machine-knitting, leatherwork, lacemaking, massage, secretarial skills and child care. Handwork and traditional crafts, in particular, are areas that are regularly stressed, not only here but through other official and voluntary bodies, as appropriate areas of training for women, and may well be offered as free courses paid for by the state through the Federal Employment Service (Levina 1994a: 11). In the promotion of traditional crafts to women, there is an unmistakable element of nationalism: whether there is any viability in acquiring these skills for women themselves, their continuation is habitually presented in an extremely positive light as an essential part of Russian regeneration. Realistically, as course organisers at the Union of Russian Women admit, programmes of this type are not likely to have a major impact on women's employment prospects, especially when two-thirds of the trainees are engineers, economists and technicians (Ebzeeva 1993). A mere 8 per cent of this first intake of women found work in their chosen sphere and it might be expected that this proportion will fall even further as greater numbers of women with skills such as these enter the labour market. Indeed, it can be argued that the purpose of these courses is to take women out of the formal labour force, rather than keep them in. Certainly, the informal sector, as we discuss further in Chapters six and seven, is the only place where skills such as these are likely to find a ready application.

Realism, in terms of job prospects, is evidently the factor uppermost in the minds of staff at the Dubna employment centre in planning their training programmes. Until 1993, employment centres were allowed to offer training only to people whom they were certain they could subsequently place in a job. With a change in policy, retraining was to be offered more widely in a range of skills which, in the view of local employment centre staff, were likely to be in demand. Courses have been run at Dubna in several of the skills listed above, but there is a clear attempt to relate this to job placement, business start-up or to a broader social rationale. With careful placement in training and monitoring of courses the success of the programme at Dubna has been much better than the rates cited above. By the spring of 1994, 83 per cent of the unemployed who had completed training courses in the previous year had found work.

The distance of Dubna from Moscow and other towns with significant numbers of colleges and further education institutions immediately raises problems for the unemployed, especially for women with young children. As a result, the Employment Centre has set up courses in association with a local vocational training college and two other training centres. One of these has a 'Practical Business School' serving the needs of new commercial firms requiring managers and brokers. The Employment Centre engages in screening potential trainees through a process of psychological profiling in order to guarantee as far as possible that the firms will receive staff who are both trained and, as Marina Zhuravleva, head of retraining, put it, 'psychologically prepared for business . . . for work in modern economic structures' (Zhuravleva 1993).

On a very different note, and one which is far more likely to involve women, are two-month courses for work with children. These have been aimed particularly at school-leavers and at women with pre-school children, both groups which have become increasingly difficult to place. In the first half of 1993, half the women with pre-school children who completed a training course at Dubna chose to move into this area. On completion, 23 per cent of the whole group found jobs, a figure which was expected to rise over subsequent months. In the case of the school-leavers, the rationale was primarily social: to catch them quickly and provide them with some kind of vocational qualification before they had had time to start hanging around on street corners. Contacts had been developed with a firm which could offer them work and most had taken up employment, although not necessarily using their new skills. Whether they used them or not was not seen by Yuri Vetokhin and his staff as the prime object of the exercise: 'The important thing was to give them a push right from the start. . . . It works, not so much economically as psychologically' (Vetokhin 1993).

Other aspects of the Centre's work also have a strong psychological element, either directly through counselling, or through course content and work experience placements. Some, though not all, of the courses in handwork fell largely into this category. Strictly vocational sewing courses were on offer and, although they were not expected to produce highly skilled tailors, they were chosen by some unemployed women because there were orders for certain items which would provide them with work directly. A course in embroidery which was running in the spring of 1994, however, fell into a rather different category. Opportunities to make money from the kind of work the embroiderers were producing would almost certainly be few, but what the course was undoubtedly doing was providing a focus where women could come together and support each other and, through the approach of the course tutor, receive a much-needed boost in confidence. Dealing with the stress of unemployment is something which the Centre regards as part of its remit. As several of the women we spoke to made clear, there is a sense in which this permeates the Centre's entire approach and is something for which women who are out of work may feel extremely grateful. At its most conscious, it is apparent in the use of the staff psychologist's time to provide counselling, direct help which was received by nineteen mostly older women in the first half of 1993.

The most extensive of the courses on offer to women, the course in accountancy, is, however, intended to lead directly to well-paid employment. Not surprisingly, this is the most popular course with unemployed women who have higher education, since it is the only one which has the potential to keep them in professional employment. Although accountants are very much in demand in new commercial firms, it is by no means a foregone conclusion that anyone who retrains will find work. Job advertisements frequently ask for a minimum of three years' experience or at least demand well-qualified staff. In Moscow, most of the accountancy courses on offer last for just one month and have no screening procedures for entrants. The results of such an approach were ironically described by one of our Moscow interviewees, an unemployed former engineer. Having worked, after retraining, as an accountant in a small firm which subsequently folded, she could not find another job in this area:

> You know what it's like in this country, all the engineers have turned into accountants! We've all done one-month courses – we studied for fifteen years to become engineers and in a month we've turned into accountants! . . . The thing is, there are loads of people like us now. There's a demand for qualified accountants, the demand is very big, but if you look in the paper they want five years' experience, five years in a bank, experience of hard currency transactions, etc., etc.

[30]

It was in an attempt to avoid problems of this type that Dubna Employment Centre took the unusual step of setting up a ten-month course which would include a one-month work placement.

Ninety per cent of trainees on the first ten-month course in 1993–4 had a higher education, while two of the students had already completed a two-month accountancy course but found it inadequate. The ten-month course was of a far higher quality, including a study of finance, credit, tax law, computerised bookkeeping, insurance and basic economics. The course had not, however, been without its problems, which had led to some discussion as to whether it might be better to train new graduates who might be more willing to learn, rather than women who already had experience of a profession. Similarly, women who had recently been made redundant were felt to do better than those who had been out of work for some time: women who had become demoralised were often psychologically unprepared to change direction. Although all potential trainees had done psychological profiling before being accepted, it was felt that some unsuitable candidates had still found their way onto the course. As a result, while all the trainees would pass the course, only half of the students were likely to be recommended to employers on completion. The implication of this decision was that a number of students lacked either the application or appropriate personal qualities for a career as an accountant. It was apparent that, in taking this view, the Employment Centre was concerned for the sake of future trainees to maintain its own reputation with local employers as a provider of good quality staff, despite acknowledging that failure to find work on completion of a training course could be a severe psychological blow.

The work placement was financed by the Employment Centre and provided a good deal for local firms who received a free audit of professional quality in the process. For the trainees themselves, however, it could be something of a double-edged sword. Course tutors subsequently recognised that some students were ill-prepared for a work placement, on occasion met with critical attitudes from their employers and, consequently, wanted to give up the course entirely. For those who did well, however, the placement was an essential element in restoring confidence. One unemployed woman, for example, who had been in a state of some distress in the summer of 1993 had received two firm job offers after placement: the resulting sense of achievement and satisfaction made her almost unrecognisable. Some firms were clearly impressed with the quality of the trainees and offered work immediately, either to the trainee on placement or after visiting the course to select a new member of staff from the available pool. As the course neared completion the Employment Centre was actively looking for work for the trainees. Three of the trainees were already working professionally and half had jobs to go to, a success rate substantially better than average for Moscow Region. In addition, there were plans to set up an accountancy firm, initially with five or six of the trainees. As enterprises have traditionally employed in-house accountants, this is something of a new departure in Russian terms. The course tutor, who would be in charge of the firm, estimated that, with 150 small businesses already operating in Dubna, as many as fifteen accountants could be employed full time by a firm such as this within two years.

While it is clear that great care is being taken at Dubna to maximise their successes in finding work for the unemployed, there are elements of the Employment Centre's achievement which are less tangible but just as real for their women users, most notably the sense of support and respect which those using its services receive. To anyone familiar with job centres and benefit offices in Britain, the Dubna Employment Centre can scarcely fail to impress as a haven of humanity and sensitivity. The key issue in this, however, is surely one of scale. Using these services in Britain is depressing primarily because so little hope can be offered. Administering a combination of mass unemployment and punitive benefit policies year in, year out has a debilitating effect on staff as well as the unemployed. For the staff at Dubna, some of whom expressed shock at the severity of British regulations, this is yet to come. While the numbers remain manageable, concern for the individual is still possible, but with Britain now advising the Federal Employment Service on how to prepare for mass unemployment it is difficult to be optimistic about the future. One can only hope that Dubna will be able to preserve the best of its approach as the situation becomes more difficult.

IN CONCLUSION: WHAT DO WOMEN WANT?

Dubna's solution of offering effective programmes of professional training and support in finding new jobs appears one of the best options currently on offer to women who are unemployed. Yet, clearly, not everyone can be an accountant, nor would they want to be. On this issue of personal preference the realities of the new labour market come into conflict with what women want for themselves. The offer of retraining certainly does not meet with universal approval. No doubt one of the reasons why so many women who have been laid off fail to approach an employment eentre is their reluctance to change direction. For older women, in particular, it is asking a great deal to retrain, especially in a country which has had no tradition of people changing profession in the course of a working life. For highly skilled women who were committed to their work, it may simply appear out of the question:

> Right, you're forty, and now they come and tell you that your profession, that you, are no longer required and that you can retrain. What are you going to retrain for? Nothing. You'll sit at home and think, 'I can't do this and I can't do that, I can't face a new workplace because I hated the person sitting next to me in the last one' – there are psychological barriers like that. I'm forty-eight, I can't retrain. I don't want to study any more. I've had study up to here. I've been in every higher education institution in Moscow, right up to Moscow State University!
>
> [32]

It is not, however, only women in this age-group who express attitudes of this type. Even women in their mid-twenties expressed great unwillingness to think of any change of direction: 'It's too late for us to learn something else. What would we do?' [25].

These comments are in line with the findings of large-scale 1992 Russian studies suggesting women are just as negative about retraining as they are about accepting unskilled work (Rzhanitsina 1993: 81–2). All of this does little more than reflect the shock of an entirely unexpected situation. It would be unrealistic to expect women who have invested years of their lives in being engineers, scientists or economists to embrace happily a completely different future. Changing direction is something they may well do if they see no alternative but it is scarcely an option to look forward to. The desire to remain as they are explains the attraction of employment creation schemes set up by women's organisations. As we shall see in the next chapter, turning to a stopgap form of employment may be very welcome to those who retain hopes of returning to their former profession.

5

CREATING EMPLOYMENT: THE RESPONSE OF WOMEN'S ORGANISATIONS

As the impact of the new economic realities on women began to become apparent, women's organisations started to respond by attempting themselves to create employment opportunities. The organisations involved were many and various: some were offshoots of the former women's councils (*zhensovety*) which had operated under the umbrella of the Soviet Communist Party, others were new autonomous groupings with a range of aims and viewpoints. It should be stressed that by no means all, or even a majority, of the ad hoc women's groups which have sprung up in Russia embrace a feminist perspective. While all would perceive themselves as acting in women's interests, only a small minority would either ally themselves with mainstream western feminism or espouse views with which western feminists would feel entirely comfortable. That this should be so is scarcely surprising in view of their isolation from mainstream feminist debates and their prolonged exposure to anti-feminist and pro-natalist propaganda under the Soviet regime. Nevertheless, it says much for the confidence and seriousness of these organisations that they responded to changing conditions for women by attempting to become directly involved in employment creation.

One of the most striking aspects of the approach developed by these organisations was its concentration on homeworking. To western women, for whom homeworking implied one of the worst forms of exploitation the market had to offer, Russian women's enthusiasm for its possibilities could appear perverse, naive, even dangerous. As with so many aspects of Russia's post-Soviet development, the difference in perspective reflected both questions of definition and of practice in the recent Soviet past. Some women's organisations clearly perceived homeworking as a desirable element of Soviet policy to be retained for the good of mothers and children; others simply took the practice and proceeded to use it in a creative way for quite different purposes. In both cases, their actions stemmed from a very Soviet perception of homeworking as a benefit and support for women.

PROTECTING MOTHERHOOD – HOMEWORKING UNDER PERESTROIKA

When considering the Soviet legacy on homeworking, the very term causes some difficulty. Looked at from a British perspective, the word is imbued with negative connotations. The employment of outworkers in the UK in the production of soft furnishings, garment-making or tasks such as filling envelopes remains an unregulated and extremely low-paid activity (Allen and Wolkovitz 1987). The oppressive and exploitative nature of this work undertaken predominantly by women is in sharp contrast to more recent developments in the area of home-based work. With the advent of information technology, the concept of homeworking, in North America at least, has come to be associated with increasing numbers of well-paid white-collar workers. As this form of home-based employment becomes more common in Britain, the term 'teleworking' is being employed to distance this activity from the low level of skills and status that is implied by homeworking (Kinsman 1987).

Turning to the present situation in Russia, the concept of homeworking (*nadomnyi trud*) inherited from the Soviet Union's planned economy, while close to the traditional form of outworking employed in Britain, nevertheless has specific characteristics of its own. Homeworking for women became the subject of state and trade union regulation in the USSR in 1981: from this date it was to be offered primarily to pensioners, people with disabilities and, where necessary, to 'women with children under 15' (Polenina 1990). It was surely no coincidence that this took place in the same year that the major piece of Brezhnev-era legislation on 'strengthening the family' was placed on the statute book. The introduction of the regulations on homeworking did not, however, signal a major shift in employment practice. Enterprise managers who were expected to agree homeworking contracts showed little enthusiasm for a form of work organisation which could not be guaranteed to show results in productivity terms and would undoubtedly create complications. Even at the level of propaganda, the Party was in no hurry to promote a wholesale change in the working environment. Good intentions had been shown by making homeworking available: the implementation was left to individuals on the ground and, understandably, with the demands of the plan still paramount, little change could be observed.

In 1987, however, with a new administration and a significant change of emphasis, homeworking received renewed attention. The changes in legislation which offered mothers extended leave and enhanced rights to work part time and flexitime also made provision for women to work at home and, moreover, allowed women on maternity leave to engage in homeworking without losing benefit. From the perspective of a planned economy with a commitment to full employment, women could feel confident that returning to work full time when their children were older would pose no major problem. It was, of course, well documented that women's promotion prospects and average earnings were considerably diminished once they had had children, but the fear that they might not be able to move back into the workforce at all, or that they would be faced with a massive drop in status and income, was, in Soviet conditions, entirely absent from their calculations. In these circumstances, a temporary move into homeworking offered, in effect, the Soviet equivalent of a career break.

Moreover, homeworking was, in theory at least, an officially scrutinised and carefully regulated sphere of production. Any woman seeking this type of work would find her home subject to an inspection by members of the parent enterprise's management and trade union committee to ensure basic health and safety standards could be met. She would then be entitled to a written contract setting out terms and conditions. In addition to the agreed piece-work rates, homeworkers were eligible for annual bonuses and a minimum fifteen working days' holiday per year (Polenina 1990: 105–6). Where women believed that the regulations would be followed it was not difficult to see the attraction of staying at home.

Indeed, journalists looking into whether the new work regimes had much to offer women often began their articles with a glance at the alternative:

> You'll be getting up again tomorrow at the crack of dawn, making the breakfast, depositing sleepy children at school and nursery, dragging yourself onto a packed bus and just about getting to work on time. Then you'll be wondering all the time whether your tired child is alright in the nursery and whether he's had anything to eat. In the lunch break you'll race around the shops, eating your sandwiches on the way and after work you'll pick up the heavy bags and rush off to the nursery. Then you'll spend all night standing in the kitchen, and there's the washing, the ironing, looking after the children, checking the homework. When is there ever time to read or watch television? When on earth are you supposed to do it all?! Of course, we women have come a long way in our emancipation

– but then why is it so hard to wake up in the mornings, why are we unpleasant to our families, why do we yell at our children out of sheer tiredness, get upset in queues and at work or get into arguments on the bus over nothing?

(Dudukina 1988: 9)

As this writer suggested, it certainly did present a very curious picture of 'emancipation' in which, for so many women, the husband was completely invisible or, alternatively, expected to be waited on hand and foot. In these circumstances the advantages to women of home-based employment were self-evident.

The development of homeworking, despite the potential demand, was, however, both slow and spasmodic: across the Russian Republic in the late 1980s a total of about 250,000 people were engaged in homeworking. Nevertheless, examples of factories offering well-organised schemes could be found from Moscow to Siberia, mostly in the consumer goods sector, and especially in the production of clothing (Polenina 1990: 106). The experience of Riazan was frequently cited as a town where homeworking was flourishing under the watchful eye of the local Communist Party. Five centres in Riazan organised hand- and machine-knitting, sewing, toy- and souvenir-making and basket work and had a growing waiting list of women, both blue- and white-collar workers, united primarily by problems over child care. On average, women were working for the Riazan enterprise for around three years and then returning to their original jobs once their children were safely at school. Those who were quoted in the pages of the press expressed satisfaction with their level of earnings and, above all, with the convenience:

I've got a little boy of four and I couldn't get him into a nursery. Now I sit at home and knit and I don't regret it at all. I work in the house and sometimes outside when I take him for a walk. I earn 114 roubles a month and I'm very happy with that.

(Dudukina 1988: 9)

At a time when the minimum wage was 70 roubles, homeworking in conditions such as these appeared a rational and sensible choice.

Nevertheless, the Riazan experience, as so often with models of exemplary practice in the USSR, could not be repeated everywhere. Even here, difficulties were reported with premises, transport, equipment and raw material; across the country as a whole, inadequate transport and a lack of technology suitable for domestic use were major problems (Mashika 1989: 135). In addition, funds were being wasted in Riazan providing free training in hand- and machine-knitting and sewing for potential home-workers who then used their skills working for themselves. Almost two-thirds of the women trained in Riazan in 1987 subsequently declined to work for the parent company (Dudukina 1988: 10). The reasons for this lay in the attraction of newly legalised individual and co-operative activity: women who had learned their skills at the state's expense evidently felt under no obligation to be employed in a state enterprise. By the end of the decade, 90 per cent of women co-operative members in the USSR were homeworkers (Musaeva 1990b: 12).

In the face of the development of co-operatives, even enterprises such as the Riazan company offering relatively good rates of pay were evidently not seen as competitive by women looking for this type of work. Prior to the advent of co-operatives on a significant scale, however, women looking for homeworking had effectively been at the mercy of state enterprise managements, whatever the intentions behind government regulation. Journalists on *Rabotnitsa* magazine, for example, observed that most of the letters they received from women homeworkers complained of poor piece-work rates and exploitative factory managers. If, as the press maintained, the planned economy's pricing system was to blame, the results might be little different from those familiar to homeworkers in market economies. Rates such as 96 kopecks for 200 bra straps had women working at home round the clock, seven days a week to make 40 roubles a month (Vladimirova 1987: 14). Even where conditions were better and the work more varied than this, homeworkers were often expected to fulfil their plan, just as if they were factory based. Women might well value the fact that they could order their day as they wished, yet, when they were working, an extremely intensive level of activity was likely to be required to fulfil the enterprise's requirements (*Nasha sovremennitsa* 1989: 42).

In addition, the psychological pitfalls of home-based working were beginning to affect Soviet women for the first time. Women who had grown up with the expectation of working full time with only short breaks for childbearing, now found themselves facing the unaccustomed dilemma of when to go back to work. Was it when your child started school, or did they need you around through their first year at school? And after that, would you want them to become a latchkey child or, later, start getting into trouble with other teenagers? After all, as journalists observed, 'every age brings its problems and it seems that a mother is needed not less, but more and more' (Vladimirova 1987: 15). And in all of this, what happens to the mother's life and her career? Questions familiar to western women were presenting themselves unexpectedly as the fruits of perestroika and its policy of 'choice'. In promoting homeworking the official emphasis was overwhelmingly on women's responsibilities towards their families and the reduction of stress in fulfilling the mass of unpaid work in the home. With these ends in view, few were asking questions about how skilled technicians, engineers and economists felt about being offered the choice between sewing and knitting if they had had the misfortune to bear children who were perpetually ill. Indeed, the assumption often appeared to be made that, if nest-building was an inextricable part of the female nature, then any woman would not only be able to knit and sew but would find these activities intrinsically fulfilling. In a rare break with this school of thought, D. Vladimirova, writing in *Rabotnitsa* in 1987, wondered how economically rational it was for professional women to be retraining as garment-makers: 'We're not used to thinking like this, but isn't it possible for an economist or engineer or teacher to work from home?' (Vladimirova 1987: 15).

It was, however, on the issue of economic rationalism that all of the 'special work regimes for women' were to prove so damaging. By early 1988 it was already becoming apparent that, with the advent of cost accounting in Soviet enterprises, it made sense for managers simply to shed potentially troublesome workers and avoid employing others. The development of such a climate in Soviet enterprises did not bode well for women who had opted for homeworking while their children were small. Oddly enough, those who saw clearly the impact of perestroika on women's competitiveness in the labour market nevertheless were likely to continue to advocate the very forms of activity that were causing all the trouble. Zoia Pukhova, head of the Soviet Women's Committee, who had been trenchant in her criticisms of the effects of economic change at the 19th Party Conference in 1988, remained a staunch supporter of the extension of homeworking for women with young children. Indeed, she viewed it as an innovative approach to the problems posed by this 'undesirable' group of workers and castigated managements which took the easy way out and simply got rid of them:

This is nothing but a bureaucratic approach which contradicts the very essence of our socialist society and aims a blow at the idea of perestroika which has been conceived and carried out to improve our whole society and the life of each and every one of our citizens.
(Gavriushenko 1988: 10)

Unfortunately, such a sanguine view of economic restructuring could scarcely be borne out in practice. In the search for economic efficiency, it would no longer be the concern of factory managements to provide safety nets for workers they did not need. In the heady days of 1988, however, one could perhaps be forgiven for failing to see the edge of the precipice. Sadly, being 'indifferent to the fate of real people', as Pukhova put it (Gavriushenko 1988: 10), was likely to become increasingly common as the planned economy descended into chaos and market forces began to rule the day.

RUSSIA AND THE MARKET: HOMEWORKING AS EMPLOYMENT CREATION

As overtly discriminatory redundancy and recruitment policies became the order of the day in the new Russia, women's organisations began to look to homeworking as a means of easing the situation for women. Yet the terms in which much of the discussion of this subject were couched often seemed oddly discordant given the new economic realities. Prominent advocates of homeworking – which included by now some major women's organisations – appeared at times to be caught up in something of a time warp. Though it was abundantly plain that full employment and extensive social welfare provision were vanishing, the notion of 'protecting' women as mothers was evidently so deeply engrained in Russian thinking that it continued to dominate the debate even as the developing market was rendering it meaningless. Understandably, perhaps, for generations which had no experience of unemployment or a competitive labour market, there often appeared to be a lack of urgency and a sense of unreality in discussing how women were to deal with the new economic imperatives.

At the Second Independent Women's Forum, for example, an avowedly feminist gathering held in Dubna in November 1992, participants discussing unemployment were strongly advocating that women should be retrained to work at home on the grounds that this would not only provide them with income, but also allow them to spend more time with their children. The retraining they had in mind followed closely on the standard model of appropriate home-based work developed in the former USSR: the fact that this was to be offered to redundant engineers and economists failed to raise any eyebrows among the Russian women present. By contrast, this archetypal Soviet approach at a predominantly feminist conference was a source of some consternation to western participants who envisaged their Russian sisters walking wide-eyed and innocent into the horrors of exploitative piece-work rates and long-term impoverishment. Certainly, there was little apparent concern or, indeed, comprehension of how market forces might make 'spending more time with the children' a luxury women could not afford.

Nevertheless, numerous women's organisations in the newly independent Russia were busy creating employment through homeworking. Some national organisations, such as the Russian Association of Women Entrepreneurs, were involved, developing a programme of outwork for women based primarily on traditional domestic skills. Across Russia, similar initiatives were being set up at local level, almost invariably offering sewing work to the newly unemployed. In the central Russian city of Voronezh, for example, the former official women's councils were still going strong and had set up a firm based on outworking. Using waste materials from local factories, their women homeworkers were producing garments, haberdashery and items of soft furnishing which were then sold within the factory gates or at fairs held by the women's council. The rationale was to provide work at home for women in the most difficult circumstances – pensioners, the disabled and those with young children (Fedorova 1993: 2; Krylova 1992: 11). Increasingly, these organisations presented their work as a question of survival and certainly some saw in homeworking the possibility of a creative approach to an extremely unpromising situation. One such organisation was the Moscow-based Missiya (Mission): the following exploration of its activities and rationale is based on interviews with the organisation's founders and a group of its employees carried out between May 1993 and April 1994.

MISSIYA: THE RISE AND FALL OF JOB CREATION

The Russian Women's Association Missiya was founded in Moscow in 1989 with the aim of promoting women to decision-making levels in the political, economic and cultural life of the country. It also had the objective of disseminating information about the international women's movement and UN Convention on the Elimination of All Forms of Discrimination Against Women. One of its founders, Tatiana Luk'ianenko, had become interested in western feminism as an economics student at Moscow University and wanted to promote its ideas among Russian women 'who knew nothing about it'. The idea of establishing Missiya took shape during her subsequent work for the USSR Council of Ministers Committee on Women's Affairs and the Protection of Motherhood and Childhood. She was joined in establishing the association by Irina Savel'eva, a former Aeroflot employee and Communist Party member who, in 1993, graduated as one of Russia's first trained social workers.

In the first instance the association received support from commercial, institutional and individual sponsors, including the Global Fund for Women, and began offering business start-up advice to individuals and to specific groups such as single mothers. A women's business school was planned, though it remained on paper only. By the end of 1991 it was felt that sponsorship was an ineffective form of support as it involved a constant outlay of time and energy on publicity and canvassing for funding. Missiya's organisers therefore decided on a very different route to expand their association and achieve the goals they had set themselves.

Missiya goes into production

In late 1991 Missiya's organisers were becoming concerned about the large numbers of women who were already finding themselves without a reliable income as a result of cut-backs in the defence industry and in Moscow's many government bodies and research institutes. At the same time they were looking for a means of placing Missiya itself on a more secure financial footing. The result was the creation of Missiya's own company, Litt. The company produced haberdashery, simple garments, slippers, soft toys and souvenirs, most of which were sold through the major department stores such as Detskii Mir and Leipzig and also through the Irish House. Missiya's organisers spent a year planning the project and, specifically, studying the potential market before determining their policy of producing cheap, high-volume lines. The prices of their goods were deliberately kept low to secure a quick turnover and, indeed, at roughly half the price of similar items in commercial kiosks, the goods were often bought up by kiosk and street traders and resold at a higher price.

If the firm's profitability was a product of its high turnover then it also reflected both the lack of waste in the production process and the relatively low overheads. As a registered small company, Litt was able to employ up to 200 workers. Some of these, both men and women, were based in the workshop that the firm rented to store materials and produce the basic pieces from which the goods were then assembled. The majority of Litt's employees, however, worked from home, with pick-up and delivery vans collecting finished work and leaving new materials to assemble once a fortnight. Intriguingly, at this stage, the entire operation brought in a satisfactory profit, despite both their low prices and their explicitly non-exploitative policy on pay.

Homeworkers were paid piece-work rates, but no targets were set; instead, they were simply asked to state how much they were prepared to do. The rates were calculated on the basis of what could realistically be achieved in a seven-hour day to produce an income on a par with what might be earned elsewhere. In August 1993, for example, rates were calculated to allow the average employee to earn 1,500 roubles for a full day's work and, hence, around 30,000 roubles per month, roughly the same as a teacher's or researcher's wage. In practice, however, most of Litt's homeworkers put in a three- to five-hour day on a regular basis. The fair rates were undoubtedly a source of attraction for potential employees and, for those who had already tried homeworking for other firms, were likely to come as something of a relief. Litt did not advertise for workers but had constantly increasing numbers of enquiries from women who had learned of the firm's existence by word of mouth.

By the summer of 1993 Missiya's founders had organised subsidiaries of Litt in the central Russian towns of Tver and Riazan and also in the neighbouring republic of Belarus. The potential appeared to be virtually limitless, as Tatiana Luk'ianenko observed:

> The market in this country is far from saturated and the factories produce primitive goods. . . . What we are doing now can be easily reproduced in various towns, i.e. buying raw materials centrally and producing a huge quantity of goods in this particular way.
>
> (Luk'ianenko 1993a)

Missiya was therefore planning to set up several new branches over the autumn and winter of 1993–4. It was intended that these daughter companies would operate as independent firms yet maintain partnership agreements with the parent company. In this way, Litt in Moscow would continue to deal with the more complex issues of marketing on the basis of a profit share with the daughter company.

Despite this rosy picture, production managers at Litt inevitably expressed concern at the impact of inflation on the business. Prices of raw materials and fuel were likely to have an increasingly damaging effect, while unavoidable overheads were becoming unpredictable: rents on their premises, for example, had been raised four times in one month alone during 1993. At the same time, it was seen as vitally important to keep ahead of the market with cheap and attractive items that people would both want and be able to afford to buy. One of their major lines, for example, was a cloth-covered hairband in black and gold which could be spotted on heads all over Moscow in the summer of 1993. Despite its huge success, it was unwise to assume that demand would go on forever: 'we can't hairband the entire country', as the stores manager laughingly put it. For reasons of both cost and diversity they were therefore planning new lines using waste from existing goods or cheap local materials, such as fur in Belarus to make soft toys.

Homeworking for feminists?

At first sight it may appear a bizarre choice for self-declared western-style feminists to be promoting an activity so strongly identified with the exploitation and marginalisation of women's labour and with reactionary programmes on the family. To understand the *raison d'être* behind Missiya's extensive involvement with homeworking it is necessary to look closely at the very specific Russian circumstances in which they were operating and to listen to their own explanations of their thinking.

First and foremost, Missiya's operation was resolutely not about returning women to traditional domestic values or encouraging them to spend more time with their children. The question of reshaping women's roles within the family was in no way part of their agenda. In fact, rather the reverse was true: Litt, as a firm offering homeworking, was set up specifically to support skilled, full-time employment for women during a transitional period for Russian enterprises. As Tatiana Luk'ianenko (1993a) explained the rationale behind its operation:

> It's a temporary form of production which gives people the chance simply to survive in this transitional period. Most of our workers are highly-qualified specialists and they shouldn't be retraining to work in shops, for example. They need to survive this period so that they can then get back into their own enterprises.

As an example of the kind of situation she had in mind she cited their initial involvement with an enterprise which, during a period of restructuring, sent its employees on three months' unpaid leave with the promise of subsequent re-engagement at an enhanced salary. Temporary employment as homeworkers with Litt allowed women to get through the three months without the pressure of needing immediately to look for a different and probably less-skilled job.

Where women had no prospect of returning to their original employment, homeworking allowed them a breathing space in which to look for appropriate work in the new economic structures. The most important issue for Missiya's organisers was that highly educated women should not be displaced and de-skilled, but that they should be supported until work appropriate to their abilities could be found. To what extent this goal would remain viable as unemployment developed was evidently a moot point, yet Missiya's organisers tended to the optimistic view that 'the country will need these women's skills in the future'.

The offer of homeworking through a prolonged lay-off in effect filled a gap which, until December 1993, government welfare provision failed entirely to address. Russia had been providing benefit payments only to those registered officially unemployed. For the thousands of workers suffering lay-offs of several months or substantial delays in receiving wages there was no entitlement to any form of income support. Employees who believed, therefore, that they would be re-engaged were obliged to forfeit the chance if they were unable to support themselves for an unspecified period, usually through street trading and subsistence farming.

In setting up its homeworking company, Missiya was therefore attempting to meet an acute social need where the social security system was failing to respond to the new economic conditions. Secondly, it set out specifically to provide a financial lifeline for those for whom street trading was an impossibility. For women in poor health or for those with young or sick children who could not arrange child care, carting goods and produce to a sales pitch and then standing for hours in all weathers might simply not be feasible. Women in these situations were completely unprotected by any kind of welfare safety net once laid off from regular employment. They were, moreover, the groups which experienced the greatest difficulty in finding alternative employment. Add to this the fact that street trading was often seen not only as physically taxing but also as psychologically demeaning, and the attraction of working from home becomes obvious.

From Missiya's perspective, then, homeworking had particular advantages in terms of what it could offer women who could see few ways out of significant financial difficulty. At the same time, given the prevailing economic climate with its very high levels of inflation and punitive levels of taxation, production based on homeworking was probably one of the few realistic options open if the aim of providing extensive temporary employment opportunities was to be achieved. Homeworking could cut down overheads, allow for low capital outlay with maximum flexibility and substantially reduce the risk of business failure. Finally, by concentrating on the production of cheap and simple items for which there was a demand, the firm could not only ensure its own profitability but also offer instant financial benefits to its employees. Unlike other homeworking ventures producing more complicated items, women working for Litt had no need to spend time training and gradually developing speeds which would allow reasonable earnings. Articles made by Litt were deliberately kept simple – 'primitive work', as its organisers frequently described it – so that women could start earning from the very first day. The uncomplicated business of assembling the items in itself underlines the fact that survival for women, offered by women as a practical response to the realities of transition, was the prime aim of the operation.

Homeworking – a stopgap or a future?

More than half of the women who have worked for Litt have had a higher education; many were scientists, engineers and economists. The entire first wave of Litt homeworkers came from Moscow's research institutes where government money was no longer forthcoming to support large numbers of full-time researchers. To these were added women laid off from the defence industries and from administrative organs. For most of these women homeworking provided a temporary stopgap until they could either return to their former jobs or find alternative employment. By the summer of 1993, however, Litt was increasingly catering for pensioners, women approaching retirement, young women on maternity leave and students, all of whom might require the support of an income from homeworking for considerably longer.

Even where survival was so clearly at stake, moving from employment as, for example, a research scientist to assembling slippers at home inevitably implies a considerable loss of status. Women's reactions to such a drastic change were not, however, as predictable as one might expect:

> At first when I was offered homeworking I didn't know whether to take it or not. I thought, 'I'm an engineer, for goodness sake!' But then I agreed to do it and found that I liked it.
>
> [4]

> I've never been afraid of physical work and I decided that I'd be happy to do this. It's ordinary women's work and I learned how to do it quickly.
>
> [3]

As the new labour market develops and people's attitudes to work change, the question of status may come to seem less significant – particularly if it is a choice between homeworking or street trading for the erstwhile intelligentsia. As one Litt employee, herself a former research scientist, put it, 'It's hard to say what prestige is nowadays. It's not linked so much to profession any more, it's linked more to money. People don't think about it, you just have to get on with things'[1].

The counterbalance to any sense of loss of face, however, has undoubtedly been the sense of relief that the firm existed, that it did genuinely provide a lifeline at a particularly difficult moment and, moreover, treated its employees with a sense of respect. 'When you come here you meet intelligent people, you can have an intelligent conversation' [6], as one homeworker put it. Or, as another expressed it, 'This firm is different because everybody can find what's right for them. If I get fed up [of this] and don't want to do it any more, they'll find me some other work. People aren't thrown on the scrapheap' [3]. The sense that this was not simply a business but a women's organisation with social and not purely commercial goals was reflected very clearly in comments such as these: if the work was an unskilled stopgap then at least a feeling of exploitation appeared to be missing.

This sense of respect for the intelligence of the women who had been pushed into homeworking led to a situation where, as the firm expanded, former homeworkers were taken on the permanent, full-time staff. In addition, members of staff who moved directly into full-time employment with Litt were women who were similarly displaced from their chosen career. In the summer of 1993, Litt's full-time staff included a civil engineer from the defence industry, a statistician from the Road Transport Ministry, a former deputy head of economic planning in a radioelectronics factory and a research biologist. All of them had been displaced as a result of cut-backs and redundancies at their former place of work from which they had been either officially or constructively dismissed. In the case of the economist from the radioelectronics factory, for example, the almost entirely female workforce of 10,000 in her factory had been reduced to less than a third by 1993. Official redundancies had, however, been few as most women left after receiving no salary for two months. Almost all the women who remained were approaching retirement and, even if skilled, were earning only 15,000 roubles per month by the summer of 1993. As the economist was supporting both her child and her parents, she had no choice but to find alternative work. She heard about Missiya by chance and was offered a job as Litt's accountant.

In the cases of two of the other women cited above, no alternative job immediately presented itself and, as they were on their own and supporting either a child or an elderly relative, both became homeworkers for Litt. Their professional training and approach did not, however, desert them when they began assembling hairbands for a living:

When you do this sort of work your mind is completely free and you have lots of interesting thoughts like how to organise things better, how to improve the transportation.

[3]

I had some ideas about how the hairbands were made and changed the method of assembly – once an engineer, always an engineer!

[4]

As a result of presenting their innovations to Litt they were subsequently employed to organise supplies, deliveries and sales as the firm expanded.

As part of the development of Litt as a focus for employment creation, Luk'ianenko and Savel'eva viewed this kind of career progression as highly desirable. For the future they were envisaging that employees might become business owners in their own right:

> We involve people and they organise themselves, i.e. the people who work for us now propose new forms of production which means that they can be business owners themselves. In another six months we will organise more branches where the business owners will be people who have initiated the production. As an association we will be on equal terms with them, we will finance them and act as partners.
>
> (Savel'eva 1993)

It is, however, undeniable that for someone who saw their vocation in civil engineering, for example, this is never going to be the same, and some still feel this acutely. Nevertheless, in current Russian circumstances it may well be by far the best that can be achieved and might, at the very least, provide some kind of stability for the future.

There were, finally, two other groups for whom the activities of Missiya appeared to offer a viable future, rather than simply a temporary support. The first was a group of women artists supported by Missiya in partnership with the Women's Art Registry of Minnesota. This project, planned to last until 1996, was launched with an exhibition of the work of the thirteen women artists of the Art-Missiya group at the Central House of Artists in September 1993. The project's second stage aimed to include an exhibition in the United States and, ultimately, a joint Russian–American exhibition at the UN Second International Women's Forum in Beijing in 1996. This group of artists were, of course, very far removed from those involved in the home production of simple consumer goods, though, in the prevailing climate, no less in need of support.

The second group in a sense bridged the gap between the artists and the homeworkers. They were a small group of women who worked from home producing *matryoshki* – the nests of traditional Russian painted wooden dolls. In their behaviour and, particularly, in their attitudes this group was entirely atypical of homeworkers as a whole. Yet they were particularly interesting as an example of the fine line that might exist between homeworking for survival and homeworking as a form of self-employment. For this reason it is worth looking at their activities in some detail.

The three women we interviewed who were working on *matryoshki* had begun this activity some time before becoming involved with Missiya. One was a research chemist, the two others were employed as an economist and a statistician in one of Moscow's many ministries. All had substantial experience in their professions and little or no background in art and crafts when they began to paint *matryoshki* as a hobby and as a way of earning extra money. Within a remarkably short time they were completely hooked and, when the cut-backs and funding problems started at their workplaces, the dolls were already providing an alternative source of income.

It was not, therefore, a case of falling back on craft production when all else had failed. In the case of this group of women there was no attempt to look for other employment for the simple reason that they no longer wanted it. The experience of the economist is particularly interesting in this respect:

> My first reaction was, who's going to buy these? What's the point? Then I started to do it and the first thing I did I sold for 15 roubles – that was seven and a half kilos of meat at the time. I was so amazed I thought I'd try some more. And it just took me over. I got to the stage where I was sitting at work and all I could think about were *matryoshki*. I resigned from work in 1990 so that I could paint *matryoshki* full time. I had to give two months' notice. Everyone at work was appalled and thought I was crazy. And it's true, I was scared to give up a job like that. At the time I was on 250 roubles a month which was a high salary – an academician got 300, but I just wanted to do it.
>
> [8]

Like the other two, she simply felt that this was the work that she should have been doing all along. For these women, the planned economy with its smooth path from school to higher education to employment in one's chosen field had provided them with a comfortable but utterly undemanding life. The *matryoshki*, curiously enough, had provided both an absorbing passion and a certain degree of romance.

Before coming across Missiya they had sold their work through a joint venture, about which they had little good to say. 'You couldn't say they had a feeling for art. All they were bothered about was whether you'd made something big and bright' [6]. In addition, they were unhappy with this outfit's exploitative approach which they contrasted sharply with attitudes at Missiya:

All they were interested in was knocking the price down, paying as little as possible and then selling for as much as possible. One five-piece *matryoshka* is the most I can do in a week, but they were always telling us to work faster. I know how much I've put into a piece and here no one's ever said that we're asking too much. We take 50 per cent of the sale price.

[6]

The profit for Missiya, then, from this work was substantial and begged the question as to why these women chose not to market their work directly.

The answer appeared to lie in the women's attitude to their work. What they loved to do was paint, not do business. They believed that Missiya paid them a fair price for the work they did and were happy that this link relieved them of the aggravation involved in selling. In this way they were not exposed to criminal elements as a more formally organised craft business might be, they gained time and freedom to concentrate exclusively on the aspect of the work they enjoyed and virtually all elements of risk were removed. Nevertheless, although working individually in their own homes, they pooled ideas and shared experiences much as partners in a business would, and, moreover, were in the habit of describing themselves as an *artel*, a co-operative association of workers.

If the *artel* functioned as an artistic collective, it also operated very much as a support group. The isolation reported by other homeworkers was overcome both by their absorption in the painting and by the regular visits they paid to each other. Although not living particularly close to each other, they appeared at times to function almost as a community of like-minded people, often starting the day late and working on through the night, discussing their work on the phone if not in person: 'when we visit each other we never take presents, we just bring along something we've painted'. Two of them had extended the *artel* by communicating their enthusiasm to their children: one had a daughter in a special mathematics school who was learning to paint *matryoshki*; another had a son who left his job in electronics to study the Palekh style of lacquer miniatures and was producing *matryoshki* while studying at art college. Although these women did not view themselves as entrepreneurs, neither could they be considered to number among the ranks of the unemployed. At this stage they saw themselves as very definitely employed and, more-over, as having found their true vocation. As far as they were concerned, it would be all to the good if this particular type of homeworking were to carry on indefinitely.

The case of the *matryoshki artel* is illustrative of the way in which definitions of work have become extremely blurred with the loss of the employment certainties of the Soviet regime. Many women who worked for Litt were officially 'sitting at home' on maternity leave, in retirement or laid off from work. Yet, in reality, they might be busier in the informal, domestically based economy supporting themselves and their dependants than they ever were when formally employed. For the chance to do this on what they saw as a well-regulated, safe and fair basis women might well feel very grateful in the increasingly cut-throat climate of post-Soviet Russia. As one woman said:

I'm extremely grateful to the women who organised this firm. There's a big idea here. In these hard times women are in the most difficult position of all, and the idea is simply to give them the chance to earn money to survive. In this benighted country this firm is for us. I dread to think what would have happened if I'd been made redundant and this firm hadn't existed. Where would I have gone? No one would have been interested in me at my age.

[3]

By stepping into this situation, Missiya provided a missing link and, in this, a measure of security both for women who could not readily find alternative employment and those unwilling to launch into business on their own. As such, the organisation of homeworking was a remarkable example of ingenuity and innovation in a far from welcoming climate. Yet, however successful it had been, Missiya's ambitions did not stop there.

The Women's Investment Fund

In September 1993, Luk'ianenko and Savel'eva launched Russia's first women's investment fund, or, to give it its full title, the Missiya First Women's Specialised Investment Fund for Social Protection. At a time when investment funds had been springing up all over the country to attract the population's privatisation vouchers, Missiya decided to set up its own fund aimed specifically at benefiting women. The objectives of the fund were seen as a logical extension of the work they had already been doing through Litt to develop production and create employment.

The benefits of investment for women were intended to be universal. Funds would be invested in small- or medium-sized companies involved in the food industry and light industries employing large numbers of women. The additional investment attracted by the fund would allow these firms to maintain their workforce and, subsequently it was hoped, to create new jobs. As these firms were producing essential consumer goods, it was believed that a market existed for their products and that a steady, reliable return on investment would soon be achieved. At the same time, becoming shareholders would allow women investors to influence the range and quality of products being made. Finally, it was envisaged that investors would receive further benefits such as preferential rates and treatment in the repair of domestic appliances.

In line with much of the rest of Missiya's work, their approach to the investment fund appeared both wildly ambitious and attractively simple. At the press conference announcing its formation, Tatiana Luk'ianenko placed the development of the fund squarely within the framework of Missiya's overall aims and objectives as a women's organisation:

> Women should remember that they are more than half the popula-
> tion of Russia, yet unfortunately, their interests and needs are not
> taken into account when political, economic and social decisions are
> made. . . . Women in Russia have a high level of intellectual
> education and considerable experience of economic organisation –
> the kind that brings real results. Despite this, women have always
> been pushed aside from the highest levels of economic management.
> We want to see women making something of all their advantages.
>
> (Luk'ianenko 1993b)

As the fund was launched, Missiya appeared to be on the crest of a wave, with the continuing development of Litt and its offshoots and great confidence that this new venture would bring the benefits of their approach to an ever broader spectrum of women. Within six months, they felt sure, some real progress would be visible.

The impact of economic change

By the spring of 1994, deteriorating economic circumstances in Russia had had a major impact on the structure and activities of Missiya. Uncertainties over the pace of privatisation, continuing inflation and punitive levels of taxation had placed question marks against many of their activities. In addition, the entire issue of the viability of production had come to seem increasingly pressing to Missiya's organisers following a visit they had made to Bahrain over the winter. While on this trip they had been particularly struck by both the intensiveness of work there and the unexpected discovery that the wages of migrant workers were even lower than wages in Russia. This had led them to conclude that, as far as consumer items were concerned, Russian workers with their lack of a 'proper work ethic', as they put it, would be unable to produce quality goods and yet, globally, had already been priced out of the market by mass production in the Far East in particular. In concentrating their efforts on cheap consumer items, they had simply not foreseen that they would subsequently be competing against imports such as these. The question of competition in an increasingly depressed market had been further exacerbated for Litt by rising overheads. Transport costs to service the homeworking operation were rising alarmingly and they had been threatened with a major rent rise (a fourteenfold increase), on their stores premises which had put the entire organisation in jeopardy.

In response to all of this they had decided on a massive cut-back in their Moscow operation. Homeworking in the capital was being effectively wound down and transferred out of town where costs were lower. In the process the distinctive feminist ethos of the company was being lost: one of the new offshoots, for example, was employing primarily disabled homeworkers, thereby making it eligible for tax exemptions. This change of emphasis was, however, at its most apparent in the new organisational structure of Missiya. Litt had been divided up and transformed into a series of new firms with a significant change in profile. Among the new outfits were a design consultancy which continued to pursue the American links for the women artists and firms offering accountancy services and even political lobbying. Most of the employees were women but three of the new managers were men because 'our problem has been finding people who can take responsibility, independent people'. On this basis the previous staff had been disbanded, some once more having to find alternative employment for themselves. The overall organisation of Missiya itself had been reduced to the original two founding members, Luk'ianenko and Savel'eva.

While Missiya's founders had taken the initiative to carry out this radical restructuring and, in the process, to salvage what they could in a difficult economic situation, their employees were inevitably less well-placed. For the several hundred women in Moscow who, at any one time, could turn to Litt to see them through a difficult period, the chances of obtaining homeworking at fair rates had been dramatically reduced. For rather different reasons, though as a result of similar economic pressures, the *matryoshki* painters had also seen their lifeline disappear.

The artistic end of Missiya's operation continued to have an interest in craft production, though, by the spring of 1994, the firm and its former employees had gone their separate ways. For all concerned the problem was the same: a lack of demand and a saturated market. Predictably, in view of the alacrity with which Russian organisations had been promoting home-based craft production as an all-purpose panacea, there were potentially too many producers even for a country with a thriving tourist industry. For Russia in winter, at a time when the foreign media had been full of health scares, crime reports and plane crashes, the market had simply collapsed. For Missiya's *matryoshki* painters who had talked so proudly of their little artistic community and sense of vocation, the disappointment was palpable. They were still painting as a hobby and hoped the summer would bring some foreigners back, but the prices they could command for their work had in no way kept pace with inflation and could not provide a living wage. As a result, one was trading clothing, one was giving chemistry lessons and the third was working as a cleaner.

The economic realities which had led to the restructuring of Litt continued to cause problems in the areas which remained. Problems with their American partnership were putting their planned US exhibition of Russian women artists into doubt, while the many words of encouragement spoken at the Moscow exhibition had failed to translate into financial support or practical co-operation. The Women's Investment Fund, meanwhile, had been suspended due to concern over the future of privatisation and, in the existing climate, an inability to guarantee people's investments. All in all, the evaporation of Missiya's buoyancy and idealism appeared inevitable given the circumstances in which they were attempting to operate. As a feminist organisation in a country which has no voluntary sector in the western sense, or concept of partnership between governmental and voluntary bodies, Missiya had been obliged to act like a private company and, as a result, just like any other private company, it had been forced to bow to market pressures.

Missiya has been by no means the only women's organisation to offer homeworking to women who have been displaced in the process of economic change and it would be misleading to suggest that all either have or will follow the path that Missiya has taken. Nevertheless, it is salutary to observe how an organisation which has clearly been immensely successful has found itself overwhelmed by the economic pressures which dog production in Russia. In a sense, the activities of Missiya can be seen as exemplifying this transitional period in which the assumptions and behaviour applicable to the old system can, for a time at least, be adapted to fit the new. Whether, in the face of market pressures, it is possible for any commercially based organisation to retain a distinctive social role is, at the very least, dubious. For the women who worked for Litt, however, the implications are serious. Though the work was intended to offer temporary support while women found new employment, it was clear that, given the realities of the developing labour market, many would come to rely on it for prolonged periods. What should have been a stopgap inevitably turned into a way of life when there was nowhere else to go. In these circumstances, when women can no longer rely on organisations to create a safety net for them, they have little alternative but to attempt to create one for themselves.

6

WOMEN AND BUSINESS

As business has developed in Russia since its independence, women have become increasingly involved in running new commercial structures and privatised concerns. The majority of these women are concentrated in one of two spheres: either they are former state enterprise directors now managing their newly privatised businesses, predominantly in the service sector, or they are commercial directors, managers and PAs running small enterprises or joint ventures set up by others. There are still relatively few women who have set up businesses of their own. In the absence of official figures, estimates suggest that, by 1993, between 1 and 3 per cent of the new class of entrepreneurs were women (Khotkina 1993: 20).

There has, however, been considerable discussion in the Russian media of the prospects for women's businesses and, moreover, much encouragement of women facing redundancy to regard self-employment as a way forward. It is, therefore, the promotion of women as independent entrepreneurs and the significant problems which this entails that are the focus of this chapter. As will become apparent, the problems women face in attempting to set up in business on their own make the definition of 'small business' in the present Russian context extremely problematical. Many women are involved in home-based activities, buying and selling or offering services to supplement their incomes on a more or less regular basis: this issue will be dealt with in more detail below in Chapter seven. For the purposes of this discussion, therefore, we are taking 'small business' to mean either a firm set up by one or more women, usually in premises of its own, which may or may not employ others, or home-based self-employment which may draw in the assistance of other family members. In either event, the defining feature is that the business is intended ultimately to provide permanent full-time employment and an adequate income for the woman involved.

117

THE COMING OF THE MARKET: OPPORTUNITIES FOR WOMEN?

A year before the failed coup of August 1991, which heralded the demise of the USSR, the parliamentary deputies of the Russian Federation had voted in favour of both Russian sovereignty and a rapid transition to a market economy within Russia itself. The major Soviet women's magazine, *Rabotnitsa*, greeted this event not only with an interview with Boris Yeltsin and a lyrical editorial on the revival of Russia, but with the launch of a new feature, the 'Business Women's Club'. In the juxtaposition of these three pieces, the magazine was nailing its colours firmly to the mast and seizing the initiative presented by a new economic programme to challenge its readers' thinking (Os'minina 1990; Skliar 1990; Musaeva 1990a).

Based on letters from women who were already feeling the chill winds of redundancy and wondering perhaps if they would be able to set up something of their own, the feature was addressed to those who wanted to 'change their lives, to become a real business person'. It went on with an 'am I the entrepreneurial type?' quiz, information on management courses and answers to legal queries. Over the following year the feature continued with information and advice and was joined in early 1991 by similar coverage in the major magazine for rural women, *Krest'ianka*. In much of this writing, its authors were at pains to place themselves alongside their readers in admitting their own sense of uncertainty at how they would face the future without the security of the Soviet system's 'job for life'. More quizzes, with titles like 'What if I lost my job tomorrow?', posed unfamiliar questions such as, 'If you have higher education, could you imagine becoming a market trader or a child-minder?' or 'What talents and skills do you think you have?' ('Chto my umeem . . .' 1991: 4). In these early days the media was preoccupied with two major issues: what kind of business should women be looking at, and, more fundamentally, should women be going into business at all?

BUSINESS AND FEMININITY: A PERFECT MATCH?

In their discussions of the demands of the alien world of business, those offering advice on the pages of the press quickly turned their attention to the personal qualities required of the successful entrepreneur. Women with some experience of business were anxious to point out the potential pitfalls and help readers avoid ill-advised decisions. As Elmira Medzhitova, head of the Union of Women Entrepreneurs, was quick to observe, 'Being an entrepreneur is not everyone's cup of tea. A person who is not prepared to take risks, who doesn't know how to take independent decisions and bear the responsibility for them shouldn't go into business' (Kariakina 1991: 23). Psychologists asked to describe the qualities of the successful entrepreneur came up with lists of adjectives such as bold, success-oriented, competitive, aggressive, emotionally stable, independent, self-motivating and creative. Given the heritage of Soviet pronatalism with its lists of 'natural' male and female characteristics, it was inevitable that the next question was whether women should be involved in business at all. Nor was it any surprise to learn from the experts that business was 'psychologically closer to the male character . . . although women can be good managers in small- and medium-sized business' (Meliia 1993: 4).

When psychologists were offering prescriptions of this kind there was little to prevent the non-specialist from jumping on the psychological bandwagon. Questions to businessmen as to why women had been relatively slow to set up their own ventures were liable to meet with a response couched in the following sort of language:

> Women are more conservative, more cautious than men – these qualities are part of women's very nature. They find it more difficult than men to decide to 'change their life', to plunge into a new sphere of activity. But then women are better at adapting to various extreme situations than men and have a higher level of endurance.
>
> (Musaeva 1990b: 12)

Women, both psychologists and lay people alike, were also drawn into this game, as were successful businesswomen who were inevitably quizzed by journalists about their 'femininity'. Thus, women were to be found extolling intuition and emotionalism as maternal qualities which could give women the edge in business, both in ideas and in handling people (Kostygova 1991: 10–11).

Just occasionally, a successful businesswoman would resist questions about her character or stand the stereotype on its head, as in this comment from Nadezhda Shuliat'eva, president of the Russian Union of Small Enterprises, when asked if she had a 'masculine character':

> It depends which way you look at it. If we're going to be frank, then our men (not all of them of course) are pretty cowardly. They go whichever way the wind blows. They don't take a principled stand. So I think I've got a feminine character – I'm a fighter.
>
> (Shuliat'eva 1992: 4)

If responses such as this suggested that some women were keen to shrug off the discussion of appropriate psychology as stereotypical nonsense, there was, none the less, a serious element for women in this discussion. The commonplace stereotypes of male and female qualities reflected the discriminatory climate in which women had been operating under the Soviet regime. Its legacy had both significant psychological consequences for women themselves and also coloured attitudes towards them on the part of the men who dominated the new business world.

Women called upon to discuss the new economic climate observed that, if women were unsure of themselves and their capacity for business, there were reasons which went well beyond notions of the 'essential feminine'. Some felt that the education system had a lot to answer for in teaching girls how to respond to orders rather than take initiative for themselves: 'As a result, women just don't have the reserves of self-confidence which are absolutely essential for business' (Babak 1992: 24). By the same token, women in the workplace in the USSR had had relatively little experience of management. The discrimination they had experienced in Soviet enterprises was therefore having a knock-on effect in the new Russian business world. As Larisa Babukh, managing director of a management training agency put it, 'There's a psychological barrier which expresses itself as low self-esteem. . . . We've got used to being in subordinate roles' (Babukh 1992: 7).

Some of the women who discussed these issues in the media were very wary of presenting yet another damaging stereotype of the diffident, unconfident woman not knowing how or where to begin when substantial numbers of women were already successfully making headway in business for themselves. What was needed, in their view, were more positive role models and plenty of publicity for women who were successful (Babak 1992: 24; Centre for Gender Studies 1993: 19). At the same time, women might achieve more with a frank appraisal of the problems they faced in attempting to gain a foothold in a male-dominated environment – 'the tyranny of grey flannel', as Nadezhda Shuliat'eva put it (Semenova 1992: 1).

Successful women interviewed in the national press made it quite clear that women were not seen as equals in the business world. Although they were often at pains to make the customary point that the market itself was gender neutral, they would immediately put forward the contradictory assertion that women began with substantial disadvantages, not least the attitudes of men towards them. 'Business in our country is a male affair with extremely strong patriarchal traditions', is a not untypical comment which, at first sight, appears somewhat curious given the very recent advent of private business (Gorbunova et al. 1992: 9; Bragina 1992: 6). Yet such observations were based in part on the nature of the new business elite in which former Communist Party functionaries played a prominent role. Neither they nor, as one woman commentator put it, the 'new "hard-boiled" entrepreneurs' had, in their view, much time for women (Engert 1993: 6; Vovchenko 1992: 1).

That they did not, it was felt, did little more than reflect opinion in society at large. Thirty per cent of participants questioned at the 'Women and the Market' conference held in Moscow in the autumn of 1992 believed that 'general mistrust of women' was preventing women taking their place in business. Others spoke of the contempt and prejudice of public opinion which translated into very real obstacles when women attempted something of their own (Gorbunova *et al*. 1992: 8; Vovchenko 1992: 1). The obstacles, moreover, might well begin at home: women journalists and sociologists alike observed how few women were involved in family businesses and how most preferred to make partners of their women friends rather than their husbands. The reasons, they suggested, ranged from the low expectations women had of their husband's involvement in the family to men's outright hostility to their wives' business activities (Vovchenko 1992: 1; Laputina 1991: 13).

Meanwhile, some of the most popular newspapers were scarcely helping matters by building a new negative stereotype of 'the businesswoman'. *Argumenty i fakty*, for example, saw fit to publish a frivolous response to a reader's question about finding a good wife in which businesswomen were described as 'hard to miss, energetic, talkative, shrill and don't know how to flirt'. It was, the piece insisted, no good expecting home comforts from a woman like this ('Kak vybrat' nevestu?' 1992: 1). More serious, and probably more damaging, were articles from self-styled experts. One of these, a woman doctor who was described as working on 'the sexual characteristics of the businesswoman', castigated women with careers for neglecting their children and damaging male sexuality. In an interview reminiscent of the height of the Soviet pronatalist campaign, she expressed great concern at the future prospects of little girls who preferred toy cars to dolls, blamed their career-oriented mothers and went on to advise businesswomen to content themselves with sexual partners, rather than a husband and children (Proshina 1992: 7).

Women attempting to set up in business, then, were faced with the negativity of a society which regarded the expression of sexual stereotypes as merely a statement of the obvious, the prejudice of men who dominated the business world and their own lack of confidence and managerial experience. Summed up in this way, it could be said that such factors differed only in degree from the experience of women in many other societies. Where they became particularly significant, however, was when placed within the very particular psychological landscape that was Russia at the beginning of the 1990s. Falling living standards and unemployment were the economic manifestations of a far broader crisis: the total collapse of a way of life, the loss of the old certainties of the Soviet regime and the consequent moral vacuum of an anarchic period of 'transition'. In these circumstances, perhaps inevitably, concepts such as family and nation began to exert a greater hold on the popular imagination and to ensure that women would not easily break with the legacy of the Soviet regime in attempting to enter the uncharted waters of Russian business.

A SUITABLE BUSINESS FOR A WOMAN?

If the Russian version of pop psychology was quick to tell women whether or not they were suitable candidates for business, it was perhaps inevitable that its pundits should also concern themselves with telling women what kinds of business to go for. 'Women are better at painstaking work which demands patience and care. . . . The most important thing is to find yourself an area of activity which takes account of the women's sphere' (Musaeva 1990b: 12). The service sector, catering and garment-making were all held to be particularly suitable for women as these activities

> can be termed 'person to person', where personal contact and communication between those offering and those receiving the services is the most important thing. As psychologists have observed, men are happier working in what might be termed the 'person–machine interface', in construction, the repair of complex technology, computer firms and so on.
>
> (Kostygova 1991: 10)

In their preoccupation with female qualities and appropriate activities, none of the experts airing their opinions in the media appeared to have noticed the blindingly obvious: the first major wave of women thinking about business opportunities were overwhelmingly engineers and other technical specialists.

Nevertheless, women were consistently urged to consider the skills they had when contemplating business and, in the first surge of discussion of this issue at least, this almost never included their professional skills. Instead, women were urged to sit down and make lists of all the things they could do, all of which were firmly based on domestic skills and hobbies. Psychologists explained how they went out to enterprises planning mass redundancies to help women cope with the future and suggested that their knowledge of sewing, knitting, cooking and child care would usher them into a new life. Others developed these ideas further in women's magazines: start a cafe, open a sandwich shop, set up a home laundry or a hairdressers, think about child-minding or dog sitting, don't be afraid of cleaning, if you can knit or embroider 'your skills are simply priceless' (Babak 1992: 24; Kariakina 1991: 22). If all of this was intended to encourage, it must nevertheless have come as a shock to women graduates with professional careers. If in fact it truly represented the only genuine practical means of survival for women in the new economic circumstances, it was a damning indictment of the conditions in Russia which produced such an outcome. Finally, it presupposed that combating unemployment in this way was a viable proposition as the market developed – a moot point at the very least.

In the many pieces of journalism which attempted to tackle the theme of how women should greet the coming of the market, few commentators questioned the nature of the businesses proposed. Ol'ga Laputina, writing in *Rabotnitsa* in 1991, was one of the few who did, wondering what kind of future lay in store for the country as a whole if its best educated women were moving *en masse* into baking and sewing. After the 'period of developed socialism' and the 'period of perestroika', society, or more particularly women, she suggested ironically, had now progressed into the 'period of pie-making' (Laputina 1991: 12). Writing eighteen months later, when the scale of the de-skilling of women was becoming ever more apparent, Galina Semenova, vice-president of the organisation 'Women and Development', could be rather more forthright:

> The problem is not simply that patriarchal views are alive and well, but that out of the huge mass of professions which could improve our quality of life, provide women with good incomes and broaden the market's sphere of activity, we are offering them a choice which is narrow, unadventurous and unproductive.
>
> (Semenova 1992: 1)

In a similar vein, Galina Yakunina, economist and businesswoman, spoke of the senselessness of retraining high-quality specialists instead of redirecting their existing knowledge, skills and contacts straight into the business world (Krylova 1992: 10). By the end of 1993, however, very little had changed, except perhaps the nationalist language in which dismay was sometimes expressed. Moscow's employment department was still offering free training in crafts and handwork at their regular jobs fairs and displaced engineers were still trying to make a living out of lace collars and artificial flowers. Asking the obvious question about the lack of demand for their knowledge, *Rabotnitsa*'s correspondent concluded, 'this is likely to lead to the degradation of the nation, if all the mothers of tomorrow's schoolchildren only know how to knit and weave' (Levina 1994a: 11).

Yet the truth of the matter was that, in the embryonic state of the market in Russia, it was far from apparent how women's existing knowledge and experience could simply be transferred into new commercial ventures. At the same time, baking pies, or some similar activity, might at least provide some immediate, much-needed income. Given the circumstances in which they found themselves, it was plain that women who were setting up independent businesses of their own were indeed very frequently basing them on traditional domestic skills. Sewing workshops, in particular, featured heavily in the press, along with advice on how to start out as a seamstress. Women's business fairs and exhibitions were dominated by garment-makers and craft producers, often reviving traditional Russian skills and patterns. The problem, actual or potential, lay not in the quality of the work of women new to these businesses, but in the sale of their produce. Pinning one's hopes on the revival of traditional crafts was, as we have seen in the case of Missiya's *matryoshki* painters, a very risky thing to do. Encouraging women to find their salvation by turning other forms of handwork into a business might very well run into similar difficulties.

One of the most common complaints made by women during the last two decades of the Soviet regime was of the lack of development of the USSR's service sector. A shortage of retail outlets, cafes and restaurants, laundries and repair shops, not to mention the dire quality of services offered by many of those which did exist, made it virtually inevitable that services would not only be seen as a suitable area for women's business, but also an inexhaustible market. Russians were so starved of services taken for granted in the West that it was assumed they would inevitably rush to patronise almost anything that anyone cared to set up. 'Our market is so empty that you can do whatever you like', was a very common observation in the first couple of years after the collapse of the USSR. Yet even then it was becoming apparent that this was not necessarily the case. In the first place, as we shall see (pp. 137–8), setting up the kind of service centres women fantasised about proved to be far from simple. Secondly, the kinds of activities women could manage to engage in immediately began to look less viable as soon as they became a mass occupation. Thirdly, and most deadly of all, the overall nature of the market itself was changing.

That literally hundreds, if not thousands, of women had taken to heart the exhortation to 'think about your skills' was very apparent from the mass of work on sale at craft fairs, exhibitions and markets and from advertisements placed in the press. In just one 1992 issue of the broadly feminist newspaper, *Novaia zhenshchina*, for example, no less than sixty-five Moscow women were looking for orders for handwork and crafts, thirty-three of them producing knitwear, twenty-one offering embroidery ('Bank dannykh' 1992: 5). While it is possible that sufficient buyers were still there at this stage to ensure a reasonable income for growing numbers of women knitters and embroiderers, it was doubtful that this situation would last indefinitely. Early in 1992 economists offering advice on business plans in women's magazines were warning that, if the economic reforms were a success, there would be more and more small businesses offering similar goods and, at the same time, increasing levels of cheap foreign imports flooding for the first time into the Russian market. In addition, the dramatic fall in living standards which had occurred by 1993 was depressing the market overall. When more and more households were struggling to make ends meet, fewer and fewer were likely to be placing orders for non-essential clothing. Indeed, they were more likely either to start making their own or join the ranks of those offering garment-making services. The problems of increasing supply and shrinking demand were beginning to make suitable businesses for women appear rather unsuitable after all.

As the myth of the service sector gold-mine was beginning to evaporate, women were also starting to find that there were other myths of the market about to explode. Perhaps the most potent of these had been closely linked to the search for the suitable business and formed part of Russia's own ideology of enterprise. So much of the discussion of business had suggested that, given the right attitude, it was actually quite easy to be a success. All you had to do was think what skills you had and there was your business. The notion that, with the market, all doors were open to the person with vision and drive had been offered to the displaced women engineers of Russia, just as it had to redundant British steelworkers, miners and shipbuilders in the heady days of Margaret Thatcher's 'enterprise culture'. 'There are enormous possibilities. You need just a little bit of imagination and thought', as Konstantin Borovoi, head of the Russian commodities exchange, disingenuously announced to the readers of *Rabotnitsa* in 1992: 'Hurry up and buy or lease a little shop, perhaps, or a bakery or a cafe' (Krylova 1992: 10). But, as women were increasingly finding out, following this advice was a good deal more complicated than it at first appeared.

HOW TO START – A QUESTION OF KNOWLEDGE

In a developed market economy, people intending to start a business can find a range of agencies waiting to offer advice, information and specialist services. Despite all of this, setting up in business remains an extremely daunting affair, not least because the mere existence of these services cannot guarantee anyone against business failure. In Russia, not only are such agencies very thin on the ground but the legislative and financial frameworks in which they are operating are having to be virtually invented from scratch. Add to this the fact that engaging in private business was until very recently a criminal offence and it is not surprising that women writing into the press for help frequently describe themselves as 'business illiterates' or 'people of the old psychology' (Virkunen 1991: 16).

Understandably, as Russia began its transition to the market, there appeared to be a high degree of bewilderment at what business might involve. Irina Korchagina, editor of *Novaia zhenshchina*, for example, observed that half their postbag came from women asking how to start a business or, even more revealingly, both what kind of business they should engage in and, simultaneously, how to find a foreign sponsor (Korchagina 1992: 6). This was producing some curious phenomena, such as women registering businesses to do 'everything that's legal', as Larisa Babukh put it. Outfits such as these would appear from time to time in the advertisement columns, offering perhaps a dozen different activities from selling fruit juice to organising modelling competitions ('Bank dannykh' 1992: 5). Lacking a clear focus, such businesses were doomed to a very short life indeed (Babukh 1992: 7).

In response to readers' queries, magazine features began to offer systematic advice on legal issues, the procedures for business registration and how to prepare a business plan. The information was very necessary. While a whole range of booklets on market terminology and the basics of accountancy were beginning to flood city bookstalls, finding one's way around this sea of print was, for the novice, utterly confusing. There were no straightforward mass-produced handbooks on business start-ups readily available, either from government institutions, advice agencies or even from commercial banks. It was in this climate, therefore, that a number of organisations run by women began to offer business start-up training. To explore further the problems encountered by women in setting up small businesses, the work of one of them, Guildia Small Business Development Centre, is looked at in some detail below.

Guildia – training for business

One of the regular contributors of advice to *Rabotnitsa*'s business features was Irina Razumnova, economist and senior researcher at the Academy of Sciences' USA and Canada Institute. As a specialist on western small businesses, she set up the Guildia Small Business Development Centre in

Moscow in 1991 together with a group of fellow researchers. While offering information and advice both to people considering business start-ups and those seeking to develop their skills, Guildia itself has not been immune from the pressures experienced by its customers. The development of this organisation and the problems encountered by its founder and staff are in themselves highly illustrative of the climate in which women attempting to set up projects of their own are obliged to operate.

Guildia was officially registered in 1991 and offered its first training course in October of that year. From the very beginning, funding of its own operation has been a constant headache. Having visited America in 1989 as a guest of the US Small Business Administration, Razumnova subsequently approached the then Soviet government with a view to setting up a similar organisation in Moscow. Responses both from them and, with the demise of the USSR, Russian government agencies have been uniformly negative, a fact which Razumnova puts down to the continuing dominance of the former political elite. Although some initial support was received from the municipal authorities in Moscow, once western sponsorship was negotiated Guildia chose to register as an independent joint-stock company.

Significant western sponsorship came from what might appear to some an unexpected quarter. Avon Beauty Products signed a partnership deal with Guildia in June 1992 through which Avon would provide financial support while, in return, Guildia would help Avon break into the Russian market. Through the US Small Business Administration, Avon has its own programme of encouraging women entrepreneurs, most visibly with its 'Women of Enterprise' Awards, a fact of which Irina Razumnova was well aware. Clearly, Avon was not interested in a Russian link through sheer altruism, but Guildia's founders were entirely pragmatic about the deal: while Russian support was conspicuous by its absence, Avon money paid for repairs to their premises, provided a security guard, helped with the lease and subsidised course fees.

Additional overseas help came directly from the Canadian government in the form of computers, a fax and a photocopier. Other than this, Guildia's very pleasant offices are the result of the staff's own painting and decorating efforts, while the courses and training packages have been put together by them from scratch. The lack of a wage for the first six months led to a staff turnover of 70 per cent, yet, despite all this, the group of between five and eight women have been responsible for a centre which, in its first two and a half years, put over a thousand people through its courses.

Guildia's staff is exclusively female – 'it's hard work, men just wouldn't stick it' – and 79 per cent of its customers are female, yet this does not, in their view, make it a women's organisation. Much of this reflects Irina Razumnova's personal perspective:

> In general I'm against the feminist movement. I don't like this division of people into women and men because, in this country, the men are probably in a worse state than the women. They are weaker: all the best men were destroyed in our country and the women have turned out to have more zest for life and a greater capacity for business.
>
> (Razumnova 1993)

As a result, Guildia does not regard itself as in any way part of a developing women's movement. Attempts at co-operation with women's organisations have proved fruitless and are described as 'a waste of time'.

Guildia's rationale places its commitment to business development at the head of its list of priorities: to develop a Russian version of the US Small Business Administration, to galvanise into action the 10 per cent of the population who, they believe, are the potential entrepreneurs and, in this way, to create 'the new middle class, the third estate'. Guildia's slogan, 'independence and prosperity through knowledge' admirably sums up its *raison d'être* and political perspective. Nevertheless, because this is Russia and not Britain, Guildia's activities and the attitudes of its staff do not comfortably fit in with the 'new right' line that all of this suggests. As we shall see, behind the business rhetoric lie considerable reserves of humanity and compassion, elements to which their women customers, often coming from difficult backgrounds, are particularly sensitive.

That the vast majority of Guildia's customers are women inevitably reflects the realities of unemployment or fear of redundancy in Russia today. It has also, in part, reflected Guildia's recruitment methods. Lacking funds to pay for advertising, Irina Razumnova set about writing articles in *Rabotnitsa* and other papers, and getting herself regularly interviewed in order to bring the organisation's existence to the attention of a broad public. The success of this policy was attested to by the arrival in response of some 1,500 letters from all over the former USSR. The letters overwhelmingly came from women, ranging from schoolgirls thinking about their future to pensioners wondering how to supplement their income. The following letter is extremely typical:

Dear Irina Razumnova,

I don't know whether this letter will get to you. I read about you in *Rabotnitsa* a year ago but I couldn't make up my mind to write to

128

you, although I kept the magazine. I was hoping to find a job but I didn't. I've been out of work for nearly a year and I would love to start my own business but I haven't got much confidence because I don't know anything at all about business. How can you be confident when you're completely in the dark? I'm a graduate of a food industry institute but I've never worked in this area because of my son's illness. The family moved to a small Siberian town and I couldn't find work here either.

I've dreamed of setting up a small children's cafe for a long time. I'm not on my own, I've got friends who would be glad to help me. If you have any correspondence courses on business I'd like to take part. Please help me get on my feet because that's so hard to do nowadays. I'm pinning my hopes on you.

Yours sincerely, Irina

As Irina Razumnova remarked, 'We answer all the letters because each one is a cry for help.'

On the basis of the letters an extramural course was developed with a learning package of legal documents, information on marketing, account-ancy and so on. Within eighteen months some 300 people had completed this course. Meanwhile, at the Moscow centre, substantial numbers of people were taking part in a range of courses, the principal ones being 'How to start up your own business', 'Small business management' and 'Financing and accounting in the small enterprise'. In 1993 the range on offer was extended to include more advanced courses, notably the University of Western Ontario School of Business Administration's 'Leader' programme which had already run successfully in Eastern Europe.

For all of the basic courses the guiding principle was that they should be cheap, and thereby accessible. As a result, most of their customers were people who would not receive funding for training either from their enterprise or from a commercial business. In addition, up to March 1994, 18 per cent of those attending the most popular courses had either free or reduced rate places. The disabled, the unemployed and women with large families all received free tuition. The Moscow courses were not, however, the end of the story. From 1993, Guildia began to work with employment centres, the first being Dubna, providing bespoke courses, funded by the centres, for local unemployed women. The first six courses, in towns across Moscow Region, were offered free to 308 women. There were plans to set up a business club to provide on-going support to people who had been on their courses, a business consultancy and, above all, a series of centres in other cities to train teachers of business skills and develop start-up courses in the provinces.

The forty-hour start-up courses at the Moscow centre cover basic questions of law, finance, accountancy and taxation, as well as the issue of security discussed by Interior Ministry representatives. The one-day seminars offered by the employment eentres cover similar, though obviously less extensive, ground. Whatever the format, the courses include elements of personal development or what, in the Russian context, is always described as 'psychology'. Beginning with these sessions is seen as very important, given that people attending the courses are often initially very disorientated, especially those newly ejected from full-time work in a climate where business may seem to operate by the laws of the jungle. In such a situation, a sense of stress and bewilderment at both their unaccustomed situation and uncertainty as to what is now possible is probably inevitable; as such, these are issues which Guildia's trainers are evidently at pains to address.

Certainly, women we interviewed who had attended Guildia's courses spoke highly of their overall quality and content but particularly valued their effectiveness in personal terms:

> We worked with the psychologist for two days. The classes were extraordinarily useful. I've studied psychology but I couldn't look at my own capabilities in the way the psychologist made us see them. . . . We made an assessment of ourselves and then we all assessed each other anonymously. When I got my piece of paper I was amazed. People had assessed me much more highly than I assessed myself. They thought I was a reliable person who would be able to take risks but at the same time use my head. It made me think that I could use this.
>
> [9]

Women on the one-day Guildia seminar in Dubna experienced similar benefits. If knowledge is indispensable for would-be entrepreneurs, the need to overcome the sudden paralysis induced by redundancy is at least as pressing. The women leading the Guildia seminar were praised by the local press for their knowledge, sincerity and ability to create 'an atmosphere of trust, optimism and emotional uplift' (Altynova 1993: 3). Participants decided to form a women's business club to explore ideas further and later described how Guildia had both broadened their horizons and given them the required 'psychological push', a phrase which recurred frequently in women's descriptions of how Guildia worked. For some of the unemployed women, the importance of this lay in breaking out of their own isolation. 'The contacts I've made help me psychologically. I know that I have to live in a different way and I'm searching, I'm fighting' [18].

Nevertheless it would be misleading to suggest that the psychological uplift of a business start-up course is enough in itself to counteract the many very clear practical difficulties women face. At the end of the day neither Guildia nor any other organisation is able to transform the Russian economy single-handed. When the realities of business start-ups become apparent the result, for some, may be a profound sense of impotence and depression:

> How can courses like this help you? I didn't know any of it so I found it interesting. . . . But things are very unpleasant now. I thought that it would be an interesting time to live. I thought I'd be able to join in, I've got experience of life, but it's not like that at all.
>
> [11]

As this woman discovered, there is a lot more to starting a business than glib exhortations to 'think what skills you have' would suggest. Her comment mirrors the far higher levels of disappointment registered by would-be women entrepreneurs than by men in surveys conducted by the Russian Academy of Sciences. As the authors of these studies comment, the realisation that success depends not on one's own abilities but on 'how close one stood to state distribution networks' can be very difficult to cope with (Rzhanitsina 1993: 120). As a result, even women with good ideas, confidence, drive and the thorough grounding of a programme such as Guildia's behind them were likely to find themselves defeated by the new business climate in Russia.

STARTING UP – THE PROBLEM OF CAPITAL

In Western Europe the proposition that women experience greater difficulty than men in obtaining capital for business start-ups has been widely discussed. In particular, the negative attitude of banks towards women as suitable risks for lending has over the years come in for a good deal of criticism (Allen and Truman 1993). Women who have succeeded in obtaining adequate credit have stressed the necessity of looking the part and being well prepared with a detailed business plan and cash flow forecasts. As business came to Russia, the media were keen to pass on the wisdom of likely western role models. Much was made, for example, of Anita Roddick's appearance at the conference on 'Women and the Market' in Moscow in late 1992 with her stories of turning up at the bank in T-shirt and trainers with two children in tow and, when she was turned down, returning in high heels with a business file to claim her start-up loan (Gorbunova *et al.* 1992: 9). Yet the situation in Russia is such that no amount of smart dressing has resolved the issue of finance for hundreds of would-be women entrepreneurs. Many Russian women have no problems with looking efficient and presenting their case articulately. Where they do have major difficulties is with the banking system as it stands.

From the very beginnings of the move towards the market, women were expressing their concern over the issue of start-up capital. At a meeting of women entrepreneurs held by the Soviet Women's Committee in 1990 this was the primary problem raised. The response of Pavel Bunich, deputy chair of the Supreme Soviet Economic Reform Committee, was that the entire country was in this position: people should stop expecting hand-outs, start using their brains and, above all, go to a bank (Bunich 1990: 13). As a recipe for success, however, this piece of advice became increasingly difficult to follow as the economic reforms produced soaring rates of inflation. By 1993, Russian commercial banks were offering primarily short-term loans to businesses with interest rates of around 200 per cent per annum. For a completely new business with no guarantee of immediate returns such rates were simply prohibitive.

Nor was it any longer true to say that everyone was starting from the same place. In the new world of business there were some very familiar faces as the former Communist Party elite transferred their dominance and their networks into this newly lucrative sphere. As women had been largely excluded from the ranks of Party functionaries, particularly at the higher levels, doors were now remaining closed to them as business developed. Moreover, this exclusion from political influence was producing a further significant economic effect. As Ol'ga Vovchenko of the Research Centre for the Social Protection of Family and Childhood, put it:

> Women got practically nothing during the 'great carve-up' when Party and other property was 'divided up'. It was mostly men from the nomenklatura who carried out this expropriation of the expro-priators. Women were left with small-scale market trading which scarcely gives an instant effect.

(Vovchenko 1992: 1)

Women entrepreneurs whose success stories were featured in the media had, however, often started out in just this way. Selling a fur coat, retailing a lorry-load of tomatoes or plunging into a whole range of unspecified transactions were described by women such as these as the only possible way of building sufficient start-up capital. Some journalists, commenting on the realities of business for women took the no-nonsense line:

Earn your initial capital by selling two dozen pies. . . . You have to realise that you have to do what's necessary before you can do what you want, and if you really don't want to get your hands dirty you'd be better off not going into business.

(Korchagina 1992: 6)

A more sober analysis of what exactly this might mean produced the stark conclusion that, 'it could take years before the lucky woman concerned will have saved up a critical mass of money' (Vovchenko 1992: 1). Certainly, two dozen pies were scarcely likely to do the trick: whatever the quantity it was all a very far cry from simply walking into a high street bank in a smart suit.

In these circumstances, what was certain was that women clearly felt a sense of exclusion from the new opportunities that were presenting themselves. As far as bank loans were concerned, the question of discrimination which undoubtedly existed and was raised, for example, by women entrepreneurs at the Second Independent Women's Forum at Dubna in November 1992, was not dissimilar, except perhaps in degree, to the situation obtaining in many other societies (Centre for Gender Studies 1993: 19). The major problem was rather whether anyone at the very start of their business would actually want a loan on the terms being offered by the commercial banks. Where discrimination was most clearly perceived was over the question of loans from state banks with comparatively low rates of interest. Women complained that it was impossible to get hold of this money without contacts and that, moreover, the banks would not lend money to businesses such as small-scale garment-making. The result, as one woman involved in attempting to set up such a business perceived it, was that 'loans on preferential terms, where interest is at 7 or 12 per cent, are available for some forms of men's business, but there are none for women's business' [16].

Whether women should be seeking special measures to combat the problems they faced over start-up capital was a source of some debate among actual and potential entrepreneurs. While this was generally agreed to be the most pressing question, views differed as to how to tackle it. On the popular premise that the laws of the market were the same for everyone, some prominent women were highly critical of proposals which might in any way prioritise women. 'I am an entrepreneur first and a woman second', as Elena Medvedkova, one of Russia's most experienced business-women, put it (Gorbunova et al. 1992: 9). Others, however, took the view that there was no sense in not recognising the 'mass favouritism' accorded to men in business and attempting to do something to redress the balance

(Semenova 1992). If state help was not forthcoming, then the creation of a national women's bank might be the answer. However, setting up an affiliate of Women's World Banking, for example, was estimated by its president, Nancy Barry, in 1992 to be likely to take five years while the legal and financial frameworks were created (Buehrer 1992: 9).

Participants in the 'Women and Business' workshop at the Dubna Forum concluded, however, that only the design and implementation of governmental national and regional programmes for women's small businesses would address the discrimination women faced. In 1993, there were at least some tentative beginnings of government involvement in encouraging small business, if not aimed directly at women. The Federal Employment Service announced measures to assist the unemployed wishing to set up in business for themselves. Employment centres were to offer initial advice, including free specialised consultations where necessary, pay business registration costs and provide the equivalent of twelve months' unemployment benefit as a lump sum. These benefits were to be made available primarily in what were termed 'priority activities' for the region concerned and to those who were likely to experience the greatest difficulty finding alternative employment through normal channels ('Vy bez raboty . . .' 1993: 7).

Inevitably, as women formed the majority of the unemployed and were experiencing considerable difficulty in finding new jobs, they were likely to become key recipients of this initial programme of state aid. As Yuri Vetokhin of Dubna Employment Centre commented, 'It's not much, but at least it's some sort of support.' In Dubna, following the establishment of the women's business club after the Guildia seminar, a small business making knitwear was set up with the support of the Employment Centre. In addition to the subsidies and benefits set out directly in the legislation, the Employment Centre had also purchased good quality knitting machines and other equipment which the women were then purchasing through a one-year leaseback deal with the Centre. The value of this arrangement to the women who had set up this business was substantial, especially in the light of the alternatives on offer. In October 1993, for example, the women had been offered a one-year commercial bank loan to cover their start-up requirements at an interest rate of 240 per cent, repayable from the first month of operation.

In the course of 1993, employment centres across the country had become involved in setting up initiatives of this kind. In the Urals city of Perm, for example, a particularly successful 'Social Centre' had assisted the creation of nineteen women's small businesses, while in Moscow itself, the pilot 'Business Incubator' scheme had supported the creation of nine

(Levina 1994a: 11). In both examples, the women involved had received both financial and practical help with the promise of on-going support. Yet, even with the direct intervention of a state agency, there were still problems: in Moscow, for example, the director of the 'Business Incubator' complained that the local authorities had reneged on an agreement to provide subsidised premises and were expecting the fledgling businesses to pay full commercial rates (Levina 1994b: 11).

Whether significant numbers of women will be able to benefit to the same extent from the legislation on business start-ups will undoubtedly depend on the extent of the funds on offer, as well as the goodwill and readiness for innovation on the part of employment centre staff. None of these provisions, however, assists women who are not officially registered as unemployed. This inevitably gives rise to a situation in which women are able to put together all the elements of a business idea except for the necessary capital, as one of Guildia's customers explained:

> We already have a workshop and nearly all the staff. We know who's going to do what. We've got suppliers. We've got everything except money. We'd only need a few million to get started. We could sit down and work right now but we can't even begin. All the documents are in order. . . . They told us on the course that a branch of an international women's bank is going to be opened. Perhaps we'll be able to get a loan from them.
>
> [9]

Until such a facility is available, it appears that, as this woman was to find, no amount of advance planning can be made to work without capital. Ultimately, as in this case, women with good ideas and plenty of willing partners are likely to find themselves giving up the whole idea as simply a pipedream. In a situation such as this, however, if a women's bank ever were to be set up in Russia there is a high probability that it would simply be swamped by women who have been unable to find support through any other channels.

STARTING UP – FURTHER OBSTACLES

While the problem of capital is undoubtedly the single most pressing factor faced by women attempting to break into business, it is both compounded and extended by a range of issues all of which have financial repercussions. If women are able to surmount the first hurdle, the obstacle race continues through the processes of organising registration, finding premises, paying taxes and dealing with racketeers, none of which come cheap.

From the perspective of a developed market economy, the very concept of registration as it exists in Russia today appears expressly designed to keep the country in a perpetual state of 'transition'. As a bureaucratic invention it is a masterpiece of prevarication, allowing for the maximum possible interference in supposedly free enterprise. The system in place was first developed during the final phase of the USSR's existence and continues to reflect the ambivalence towards autonomous activity which characterised that period. Before the demise of the USSR aspiring entrepreneurs were required to present their local authorities with documentation outlining the economic rationale for their project's existence before permission to start up would be granted. Subsequently, this demand was dropped, but local authorities still expect to see the project's charter and brief curricula vitae of its founders. On payment of the appropriate fee, the business then requires police permission for an official stamp, registration with the tax office and a bank account before the registration process is complete. If all of this sounds reasonably straightforward it should be borne in mind that, in Russian conditions, simple bureaucratic procedures are apt to turn into exhausting paper-chases designed to deter all but the most determined.

The entire procedure has to be completed within a month, otherwise the temporary registration document becomes invalid and the aspiring entrepreneur has to begin all over again. Yet it is very much a race against time: offices may only open on certain days, fail to complete the paperwork speedily, demand numerous extra copies of documentation or simply refuse to proceed further. The apparently simple procedure of opening a bank account may be rendered impossible by a bank's demand for a substantial initial deposit: a ploy no doubt designed to avoid dealing with customers of limited means. In addition, all of the steps in this process can only be completed consecutively:

> A bank will not open an account without the certificate from the tax office, and the tax office will not issue a certificate unless you have an official stamp, but the police will take their time issuing the authorisation for the stamp even though you are only organising a service centre and not manufacturing weaponry.
>
> (Rzhanitsina 1993: 34)

In circumstances such as these it is not difficult to see the potential for abuse of the system.

The registration process itself is therefore liable to be a significant element in swallowing up whatever start-up capital is available, as the editor of *Novaia zhenshchina*, Irina Korchagina, ironically observed:

136

The registration process in this country is made up of lots of different stages and at every stage there's another bureaucrat gazing longingly at your hands. If you haven't learned to pay bribes yet it's no use complaining if your documents sit and stew for months on end.

(Korchagina 1992: 6)

All this, of course, is in addition to the registration fee itself, without which business cannot officially begin. If women have learned that corruption is an unavoidable aspect of an already expensive process, it may not simply be the cost which worries them. Distaste at the entire notion of delivering backhanders may be a further factor deterring women who feel they lack the support networks men enjoy. As one of Guildia's customers put it, 'You can understand intellectually that you've got to move into a new life now that the new market relations have begun, but you want it to be on a legal footing and not have to bribe everybody' [10]. Galina Semenova of 'Women and Development' evidently knew exactly what this woman had in mind when concluding in a 1992 article that it was not 'fear of the new' that stopped women going into business, but 'fear of new humiliations' (Semenova 1992: 1).

In the same way, finding suitable premises is not simply a matter of touring the estate agents and negotiating a lease. However complex and drawn-out the process of conveyancing business leases may be in the western context, it is usually fair to assume that, at the end of the day, premises will be made available. For those who set up businesses at the end of the Soviet period, it was not unusual to receive assistance from the local council in locating premises or even simply to be allocated a place in which to begin. Women attempting to establish a business in the post-Soviet era, however, have had the new forces of privatisation to contend with and, lacking contacts and capital, have been unable to secure a major stake in business properties. A significant exception to this rule has been women managers of former state enterprises and retail outlets who have been able to organise a management buy-out during privatisation. Yet, apart from this relatively small group of women, commentators have frequently observed that 'privatisation has passed women by' (Vovchenko 1992: 1).

The implications of this for women who have been encouraged to think of starting businesses in the service sector may be severe. Years of experience of the dearth of services in Russia makes women well aware of the potential demand for well-run and attractive cafes or one-stop service centres offering a range of facilities. In the wake of privatisation, however, women are likely to be brought to a standstill by their inability to obtain premises at rents they can afford. One of Guildia's customers described a very typical set of circumstances:

> I've had a definite plan for the last six months. Just about everybody in my town uses household services in Moscow, although of course Moscow isn't all that far away. We haven't got a decent service centre or hairdressers or dry-cleaners and it's very inconvenient for women with children. So I'd really like to set up something like a women's salon where there'd be a hairdressers and a beauty parlour, some-where women could go to look nice and buy things at the same time, a place with a crèche. . . . I've got friends who would support me and work with me but everything's being leased now and it's very hard to get premises. They built a service centre in the town but when perestroika started it was frozen so it's just standing there and there's nothing in it. No one knows what they're going to do with it − it could be a night club or a sewing workshop. I can't go and ask because all I've got is my idea. No one's interested in that.
>
> [10]

As this story suggests, finding one's niche in the apparently wide open service sector may be no answer at all to women who lack capital and contacts, and, as this woman found, presents problems which are likely to remain insoluble in prevailing conditions.

Finally, for women who remain undeterred by the obstacles outlined above, there remains the question of how, if their business starts up at all, it is to continue to function in the light of both government taxation policy and the racketeering of competing mafia groups. While estimates as to the level of extortion vary wildly, with claims that protection money runs at anything from 10 to 50 per cent of business profits, the level of the government's demands on business are at least open to scrutiny. Small businesses are liable to pay taxes to federal, regional and local authorities all of which introduce changes frequently and in an ad hoc fashion. By 1994, the principal taxes were value added tax at 23 per cent and enterprise profit tax at 35 to 38 per cent which, when taken together with all the other taxes, produced a high overall tax burden and ample incentive for evasion. Common complaints by those involved in business include uncertainty as to their level of liability due to constant fluctuations, the excessive total demand which may amount to as much as 90 per cent of profits and the practice of demanding tax in advance on estimated profits: the subsequent delays in payment of rebates makes them worthless in periods of soaring inflation. Exemptions from the tax on profits apply for the first two years on a range of businesses, most notably from women's points of view on those producing consumer goods. Nevertheless, taxation is habitually described as 'stifling' and 'completely crazy' or, in Irina Razumnova's view, 'expropriatory', resulting in 'bankruptcies rather than prosperity' (Razumnova 1994).

Racketeering in current Russian conditions is something which any aspiring entrepreneur is obliged to take seriously. Payment of protection money is simply a fact of commercial life to be disregarded at one's peril. Certainly, women in commercial organisations which come into dispute with mafia groups are in no way immune from the threats to person and property which have resulted in a spate of car bomb attacks, arson and contract killings in Russia's major cities. Becoming embroiled in difficulties with racketeers provides probably the ultimate paradox in the entire question of women's involvement in business. For women who occupy key positions in commercial organisations and enjoy both high income and status, there is a frightening price to be paid if it all goes wrong. Living under a twenty-four-hour guard is scarcely the model of the successful, independent woman entrepreneur one would care to recommend to other women for emulation, yet this is precisely the reality for some prominent women in Russian business.

This fact alone, one might imagine, would be enough to deter many women from placing themselves in the exposed and vulnerable position of the business owner. Indeed, even as the USSR was collapsing, women contemplating business start-ups were already expressing fear at the un-checked activities of mafia groups, while many who had already begun businesses of their own were driven out, unable to withstand the pressures of the racketeers (Kobzeva 1992: 72; Rzhanitsina 1993: 119). From this perspective, there is much to be said for involvement in commercial undertakings at a subordinate level, and women may well perceive the sense of a trade-off made between status, potential profits and peace of mind. One of Guildia's customers who failed to set up her own business through a lack of capital subsequently found a niche for herself as manager of a commercial enterprise owned by a separate parent company. As far as she was concerned, failing to become an entrepreneur in her own right had turned out to be the perfect solution:

> I'm my own boss. I sort out my own advertising and business contracts. I'm responsible for the equipment and the accounting. It's all up to me. . . . In the end I think it's worked out even better this way than if I'd had my own firm. For a start I didn't have to worry about start-up capital or premises – I got it all handed to me on a plate. Also, we've already had a visit from the racketeers but the

139

director of the main firm sorted it out so I didn't have to get involved in something which isn't really women's business. I don't think the racketeers are so bad as a matter of fact. Now we've paid them they do protect us and we don't get any hassle from anyone else.

[9]

Continuing to be an employee, but with all the benefits of the entrepreneur in terms of independence and high earnings, if not a profit share, allowed this woman to feel quite sanguine about the activities of rival gangs. When there is no parent company, women may have no choice but to deal with racketeers, irrespective of the distaste and fear they might feel at doing this particular 'man's job'.

Concern for personal safety is a further factor which may keep women who wish to set up in business for themselves in low-profit, low-status, 'women's' spheres such as small-scale garment-making. Several women we interviewed expressed a degree of fear of profitable commercial activity precisely because of its inevitable links with organised crime, sometimes illustrating their anxiety with stories of friends and acquaintances who had 'had a bad time'. For some, the value they placed on peace of mind had a direct bearing on their choice of activity:

Commerce is very profitable but I value my peace and freedom too much to live under a sword of Damocles.

[10]

Property is all mafia-connected. Some areas are very dangerous. No one is going to target grenade launchers at us when we're sewing.

[9]

Women who were attending courses, thinking and planning carefully about any move into independent business, were clearly unimpressed by the notion of making money at all costs.

Nevertheless, for women who feel excluded from the new 'enterprise culture', it is tempting to lump both mafia activities and state taxation and registration policies together as simply one big racket. Within months of Russia's independence, describing the state as a greater source of extortion than organised crime had become a popular thing for commentators in the media to do. Women we interviewed who were out of work or struggling on meagre salaries were liable to echo this point of view:

It's not so much the mafia that stops you setting up in business as the state racket. . . . If you earn a hundred roubles the state takes ninety and despite that doesn't lift a finger to help you. All the state does is take.

[12]

It's impossible to start anything because you're just working to pay taxes. It's not just that the obstacles are enormous, it's that it's literally impossible to overcome them. You can't develop anything.

[30]

As the impact of market reform policies has come home to women, the notion of starting a business of their own, so blithely promoted at the beginning of this period of transition, appears increasingly to be flying in the face of reality.

Certainly, studies carried out by the Russian Academy of Sciences indicate that women have become more negative in their attitudes towards business since the market reforms began. A survey of nearly 600 women in the defence industry, for example, both in Moscow and in three provincial cities, found more than a third in 1992 expressing distaste at the idea of setting up a business. Only in Moscow did women show significant interest, yet, even here, by the following year two-thirds of the women surveyed were expressing negative views on the subject. Their reasons were no longer on the lines of 'it's not for women', but were entirely practical: neither the necessary conditions nor appropriate training was available (Rzhanitsina 1993: 138–40). The attitudes and experiences of the women we interviewed entirely bear this out. By the spring of 1994, they were no longer expressing any optimism that breaking into business for themselves might be possible. Whatever the propaganda, the reality ensured that, as a genuine alternative to women's unemployment, developing small businesses was a non-starter.

WOMEN IN BUSINESS: RESPONDING TO PROBLEMS

Where women entrepreneurs have met together to discuss the needs of women in business they have prioritised the need for networking to provide support and information, particularly for those new to the business world. At the 1992 Second Independent Women's Forum in Dubna, for example, women pooled information on banks and insurance services headed by the growing number of women in finance whom they had found to be supportive of women's projects. On this basis it was resolved to set up national and regional information networks and a series of meetings and seminars through which successful women entrepreneurs could help develop programmes to support women's small businesses. Some suggested that the bias against women in business could be addressed by developing services exclusively for women, though, in the prevailing climate, it was felt that self-help almost certainly would not be enough to resolve the problems.

An interesting aspect of women's networking in this area is its element of altruism, and not merely to other would-be entrepreneurs. The question of social responsibility was a very live one for women at Dubna and crystallised around a discussion of a piece of legislation from the central Russian republic of Bashkortostan (formerly Bashkiria). As a result of lobbying by women entrepreneurs and the fourteen women members of the republic's parliament, the law, 'On the Development of Women's Businesses in the Republic of Bashkortostan', provided that firms where over 60 per cent of employees were female and which had a programme for the social protection of women and children would be exempt from the tax on profits. In this way it was intended that women's employment would be safeguarded and welfare benefits retained. While this provision was not universally acclaimed at Dubna, there was a consensus that women entrepreneurs should be directing their profits towards fulfilling social needs rather than watching them disappear into the black hole of the government's coffers (Centre for Gender Studies 1993: 18–19).

This question of humanitarian aims has not been confined to the Dubna Forum, but is one that has been regularly raised by women discussing business. Successful women interviewed by the media habitually talk about the need to help others, yet are clearly not interested in simply pouring money into some unaccountable charity fund. As a result, many are involved in specific local projects directed at children, the disabled and large families and regard it as essential to maintain a direct link with the beneficiaries of their philanthropy, as Tamara Krushinskaia, head of a commercial bank explained: 'We know exactly where and to whom our money is going and it brings us enormous pleasure' (Skliar 1994b: 17). Some of the major organisations for women's business have also taken an interest in cultural development. For example, Tatiana Maliutina, president of the Association of Women Entrepreneurs of Russia, described in an interview in 1992 how her organisation had been concerned with what she termed 'the spiritual content and meaning of enterprise' since its inception in August 1991. To this end, they had become involved in programmes for the financial support of Russian culture and traditions (Krylova 1992: 11). More recently, the businesswoman, Elena Ponina, personally endowed three postgraduate studentships for women in literature, history and economics (Skliar 1994a: 18–19).

This perspective on business not only determines the marked degree of social concern among women entrepreneurs, but also affects how they run their own businesses, as Zoia Khotkina of the Moscow Centre for Gender Studies has observed:

> The new businesswomen . . . do not want their businesses to be the pragmatic, technocratic structures that men have set up. They tend to be aware that they owe something to society, and strive to give their businesses a humanistic face. Thus many of the associations and clubs which have sprung up have started funds to go towards creating new jobs for unemployed women and for charitable purposes.
>
> (Khotkina 1994: 107)

As Khotkina suggests, it is not uncommon for the minority of women who have managed to make a success of business to reject what they see as the male way of doing things. Women who take this position frequently express dismay at the 'get rich quick' attitude of men who dominate the business world and seek to distance themselves from it. As one woman entrepreneur at the Dubna Forum put it, to murmurs of approval all round, 'everywhere today there's so much dabbling and blustering'. For women who have had to work hard to get their businesses off the ground there is inevitably something distasteful about the new breed of 'businessmen' who buy smart cars, fail to invest and think that the good life means eating, drinking and sex in the sauna, while their businesses collapse around them. Where women are to be found subscribing to the notion that there are differences in male and female psychology in business, it is in this area, rather than in the popular notion of 'appropriate work for women'.

Nevertheless, whatever the intentions and, indeed, results as far as networking is concerned, it is clear that this has not as yet had a radical impact on women attempting to break into business. The Bashkortostan model has not been widely accepted and government programmes for the support of women's small businesses were, by 1994, still at the discussion stage. In the absence of accessible capital, affordable rents and a rational system of taxation and registration, the key factor in the success of women's businesses increasingly appears to be timing. For the relative few who managed to set up their projects before the country descended into chaos, running a successful business may appear a viable proposition. For those who missed the boat, the picture is much bleaker. In the final section, we will turn back to the experiences of Guildia and its customers to illustrate the way in which the situation was changing between the summer of 1993 and the spring of 1994, a period of less than a year.

FACING REALITIES – THE QUESTION OF BUSINESS TRAINING

In the summer of 1993, Irina Razumnova and the staff of Guildia were understandably well pleased with the progress they had made in the face of substantial difficulties and buoyant about their plans for the future. By the spring of 1994 the picture had changed significantly. Guildia, like Missiya, appeared to be stuck in the trap of wanting to behave as a western-style, voluntary sector organisation yet, without any form of government funding, being obliged to operate as a small business itself. As such, it was subject to all the pressures its trainees would have to negotiate. Rents on their premises which were built on church land had gone up eighty-seven times, while they were now threatened with eviction so that the church could sell off the site to a commercial institution. They had just paid over two million roubles for a new telephone line and for water charges while, at the same time, still attempting to keep their own course fees affordable. Meanwhile, sources of income had become a series of swings and roundabouts: Avon had reduced their sponsorship in view of what they regarded as political instability and their failure to make headway in the Russian market, but Guildia had then become involved in the BBC Russian radio series, 'In Business'. They were also selling information packages and individual items of business advice.

Nevertheless, the financial squeeze was making itself felt as a lack of resources continued to prevent their advertising what they had to offer and putting in train the development plans they had had. For this reason they were unable to keep track of ex-trainees or offer on-going support to their new businesses as they would have liked. They still attempted to reply to the letters they received but were unable to employ anyone to do this full time. In these circumstances they were understandably far less sanguine about their future prospects than they had been the previous summer. 'I'm not optimistic anymore', Irina Razumnova commented, 'Everything's falling apart. We keep writing letters asking for help because we keep thinking that people will get fed up of us in the end and pay us to go away' (Razumnova 1994).

The nub of the problem for Guildia was that, as their overheads increased, they were obliged to charge more for their courses and materials, yet, at a time of falling living standards, fewer people could afford the fees. As a result, there was not enough demand for a one-month accountancy course, for example, which now cost an apparently very reasonable 60,000 roubles. In addition, and potentially more worrying for the organisation, there was the fall in demand that stemmed from a generally depressed climate in which, in Guildia's view, people could see that training was unlikely to get them anywhere. As the manifold problems outlined in this chapter began to induce a widespread sense of hopelessness about business, the question had to be asked: why bother going on a business start-up course if starting a business in the formal sense was virtually impossible?

Of the women we interviewed who had attended Guildia's courses in the summer of 1993, only one had subsequently set up in business. In the circumstances Guildia's customers faced it would appear no coincidence that this was the unemployed former engineer who received the support of Dubna Employment Centre. Yet overall, if the picture is one of failure to set up small businesses, there are nonetheless brighter aspects to it. Women had certainly expressed appreciation of the psychological boost the course had given them shortly after its end, and it became clear that the effect did not necessarily diminish with time. Women who had found new openings in suitably skilled employment several months after completing the course spontaneously ascribed this to the effect the Guildia course had had. One woman, for example, who had initially expressed doubts about the usefulness of the course and had been particularly depressed about her future had later found an opening for herself as a broker and delightedly explained the role she felt the Guildia course had played in boosting her self-confidence. While some primarily expressed the view that they would not otherwise have recognised their ability to pursue an entirely new direction, others also valued the content of the knowledge they had acquired:

> I'm very glad I went to the course at Guildia, it helped me a lot. It gave me the idea and the self-confidence to try and start my own business. It helped me understand my own abilities and also taught me a load of useful stuff about advertising, accounting and so on which I really need now.
>
> [9]

Although it is impossible to draw firm conclusions on the basis of such a small sample, it was very striking that Guildia's customers were virtually the only women we interviewed who, by the spring of 1994, had overcome their employment problems and found a new niche for themselves in relatively well-paid, skilled jobs. In the light of this it appeared ironic in the extreme that Guildia itself was experiencing such difficulties and its founders expressing such pessimism.

A study of Guildia suggests that, while business start-ups may be highly problematical, there is certainly a need for training which enables women to familiarise themselves with the language and behaviour associated with the market, and, moreover, to appreciate the abilities and qualities they possess. The combination of these two elements, when offered on Guildia's start-up courses, evidently allowed some women to reorientate themselves with confidence in a rapidly changing environment. As far as business development itself is concerned, it is difficult to see how women are going to break into business in significant numbers without some form of government programme or, at the very least, a more sympathetic climate in banking and taxation. As things stand, it would be churlish to blame anyone for feeling defeated by the obstacles currently in the path of enterprise. Women who might have been inclined to blame themselves were, by the spring of 1994, more likely to be arriving at a position of acceptance, as one unemployed woman summed up:

> Look how we all supported Boris Nikolaevich when he reduced taxes on profits by 5 per cent. When I was working with all of that I realised 5 per cent is nothing and, what's more, he's put it back up again in another decree! When you start looking at taxation you realise that it's all just rhetoric. Then you can calm down and start to work out your own method of survival.
>
> [30]

For those who had not found a new role, either in business or employment, which could provide them with an acceptable income, working out a method of survival had become essential in Russia in transition. Whatever their failures in formal business or problems with employment, women, as we shall see in the next chapter, could not be accused of lacking in enterprise in the strategies they employed for providing for themselves and their families in the new conditions.

7

SURVIVAL STRATEGIES

With the shock of price liberalisation in January 1992, a new phenomenon rapidly became part of the Russian landscape: the lines of people, most of them women, trading goods on the street. For some it was a question of rifling through cupboards to make some spare cash by selling unwanted possessions: a pair of shoes, a cut glass vase, a tea set or a shawl. For others, especially pensioners, trading soon became a way of life as they queued in the mornings to buy quantities of milk and yoghurt, salami, alcohol and cigarettes at shop prices which they sold later in the day at a profit to passers-by outside stations and on major thoroughfares. Forlorn images of elderly women, buttoned up against the cold, holding aloft their meagre supplies, became within a few months a standard feature of western news reports and documentaries on Russia's transition to the market. As living standards have slumped, the pictures have become more exotic: women offering the pets they can no longer afford to visitors to a public library, or selling the braids they have saved from their youth to a specialist hair shop for more than their monthly pension.[1]

The fact that images such as these have become familiar to western eyes is indicative of the scale of the phenomenon. While the burgeoning of the commercial sector has seen the development of stalls into kiosks and kiosks into mini-shops, there has been no decline in the numbers of women selling one or two items out on the streets. The more lucrative end of the new retail trade is dominated by men who are the major owners of kiosks and small shops and the primary importers of goods from abroad. Small-scale, ad hoc, 'amateur' trading, as women themselves may term it, is the principal area of female activity. To the numbers of women selling occasional items have been added those selling produce from their allotments on an upturned box, displaying hand-made garments over their arms, cradling doe-eyed kittens and puppies or trading a whole range of consumer goods acquired through personal contacts. When wages, if they are paid at all, cannot begin to cover prices, it is scarcely surprising that the entire population appears to be caught up on a bizarre carousel of buying and selling to each other. Despite the fact that this has become such an important factor in national life, there has been very little coverage of the issue in the press, even in women's magazines. As a result, a major element in many women's lives is simply passed over in silence and all the work involved in trading disregarded and rendered virtually invisible. The material for this chapter, therefore, comes primarily from our interviews and provides at least some illustration of the strategies women may adopt to keep body and soul together.

If major cities sometimes feel like giant open-air bazaars, trading is by no means confined to these centres. 'Everyone sells, everyone trades whatever they can all the time', observed Marina Baskakova, sociologist at the Moscow Centre for Gender Studies, discussing her research in a small provincial town. By way of illustration, she described how she had recruited a local young woman to take details from the respondents in her survey while she conducted interviews.'When I asked her at lunchtime how the work was going, she said, "This is a really good job, I've sold two lipsticks this morning already!"' (Baskakova 1993). As this comment suggests, petty trading, while ostensibly a means of supplementing income, may be so important from a financial perspective that it takes precedence over all other activities for the women concerned. Whether it is pensioners getting up at 5 or 6 a.m. to travel out to their allotments or take their place in the queue at the tobacco kiosk, or university lecturers rescheduling all their classes to the evening so that they can spend the day selling clothing or fruit and vegetables, the constant factor is material need.

In a country where incomes are inadequate and the benefit system cannot fill the gap, women have been obliged to find whatever way they can to make money. For so many, especially women on their own, buying and selling and subsistence farming have been the only avenues open to them when developing legitimate business ventures has been effectively off limits:

> The only thing the whole country is living on is black market trading. You don't register anywhere, you buy here and sell there until they catch you. And this is the only thing that allows people to survive. But now that they're cracking down on this too we can't imagine how we're going to go on!
>
> [30]

While essential in low-income households, if not always for basic necessities then frequently for items above a bare survival level, trading and subsistence farming may require considerable commitment and inspire extremely mixed feelings. As became apparent in the course of our interviews, what women do and how they feel about it are very individual issues. In the course of this chapter we hope to shed some light on the kinds of decisions women take and their reactions to the situations in which they find themselves.

TRADING, FARMING AND COTTAGE INDUSTRY – WOMEN CREATE THEIR OWN JOBS

The extent to which women engage in trading, subsistence farming or home-based production for sale depends on a range of factors: their need for income, their skills, contacts and, of course, personal inclinations. While some women, for example, cannot imagine how they would survive without produce from their allotments, others insist that the time and effort involved cannot be justified if trading can bring in enough to put food on the table without ever leaving the city. Although women are understandably cagey about discussing the money they make from buying and selling, it is clear that some do make a comfortable living. For the most successful this may be the first time in their lives that the combination of cash in their pockets and goods in the shops has permitted them a choice of small luxuries.

More typical, however, is the woman for whom trading is literally a means of survival. For women with young children it may be a spasmodic activity that brings in extra income without incurring the need for full-time child care, especially if personal contacts provide access to a line of selling that is reasonably profitable:

> From the time when I was involved with the pizza firm I've still got connections. Other lads have set up a firm there now – different pizzas, they're not bad. We get them out of the fridge and take them to this shop or that – to be frank that's the only reason I can manage not to work.

> [30]

Others effectively turn trading into a new full-time job. Two of the unemployed women we interviewed, an engineer and a computer programmer, had done this through selling clothes. Neither of them had any other source of income whatsoever. One was buying items from importers of cheap fashionwear from China and Turkey and selling them on a market stall; the other was picking up clothing from middlemen and then renting stalls in three different factories which had to be paid for even if she sold nothing. Neither was making a fortune for all the effort involved, as one remarked: 'If I could get a cleaning job I'd go for it straight away, but I've looked round here and nobody wants anybody' [6].

A further variant is trading to support a specific family need, characteristically to put a son or daughter through their education. As higher education in particular has become an extra drain on the family budget, women may engage in trading to pay for private tutors to secure university entrance, for bribes or fees and to supplement an extremely meagre student grant. One newspaper article exploring the question of street trading found that this might be a goal which the women in a family would pursue together. One woman, for example, described how they were raising money to pay for her son's university entrance: grandmother was selling aprons and housecoats sewn from old material while she was offering a 'teach yourself computers' guide which she had written herself (Sorokina 1992: 4).

As this example suggests, many women attempt to make money from items which they have produced themselves, rather than become involved in buying and selling. A major area of activity is fruit and vegetables. Not all the trading of produce is, of course, the result of small-scale home production: much is imported by traders from other former Soviet republics and, increasingly, from abroad, and is an area in which men predominate. The archetypal example of this is the trade in bananas which reached epidemic proportions in major cities by the summer of 1993. From a country in which only rare and treasured sightings of a banana had been possible through the Soviet years, Russia rapidly made the banana the ultimate designer snack. Indeed, by August 1993, the number of banana traders, both men and women, had increased to such an extent that Moscow must have been the only world capital in which slipping on a banana skin was an ever-present danger rather than a music-hall joke. Nevertheless, although women were engaged in retailing fruit, they were more frequently to be found selling their own varied produce from their allotments.

From the 1960s, as rural families became a decreasing minority of the Soviet population, urban dwellers were ever more likely to spend their leisure time in the countryside. For many, their country dacha and allotment were all that was left of their family's relatively recent rural past. Others shared the allotments of other family members, acquired dachas and plots through schemes set up by their enterprises or rented privately for the summer. Whatever the method, spending time at the dacha had become a major pursuit by the end of the 1980s. It was estimated that some eighteen million families had access to allotments in the countryside through enterprise schemes alone by the time of the USSR's demise (Fedotova 1990: 31).

The dacha did not, of course, simply provide summer holidays and weekends out of the city, it was also an important source of produce for Russian families. Securing winter food supplies has always been a Russian preoccupation and one which certainly did not diminish during the final decade of Soviet rule. 'I always used to keep sacks of potatoes at home', as one of our interviewees put it, 'They were forever threatening us with famine' [3]. The intensity of cultivation inevitably varied a great deal from one family to another, but it was commonplace in urban families to be offered home-made preserves and pickles in winter and home-grown salad vegetables in summer. Many families took great pride in their self-sufficiency and the quality of the food they could provide. In addition, growing their own produce and gathering berries and mushrooms from the forest provided a healthy leisure activity and, for the children especially, plenty of fresh air and vitamins.

With the advent first of chronic food shortages as the Soviet economy spiralled into decline and then of high inflation with Russia's market reforms, the recreational element in all of this was superseded for many families by the need to ensure their own food supply and to save money. For those who were already used to allotment gardening, growing as much of the family's food as possible was an obvious place to start. By the second summer of Russia's independent existence, inflation was biting deep into family budgets and increasing numbers were being temporarily laid off from work, leaving them with both time and motive for working hard on the allotment. Those still in work packed local transport at weekends, returning laden down with produce on Sunday evenings. The depth of the population's involvement in subsistence farming at this stage in Russia's market reforms can be well illustrated by the fact that almost any casual conversation in the country's capital city would include expressions of anxiety at the effect of the constant rain on the potato crop.

The media, while ignoring the issue of trading, were quick to respond to this national preoccupation with food production. Advice columns, in the local press in particular, offered exhaustive information on plant varieties, cultivation methods and preserving techniques to ensure the maximum possible return on small plots of land. Between the endless commercials for British-made chocolate ice cream bars, television too joined in with gardening programmes, concentrating not on the frivolities of flower growing but on new strains of high-yielding peppers and carrots and easily adapted small-scale technology. Just as incongruously placed between the advertisements for investment companies on the Moscow metro were the ones for electric storage boxes – a kind of reverse refrigerator – which would keep up to five sacks of vegetables safe from frost out on your balcony through the winter.

If, during the Soviet years, growing food was about subsistence while market trading was left to genuine villagers, as times got harder more and more city people began to sell the produce from their allotments. While some managed to get market stalls, most were on the streets outside stations and shops, or lining the pavements on the edges of the markets with their produce on boxes and buckets. For an activity that was becoming so widespread for women, it received very little attention, even in women's magazines. By August 1993, however, it could no longer be ignored and *Rabotnitsa*'s lead article for the month featured a laid-off engineer in Riazan who had acquired a market stall to sell salad vegetables from her allotment. She shared with her interviewer some of the tricks of the trade, such as always wearing the same brightly coloured dress so that customers would remember her: 'I chat to the customers and tell them which are the best varieties, why a particular vegetable is good for you and the best way to eat it' (Baklanova 1993: 3). By the time this article appeared, however, the numbers of women involved had swollen to such an extent that the comments it contained must already have rung very hollow to those crowded side by side with dozens upon dozens of others selling virtually identical produce.

To the women selling produce from their allotments must finally be added those selling the results of what might be termed 'cottage industry' – both home-based production and the provision of services. Again, this may represent simply an extension of something they have been doing for a long time, perhaps as a hobby, such as dressmaking or knitting, or it may be an entirely new activity begun specifically to make money as their financial circumstances have changed. It is, of course, immediately apparent that much of this is precisely the kind of activity urged upon would-be women entrepreneurs. While, as we have seen, setting up a formal business simply may not be an option for most women, making extra money through selling home-made goods and domestic services is something many attempt to do. In the case of services, women may put together a whole range of domestic activities to provide an adequate income. One former economist we interviewed, for example, was surviving through combinations of dog-sitting, child-minding and cleaning. Although this is very definitely a form of enterprise, it contains few elements of choice. Rather, as Russian economists have pointed out, it is 'a route they are obliged to take to make additional income, a means of survival' (Rzhanitsina 1993: 141).

The big question, however, is whether there actually is any money in all of this. Just as in the provision of advice on formal business start-ups, there has been no shortage of suggestions and even training for home-based activities. The press, for example, has carried hundreds of adverts for correspondence courses in skills such as dressmaking, knitting and millinery – 'a real salvation these days', as *Krest'ianka* (*Peasant Woman*) magazine described them ('Ot podpor'ia do spasen'ia' 1992: 16). Articles have appeared giving detailed advice on how to get customers and cost articles as a home dressmaker, not to mention the question of security – 'lots of dressmakers keep a dog' (Sergeeva 1993: 4). On a more extensive scale, Zoia Khotkina of the Moscow Centre for Gender Studies has produced a booklet of '100 ideas for go-ahead and enterprising women', based on American materials, which is intended for business start-ups but is full of bright suggestions for less ambitious undertakings (Khotkina 1993).

Training women in traditionally female domestic skills which they can then employ at home is an activity that has been strenuously promoted by some women's organisations, most notably those developing out of the former Communist Party women's committees and councils. The former Soviet Women's Committee, for example, metamorphosed into the Union of Russian Women, set up its Women's Social Support Centre in May 1992 and offered courses in a range of handwork skills, crafts and activities such as hairdressing and massage. As the Centre's organiser explained their rationale:

> Our hairdressers earn money doing the hair of people they know. In this transitional period the most important thing is to survive and for that you need money. And it doesn't matter if you earn it at the workbench or at home. . . . We are giving women realistic help.

That many women can concur with such sentiments is borne out by the fact that the Centre's courses have a four- or five-year waiting list (Ebzeeva 1993).

Women who have been on courses like this may well view the results as a form of economising rather than a significant means of supplementing income, particularly when they are surrounded by people who are in the same boat, as this unemployed engineer explained:

> In the summer I went on a hairdressing course. I was interested in it and it was enjoyable. So now I cut my husband's hair, I do my own hair. We've been doing our own hair for a while and when I go out I see other people on the street and I think, 'you're doing your own hair too!' Everybody's getting their hair done at home. I

do my parents, my brother, my sister's husband – everybody comes to me for a haircut! Because doing it in a salon now costs 20,000 – think of that when you earn 100,000!

[30]

Other women we interviewed were involved in sewing and knitting or babysitting, but they either had too few customers to make much money out of it or felt they were unable to charge enough to make it pay. Two design students who had a regular clientele of friends and relatives for whom they made substantial garments such as coats, suits and jackets, saw this activity as a long-term business proposition with very obvious short-term drawbacks:

We don't get much money for it because we're still students. We charge very little because, although we sew well, we have no certificates. In fact we're doing it at a loss. Lots of girls at our college do this.

[35]

Here again, the problem was one of competition, an issue which cropped up time and again when women talked about trading. 'I started to sell things at the market in Moscow but it was dreadful. Too many traders and not enough customers', observed one unemployed engineer. 'I know how to do home repairs, so perhaps I'll have to do that. . . . I haven't found my niche yet. There are so many women like me' [14]. Here, inevitably, lies the nub of the problem. When there are large numbers of women trying to make ends meet by offering similar products and services, the price any job can command is unavoidably driven down. At the same time, as living standards become so depressed, the market cannot but shrink. In the common expression, 'nobody's buying anything', women demonstrate their newly acquired experience of the laws of supply and demand.

Another erstwhile engineer described how what she termed her 'small business' was running into problems for just this reason:

My daughter wanted a cat. . . . I decided that if we were going to have a cat we'd get a good one so that she'd provide us with an income. She's our breadwinner! That's what they used to call the family's cow – now it's a cat! . . . I sell the kittens, they go for about 150 dollars each. But it's getting difficult in that it's hard to find customers now, because people have become very poor. Anyone who can afford one has already got one. Everyone else . . . well, before, people were more or less all the same, but now it's very hard.

[31]

In this comment it is worth noting, quite apart from the issue of market saturation, the way in which this woman's concern for her family's survival extended even into the sphere of acquiring a family pet. As one unemployed engineer commented, 'Women are more active than men when they are made redundant. Women will do anything to feed the family' [19].

Whether they can make much money or not, when there is little else on the horizon women will inevitably try out whatever schemes they can to economise, to barter, to make a little money here or there. For women who have grown up with the certainties of the Soviet system this demands a completely new mind-set and throws up problems which they are evidently handling with considerable ingenuity. When there are few hand-outs to be had, women's traditional responsibility for the family's domestic needs has expanded dramatically. It is not, however, without both a physical and psychological cost.

TIME AND EFFORT

It has been asserted by advisers to the Russian government, among others, that one of the gains of the market reforms for the population at large is the free time they have acquired as a result of no longer having to stand in queues ('Poverty of numbers' 1993: 34). It is certainly true that, with price liberalisation, the shops have rapidly filled with a vast array of produce and queueing is now a result more of inefficiency than of scarcity. Yet, if this is so, can it be assumed that women have gained time as a result? The answer would appear to be that it depends on how much disposable income they have. With money, running a home has certainly become much simpler; without it, the complexities of survival are likely to make demands of women's time and energy at least as much as the 'double shift' ever did. At the very least, time not spent in queues is likely to be spent shopping around for the best bargains.

Women who are resorting to trading and subsistence farming to provide income may have differing degrees of commitment to these activities. Where they are engaged in intermittently and are reasonably profitable they may be relatively undemanding. For women who have effectively turned these activities into a full-time job, however, the demands may be substantial. The most obvious example of this are women who have become heavily involved in buying and selling. These women are likely to find themselves carting heavy boxes of goods around the city and standing for hours in all weathers trying to get rid of them.

One of the clothing traders we interviewed explained how she had found herself working a ten- or twelve-hour day when she first began selling and was simply physically unable to go on doing this. Initially, she had collected goods from a central depot and had even been given a car by its organisers to get to her various sales pitches. Now she was piling up more and more boxes of clothing in her flat and hauling them around on public transport. The other woman involved in clothes trading did not mince words in expressing her view of the work she was doing:

> The whole thing amazes me. I think if your average woman from the West had to live in these conditions she'd age twenty years in a fortnight, humping stuff around, it's really hard. And that's without the climate. The climate's really harsh here. The only thing you can say about living in the centre of this country is that we hardly have any natural disasters!

[32]

Clearly, these women had not simply lost white-collar employment and been forced to accept a drop in status, they were also now firmly engaged in heavy manual labour.

Another group of women on whom the need to supplement income has taken a particular physical toll are urban pensioners involved in subsistence farming. Many are not simply providing for themselves by growing food, but also supporting their children and grandchildren. Where there is a dacha, they may effectively take up residence for the entire growing season, taking prime responsibility for planting and tending, with younger family members joining them at weekends. In addition, the traditional female tasks of preserving and bottling fall primarily to them. As the need for food has increased the intensity of cultivation, these women have effectively turned into full-time subsistence farmers, working entirely manually with only the most basic equipment. Tied to their allotments where the range of tasks may appear virtually endless and living without basic amenities such as running water appears as yet another act of self-sacrifice by a generation of women whose lives have been far from easy. As the eminent sociologist and writer on women's employment, Elena Gruzdeva, expressed this:

> The role of the older generation is very important now. People who have gone through so much and suffered a lot through the years of Soviet power are genuinely ready to take on more to help their younger relatives. All the years of experience, struggle and patience lead them to this.

(Gruzdeva 1993)

That they are prepared to do this is testimony to their endurance, given the conditions they have to face.

What should, perhaps, be pointed out is that tending the allotment is a very different concept from the one with which we are familiar in Britain, and not simply over the question of amenities. While some people have access to plots of land on the edge of an urban area, those who live in major cities may frequently have to travel as much as 130 or 140 kilometres to get to their dacha. Travelling for two or three hours each way on the slow and overcrowded local trains had become just another feature of the weekend for thousands of Muscovites, for example, by the summer of 1993. One pensioner, standing with her bags on the Sunday night train, described how she had a job as well as an allotment and so could only travel out at weekends. Every Saturday morning she would catch the 5.40 a.m. train, then take two local buses and, finally, walk 3 kilometres to her allotment, arriving at about 11 to start tending the potatoes. Every Sunday she would make the six-hour journey back. She felt that she had no alternative because she could not afford to live on her pension.

Where allotments are closer the physical strain may not necessarily be much less, especially if there is no dacha in which to stay. One pensioner wrote into the press in January 1994 to describe her feelings at the enforced labour of farming. Every day she was cycling 12 kilometres each way to work her allotment, instead of reading and doing photography, as she had hoped to spend her retirement:

> It's turned out that work on the land is all there is. I can only do anything else in odd moments or in winter. Soon it will all start again: the seeds, the seedlings, the rows of plants, the bicycle, the road, my sore knee and my aching back, struggling against the wind. But you've got to survive somehow.
>
> (*Sel'skaia zhizn'* 1994: 3)

Worse still is the fact that thefts of produce directly from the fields have begun to hit dacha owners. In some areas, pensioners have ended up taking turns to sit up all night watching over their allotments. Perhaps the saddest aspect of the slump in living standards is the fact that so many women who have lived through war, repression and harsh working and domestic lives now find themselves in their old age deprived of a peaceful retirement.

THE DEMANDS OF SURVIVAL – WOMEN'S RESPONSES

While working on an allotment to this extent is undoubtedly a heavy physical burden and, in its relentlessness, a source of stress, there are some women for whom subsistence farming still retains an element of pleasure. Once again, this appears to depend primarily on the level of involvement. Where material need is not acute, the element of relaxation may still be strong:

> I have a dacha 30 kilometres from Moscow. We go there every Saturday and Sunday. . . . Last year we didn't buy any fruit, we had a big crop of our own. This year's been poor for apples so we're buying them. . . . Two days out at the dacha and I can switch off. I've been south twice but I prefer birch trees to palms. I really love our countryside.
>
> [12]

The sense of pleasure in open spaces and clean air, or simply a feeling of closeness to the land, away from the pollution, overcrowding and frayed tempers of the city may continue to offer something of a psychological haven to some, provided, of course, that they are not obliged to have too much of it (see also Baklanova 1993: 3).

Once the picture is clouded either by a major struggle for survival, or by the need to sell, then elements of stress are all too likely to creep in. Women express anxiety at the unfamiliar, unwritten rules of the market-place: where you are allowed to stand and how much it will cost you, how much you are allowed to charge and, indeed, if you are allowed to be there at all (Sorokina 1992: 4; Baklanova 1993: 3). If some fear the violence of racketeers, the unpredictable actions of the state and its servants may be just as bad:

> The biggest racket is the state. Nowadays, if someone is trading somewhere on the street, racketeering can affect you but, as far as I know, it's within limits. But the city police can just kick you out. They take bribes, of course, but for some of them it's just a sport to kick you out and take nothing at all. It depends on the individual, because getting permission from the tax inspectorate and from the public health department is also virtually impossible, because they take the view that it will be warm on the streets now, the food will perish and so it's not allowed.
>
> [30]

By the same token, women who have found themselves an acceptable regular sales pitch may find that the local authorities will decide to upgrade an entire area and close it to unregulated trading at a stroke. In the summer of 1993, this is exactly what happened in the area around the Iugo–Zapadnaia metro station in Moscow where literally hundreds of people lined the streets selling mostly fruit and vegetables from their allotments. As the journalist from *Moskovskii komsomolets*, surveying the wreckage after the authorities had moved in, observed, this might seem rational to the mayor's office and to those who would be able to afford the smart new market stalls, but for the 70 per cent of traders who had been selling home-grown produce it was nothing less than a catastrophe (Kas'ianikova 1993: 1).

However well organised women's involvement in trading appears to be, it cannot, for most, be assumed to equate to regular employment. There are considerable and very real insecurities related to the entire business which are no doubt inevitable for anyone effectively operating outside the law. For some, the stress involved is more than they can deal with, whatever the potential benefits:

> I'm too emotional to make any money through trading. I know, because I've tried it. I'd just lie awake at night thinking things like, 'I'll have to go there and get that, then get over there and do this', and so on and so forth, and I'd be incapable of just doing it. I was wound up like a spring all the time.
>
> [26]

Add to this the worry of finding customers, or of being left with dozens of pizzas or Chinese anoraks on your hands, and the reluctance of many to get involved in trading becomes immediately understandable.

There are, however, other factors at work in Russia which may make street trading difficult to stomach. In the very recent Soviet past this form of buying and selling was a criminal offence: where trade was state controlled, acquiring goods and putting a mark-up on them for resale was speculation, while production of items for sale by individuals, other than in collective farm markets, was not permitted until 1987. Anyone not in the first flush of youth is likely to have problems, therefore, with the very idea of trading. There are still plenty of people around who are ready to hurl the word 'speculator' as a term of abuse in the face of someone standing in the street selling. Alongside this, there is evidently a residual contempt for those who have been reduced to trade. While this remains largely a reflection of the country's unresolved political battles, it has probably not been helped by the arrogance of some of the nation's *nouveaux riches*. If 'speculation' is a word which springs readily to the tongue of those who oppose the market reforms, it is evidently ever-present in the minds of women engaging in trading (Baklanova 1993: 3; Sorokina 1992: 4; Kleiman 1993: 8–9).

To overcome their awkwardness, women use the word 'speculator' as a joke about themselves or their friends who are trading. Yet, if the laughter helps to rob the word of its power, it also betrays a continuing sense of unease. This is underlined by women who contrast their own position with that of younger people who have plunged more readily into the new commercial world. Women who are trading may feel, with some justification, that it has all been much easier for those who have grown up in the period of increasing liberalisation post-1985. With few moral qualms, and certainly without the unpleasant connotations of 'speculation', they can simply get on with making money. Certainly, young women are far more likely to express unequivocal approval of the money-making activities of their friends and see the rewards as simply a fair return on hard work. As one student we interviewed commented, 'At my institute all the young men are involved in business, opening their own firms, working as brokers. Good for them' [23].

Beyond the legacy of a past regime, there is a further psychological barrier which women who engage in trading have to come to terms with: the question of loss of status. Unlike so many of their counterparts in the West, women in their thirties and forties who have lost their jobs or suffered a major drop in their standard of living have never before experienced the insecurities of the job market. They have never encountered lay-offs and redundancies, been obliged to accept part-time work or short-term contracts, or had to change direction completely in order to earn money. The graduates among them have never experienced competition for jobs in their field or been obliged to move into a career their degree had not trained them for. Instead, most had gone through their education, been offered work in their specialism and settled down to collect their monthly wage and wait for their pension. If accepting a drop in status is difficult for anyone to face, it could therefore be argued that the metamorphosis from Soviet engineer to Russian street trader is doubly difficult. Women such as these had simply never imagined that their lives would change. They had been able to feel, moreover, whatever the realities of their job, that their position was respected in a society where the term 'intelligentsia' has the positive overtones which it lacks completely in the English language.

For these women, now so resoundingly rejected by the ageism of the new job market, standing in the street or at the market stall is a profound shock to the system. The relatively few journalists who have dealt with this issue in the press are given to using the word 'shame' to describe what women go through when taking their first steps in street trading. From the tone of their reports it is very apparent that women they have interviewed have indeed felt acutely embarrassed at facing the public, and not least their own families, in this unexpected guise (Baklanova 1993: 3; Sorokina 1992:

4). Shame is, however, too strong a word to describe the reactions of the women we interviewed. None of them used it, yet there was certainly an element of awkwardness in describing what they were doing. For the most part this was covered by jokes and heavy irony – '*I* am in *commerce* now' [6], said one with a flourish and suitable dramatic gestures. Sometimes the bravura performance seemed expressly designed to ward off any expression of sympathy, sometimes the laughter would feel faintly hysterical. However it was dealt with it was apparent that, for some women, discussing trading was touching a very raw nerve indeed.

It was scarcely surprising, then, that when they talked about their involvement in buying and selling, women would often studiously avoid describing how they felt. For those who did discuss their feelings, much depended, as always, on their view of their former profession. One woman who had held a responsible job in one of the USSR ministries compared her reactions to trading to the discomfort she had often experienced in her work, especially when sent on assignments to other towns:

> People thought that you could help them, give them something. All I could do was tell them what pieces of paper to fill in to give to Gosplan. At least this is honest work and I earn my money now.
>
> [6]

Others, however, who had lost work they valued would, behind the jokey delivery, evince palpable degrees of bitterness and distress:

> I left school with a distinction, went to a top-class institute and this is what happens! I've been on six-month courses, I even did English for six months – technical translation, I've been to lots of institutes, and look at me! It's incredibly upsetting. And it's a catastrophe for the country, a catastrophe.
>
> [32]

Perhaps more than anything else, it is over this issue that the greatest impact of change has been felt. Certainly, as a symbol of loss, it is extremely powerful: loss of face, loss, for some, of work they loved, loss of security and loss of a position in society. Trading may well demonstrate women's indomitable will to survive, but, at the same time, they are not obliged to like it.

SAVING AND SELLING – THE NEW REALITY

When women lose their jobs, especially if they are over thirty-five, they are likely to find that their chances of finding what they would regard as acceptable employment are few. Moreover, even where work is available, when wages have become so devalued taking another job may cease to present itself as a sensible course of action. This is particularly true of women with children who would have to pay for child care if they were to find another job. Two women we interviewed who were in this situation gave examples of the low pay of relatives and friends – 'you go to work and it's like you're on benefit' – and explained how being stuck with an eight-hour day and the cost of child care simply made no sense. With a judicious combination of economising and trading, better results could be obtained:

> If I wanted to get a job in my profession now, the most I could earn would be 100,000. I don't want to do it because I think I'm more useful here. I can look out for the cheapest food, I can cook myself. I do everything myself and I think that's more profitable at the moment.

[31]

Both of these women had husbands who had jobs with low to average pay and neither was registered unemployed, seeing it as too much hassle for a virtually worthless benefit. To all intents and purposes, they had simply vanished from government figures into the mass of 'dependants' or 'housewives'. Yet their families could not have survived without the range of activities they were involved in. Whatever their official status, they were certainly not sitting around idly, but were busily engaged in a well developed form of self-sufficiency.

Keeping benefit levels extremely low means that even women who have no other financial support may not see registering as unemployed as an option worth pursuing. Whatever their dismay at being involved in trading they may still see it as preferable to being pushed into retraining for a more menial future; one which, in any event, may not lead to secure employment. If trading is humiliating, retraining for the work on offer, especially for older women with twenty years' service or more as highly skilled engineers, may simply be one humiliation too far. Perhaps the most significant aspect of trading, whatever its many glaring drawbacks, is that it does allow women to retain at least some element of control. The decisions they make about what and where they buy and sell are theirs alone – as is the sense of achievement at having survived such an unpromising set of circumstances. For those who feel they have lost everything else all of these factors may become extremely important. What is certain is that, behind all the talk and the images of the entrepreneurial woman, this mixture of make-do-and-mend, of sewing and growing, buying and selling, is the new reality for far more women in Russia today. Whether it is, however, any less entrepreneurial in character is very much a matter for debate.

So, if women have very mixed feelings about the lifestyle they have been constrained to embrace, how do they cope with the fact that little else is on the horizon? For the women we interviewed, the answer appeared to lie primarily in the level of optimism they could muster for the process of reform. Those who felt sure that things would soon start to improve were able to rationalise their current activities as being purely temporary, a phase which they simply had to go through until things settled down and new opportunities began to emerge. Others were by no means so sanguine, expressing considerable cynicism about the progress of reform. Yet even women who could see no prospects whatsoever in their own future did not necessarily express a sense of hopelessness about it. Some appeared to have come to terms with their own personal situation and, having accepted their powerlessness to change it, were dealing with it with a certain measure of calm:

> In the past, people spent their whole life waiting for better times. It's as if our people have always had to go through something difficult. My grandmother, for example, was always expecting things to get better, but they never did. Now at least you can simply live for today, that's all there is, and maybe this is the sole improvement that we can see.
>
> [30]

Those who had managed to adopt a perspective in which they could take one day at a time and expect little or nothing from it were probably the most successful in adapting to their starkly changed circumstances.

Inevitably perhaps, the older women were the least likely to feel any measure of optimism for the future. A sense of both rejection and finality was very strong in the things they had to say. Yet they also expressed remarkable stoicism and determination. Women may be very unhappy at the situation in which they find themselves, yet many are managing to provide for themselves through their own efforts, without a job and without any assistance whatsoever from the state. It is an achievement in which, in a perverse kind of way, they can take some pride, as one unemployed engineer made very clear:

I've got eight years to go until my pension and no one needs me. But I'm not going to go away. I'm going to plant my four paws on the ground and I'm going to stand right here!

[32]

8

SEXUAL EXPLOITATION AND THE NEW LABOUR MARKET

If older women cope with the impact of transition by combinations of self-sufficiency and small-scale business, the young have one additional opportunity presented to them. The world of modelling and the sex industry in all its many manifestations may appear to offer those with youth and acceptable figures undreamed-of material benefits. As Russia has cast off the restrictions of the Soviet period, the potential for women to gain money and possessions by using their bodies has burgeoned.

The period of liberalisation which began in the mid-1980s had, of course, already produced a growing sex industry in the USSR: the change which has taken place in Russia since 1991 has largely been one of degree. With the abandonment of controls, pornography in particular has become extremely high profile. The sheer quantity of images of female nudes on display in Russian cities is very difficult to convey: within months of Russia's independence it had become commonplace for pornography to festoon virtually any public space where trading was taking place. In a similar way, prostitution has grown into a major racket. No longer catering primarily for western businessmen with hard currency to spare, prostitution has developed to serve the growing Russian clientele of newly rich entrepreneurs. A plethora of call-girl agencies now offer their services and advertise for new recruits quite openly week after week in the Russian press.

With political change, the backlash against the moral and psychological controls of the former Soviet system has provided ample justification for the excesses of the growing sex industry. At the same time, falling living standards and the threat of unemployment have made women far more vulnerable to activities which may appear to offer substantial financial rewards. For younger women, in particular, the attractions of western-style consumerism so suddenly and mercilessly paraded in front of their eyes are readily understandable. As the period of transition continues, the key question is whether the growth of prostitution and the continual media emphasis on images of women as sex objects is creating a climate in which sexual exploitation and abuse can flourish, not merely within the sex industry itself but also in the broader world of employment.

What is certain is that the social attitudes which underpin the current situation have not simply sprung up in some post-Soviet vacuum, but have developed directly from the Soviet legacy. Since the height of the Brezhnev era with its official concern over the birth rate, the media have produced a deluge of images and language portraying women as 'different' and 'special', their thoughts and actions irrevocably determined by their reproductive function. For the best part of a decade before the advent even of perestroika, women's characters were being habitually portrayed as inextricably bound up with their sexuality. By the time the process of liberalisation began, therefore, the 'otherness' of women had been emphasised to such a degree that to objectify them further in an overtly sexual way was but a small step to take. As the pronatalist discourse contrived to ease women out of the workforce, it became much easier to depict them not as skilled or intellectual but as domestic, decorative and sexual. In effect, the representation of women was increasingly being restricted to either wife and mother or mistress and whore. While all the efforts of the pronatalist campaign had little impact on reproductive behaviour, the same could not be said of social attitudes, as Marina Malysheva of the Moscow Centre for Gender Studies, writing in 1991, observed:

Very palpable changes were brought about in the attitudes of both men and women. Moreover, and this should be particularly emphasised, their attitudes diverged and polarised to such an extent that the gulf between the sexes in the current generation is probably greater than at any time in Soviet history.

(Malysheva 1991: 80)

Cultural change of this type, followed rapidly by massive economic upheaval, has proved to be a particularly vicious combination for Russian women. Moreover, its consequences, even for those who have no desire to use their bodies for material gain, may be increasingly difficult to avoid.

RESPONSES TO THE SEX AND GLAMOUR INDUSTRY: ATTRACTION AND RESISTANCE

It would be remarkably easy in the present circumstances to portray Russian women as simply the hapless victims of predatory males. It is perhaps worth bearing in mind when observing the attitudes of Russian women to the new sexual climate that women in the West have taken their time in responding to the issue of sexual exploitation and that, even now, there is no consensus among feminists on questions of pornography and censorship, for example. The liberalisation of moral attitudes, following a period of relative puritanism, may find women as well as men enjoying what they see as newly won personal freedom. There is, therefore, an understandable reluctance on the part of many women, as well as men, in Russia to set off once more down the path of imposing controls.

Moreover, in a society where sex education had been non-existent and where the kinds of articles on sex that appear in virtually any western women's magazine were absent from mainstream publications, soft porn magazines did, to some extent, fill an information vacuum. For this reason, no doubt, women could regularly be seen at street bookstalls buying this material for themselves. In such a situation, the issue of sexual exploitation was evidently not uppermost in women's minds. As a result, the possible effect on social attitudes of this deluge of images of female nudity was initially something very few women appeared concerned about. It was only with the explosion of pornographic material onto the streets and a marked increase in prostitution as the market reforms got underway that the question of the effects on women began to be taken seriously. In 1993, for example, the parliamentary hearing considering how the UN Convention on the Elimination of All Forms of Discrimination Against Women might be implemented in Russia concluded that 'measures should be taken to forbid the propaganda of pornography, sex, cruelty and violence' ('Predlozheniia uchastnikov parlamentskikh . . .' 1993: 3).

Nevertheless, women's responses to pornography have generally remained muted. While occasional letters have appeared in the press from young women complaining about the prevalence of images which 'make you feel like an animal' (Khar'kov 1993: 8), the emphasis has remained less on their potential impact than on their excessive and inappropriate display. Self-declared feminists writing in the press have castigated the 'outrageous display of pornography where young and old can see it in every busy place and on every street corner', comparing this unfavourably with what they perceived as the more acceptably controlled situation in the West (Aristova 1992: 7). Pornography, in effect, is all right in its place, as one student we interviewed characteristically remarked:

> It should be in special shops, not all over the place. At the moment there's too much, it's in excess. . . . In principle, I'm not against it.

If there's a demand then of course it should be met, and there'll
always be a demand for it I think.

[23]

If women would prefer not to be inundated with pornographic material
at every turn, few express disquiet at the impact it may be having on broader
attitudes towards them.

This absence of public response by women to the potential effects of
pornographic images is closely linked to attitudes towards direct participation in the sex and glamour industry. If women *en masse* are not objecting
to the vast quantities of pornographic magazines, photographs, films and
videos currently in circulation or the constant use of female nudity in
advertising and modelling, there is little disincentive to young women to
become involved in its production. Indeed, given a more liberal sexual
climate and women's dire prospects for well-paid employment, attempting
to get into the world of glamour modelling, if nothing more than that,
may appear to many to be the smart thing to do. Unfortunately, as
experience has already shown, even women who believe they are walking
into this with their eyes wide open may rapidly find themselves trapped in
situations beyond their control. In the rest of this chapter we will attempt
to explore the nature of women's involvement in the sex industry, the
'hidden agenda' of sexual harassment and some of the first initiatives by
Russian women to combat sexual exploitation.

BEING 'DISCOVERED': THE LURE OF THE BEAUTY CONTEST

As Russia began its transition to the market, the overwhelming popularity
that beauty contests had experienced in the USSR's final years did not die
down. On the contrary, with new commercial opportunities developing
by the day, the beauty contest was increasingly seen as an essential
stepping-stone by growing numbers of women aspiring to enter the world
of fashion and modelling. The attraction was obvious: as it became ever
more apparent that most Russians were not about to reap the benefits of
a more prosperous, more glamorous western-style existence, younger
women in particular began to express a sense of impatience with the
hardships of Russian lifestyles and a determination to escape the humdrum
and monotonous existence of their parents' generation. Beauty contests
served an important function, therefore, as the most accessible and most
respectable element of the glamour industry.

For many women, entering a contest must have seemed a perfect way to kill several birds with one stone: to alleviate some of the boredom by inserting a more glamorous interlude into their ordinary lives, to gain some recognition and value for their 'beauty' and perhaps, for the lucky few, to win a ticket out to a new and better life. These sentiments were reflected in the attitudes voiced not only by contestants but also by some of the organisers of these events. Aleksei Romanov, for example, organiser of the 'Miss Press 1992' contest insisted, 'As always there will be prizes of sponsorship and trips abroad, but this is not where we put the most emphasis. The most important thing is the chance to meet people and to enjoy the holiday atmosphere' (Kilesso 1992: 4). Similarly, women entering a competition organised by the weekly newspaper *Vechernyi klub* gave their main reasons for taking part as: a desire to be 'discovered', to bring some variety into their lives, to have some activity and communicate with others, to make new contacts and meet new people (Glinka 1993: 3). These women were in their twenties and thirties, the majority of them had higher education and they were, for the most part, employed in the state sector with relatively low salaries.

Vechernyi klub's contestants typify what has persistently been one of the most striking aspects of Russian beauty contests: the high proportion of entrants with higher education and professional jobs. From the very beginning of the beauty contest craze, surprising numbers of technicians, doctors, sociologists and postgraduate students had been parading down the catwalks. In part, no doubt, this reflected the fact that the contests were still a novelty and lacked the tacky associations they had developed in the West. Yet, in a country where professional jobs were notoriously badly paid, the bright lights undoubtedly had an added allure. After 1991, prospects for women with higher education were, if anything, becoming less and less bright. In the past, the professions of engineer, doctor or teacher had at least commanded a certain amount of respect and social status. As these women fell under the onslaught of the first wave of unemployment and falling living standards, they found that together with their job security and a living wage they had also lost their prestige. Women engineers in particular were having to face the fact that their qualifications were useless, that no one was interested in employing them and that their old jobs had, in many cases, in fact been a waste of time. Certainly, the situation held little comfort for new graduates in technical professions. In these circumstances, it was scarcely surprising that women with the right face and figure felt that they had very little to lose.

There is, however, a further important element in understanding the attraction of beauty contests: the pursuit of what is perpetually presented as a uniquely 'Russian' approach to the concept of beauty. Again and again the organisers, judges and proponents of these competitions insist that the beauty of a Russian woman is much more than skin deep. The jury for the 1993 'Miss Russia' competition, for instance, announced that 'this is not about having long legs, or any other stunning physical attribute. . . . A true Russian woman is not just for show. . . . Above all she must be kind, understanding and sympathetic to all' ('Chto–to zakhotelos' . . .' 1993: 1). It is surely no coincidence that this comes at a time when resurgent nationalist sentiment is rife. Such assertions by the organisers of these events bear witness not only to an eagerness to jump on the nationalist bandwagon, but also to a desire to defend themselves against any accusation that they might simply be mimicking trashy western entertainment, or degrading the mothers of the future Russia. For the women who take part in these events, this additional element means that it is not just about parading in a swimsuit or being told they are beautiful, but about being acknowledged as a 'good' person, a 'proper' Russian woman, about getting at least some praise and recognition for all that they do.

This element of moral irreproachability makes it all the more ironic, therefore, when stories leak out of the contests' unwritten rules. Contestants dreaming of glamour and fame and seriously aspiring to be 'discovered', especially to win a contract abroad as a top fashion model, often find themselves entangled in something much less appealing. Reports on several of these competitions imply that the women involved are expected at the very least to sleep with the organisers, and, if they really hope to win, probably with everyone from the judges to the lighting technicians as well. Women who finally land the sought-after modelling contracts, whether via beauty contests or through other channels, may well find themselves facing a similar predicament.

MODELLING: ANOTHER NAME FOR PROSTITUTION?

As Russian society has opened up in the area of sex and sexuality there has been a great deal of confusion around where the boundaries lie between erotic art, glamour modelling, pornography and prostitution. On the one hand, this confusion has meant that any woman entering the world of fashion modelling or beauty contests lays herself open to being treated as a prostitute by any other name. On the other, the lack of clarity in women's own minds has resulted in what can appear to be extreme naivety. Victor Ginzburg's documentary, *Neskuchnyi sad* or *The Restless Garden*, produced in 1992, was one of the first to explore the issues surrounding the explosion of sexually explicit theatre, pornography, striptease and prostitution in

Russian society, and amply illustrates the point. Throughout the course of the film, women time and again describe what they are doing as 'art' or as 'self-expression'. Attitudes such as these may make young women easy prey to any smooth talker, as the numerous stories of models 'discovered' by photographers who claim to have spotted them in a crowd would appear to testify.

In the summer of 1993, the weekly newspaper, *Moskovskie novosti*, attempted to explore modelling's hidden agenda. Their interview with a woman research biologist who had been 'discovered' by a fashion photographer on the metro described how she had given up the idea of becoming a model full time after encountering expectations of sexual favours at every turn. When refusing to have sex on her first photographic assignment,

> she was told that she was the first for many years in his line of work, who had refused to go to bed with him. That is not the way things are done. Even famous models can rarely allow themselves to refuse. Katia realised that she was not going to be a famous model.
>
> (Kolesnikov 1993: 10)

While it is impossible to ascertain the extent of sexual harassment in either beauty contests or modelling, some measure of its prevalence can be gauged from an event which caused a minor sensation in Moscow in the 'coup-season', as the papers put it, of August 1993. On the eve of the second anniversary of the coup which was the beginning of the end for Mikhail Gorbachev, traffic was temporarily brought to a standstill, not by barricades but by a demonstration by fashion models. Bearing placards proclaiming 'Models get paid, not laid!', they announced their intention to form a trade union both to regulate minimum rates of pay and to combat what they termed 'sexual terror'. Their action made it clear that the latter was extremely widespread and that some of the newest modelling agencies, in particular, were effectively thinly disguised prostitution rackets. The purpose of the demonstration was in part to draw attention to this state of affairs and in part to change the image of modelling in the public mind (Legostanev 1993: 1; 'Zdras'te: avgustovskie strasti . . .' 1993: 1).

Reactions in the media to this unexpected turn of events were, predictably, less than enthusiastic. While some of the initial reporting – by male journalists – was highly sympathetic and evidently took seriously the models' concern that 'professional issues are often resolved in bed', other reports inevitably trivialised their action. Some were openly hostile. Within a couple of days of the demonstration an extremely vicious response from one Moscow agency appeared in the popular paper, *Moskovskii komsomolets*, depicting models as hysterical, manipulative gold-diggers. The actions of agencies run by organised crime, they asserted, had nothing whatsoever to do with 'the profession' and, moreover, 'models are not children and are perfectly capable of dealing with "sexual terror" – if they want to, that is' (Volkova 1993: 4).

Nevertheless, the models went ahead with their attempt to form their trade union through the following autumn and winter. Progress was slow. In the increasingly authoritarian political climate which followed Yeltsin's dissolution of the Russian parliament, they found it literally impossible to register as a new trade union. As a result, by the spring of 1994, they were working on a constitution establishing a 'models' club' instead. This, they felt, would allow them a broader sphere of action and also, unlike a trade union, permit them to restrict membership to women only.

Whatever the final outcome of this initiative, in the short term at least nothing has changed in the world of modelling. Moreover, as criminal activity has flourished in Russia, reports have become increasingly frequent of trafficking in women: the most glaring and disturbing manifestation of modelling jobs which go badly wrong. Where this occurs it generally involves the most sought-after contract of all – a modelling assignment abroad. When foreign travel has been virtually unknown, it is scarcely surprising that women who get the chance to see something of the world and earn hard currency into the bargain may be in no mood to contemplate the potential risks. Women may also end up in situations they had not bargained for as a result of a widespread, unwarranted trust in the West. When discussing social problems in their country, Russians have been prone to assert that the crux of the matter is that their society is still underdeveloped. The term *dikii*, meaning wild or untamed, has frequently been used to describe the Russian situation in contrast to western societies which were heralded as *tsivilizovanii*, or civilised. The conviction, not only that life is better, but also that a fundamental difference exists between the way things are done 'there' as opposed to 'here', has no doubt led many aspiring models to believe their dreams: if they can only win a contract to the West they will not only automatically achieve a lifestyle which they fondly imagine to be universal in those countries, but they will also be treated with respect and scrupulous justice.

In fact, the reality for many women who do manage to secure 'work' abroad is very different. Numerous stories have been published in the Russian press since 1993 of women trapped in mafia-controlled porno-graphy and prostitution rings in Italy, Germany, Turkey and America. In some cases the women have been quite literally abducted on arrival in the foreign country, having gone there under false pretences, expecting to work in restaurants or as au pairs. Others who have secured work abroad as models find on arrival that they are in fact expected to strip, or to work as topless dancers and prostitutes ('Rabyni pod krasnym fonarem' 1993: 3).

The element which reduces women's ability to control these situations is the involvement of Russian criminal networks in such affairs. Using their links to international mafia groups, these organisations take part in the buying and selling of Russian women. There is usually a Russian go-between who sets up the original misleading contract, but, once abroad, the young women find themselves entirely alone, at the mercy of a group of foreigners, in a country whose language they often only partly understand. These women are completely vulnerable to all kinds of degradation and exploitation since they usually have no work permit, have often had their passports confiscated by their 'employers' and frequently do not have a return air ticket or any money with which to buy one. Having dreamed of a western paradise, they find themselves trapped in a living hell. The criminal connections of their 'guardians' makes escape that much more difficult. A model abducted and forced into prostitution while working at a fashion show in Italy was assured by her captors,

> that they had ties with the mafia . . . and that they would kill her if she did not do as she was told. They also added that they had good contacts in Moscow and that it would be no problem for them to make sure that no one in Moscow would want to try and find her. Vera was able to see this for herself very shortly, when, having agreed to everything and worked for the Italians, she was allowed to pay a visit to her children in Moscow. At the airport Vera was met by Russians, tough guys in leather jackets, and they followed her everywhere for the whole of the three days she spent in Moscow.
>
> (Kolesnikov 1993: 11)

The fact that women in this situation survive to tell the tale may be due only to the intervention of the police in other European countries. Reports have reached the Russian press from Turkey, Greece, Cyprus and Germany of cases where Russian women have had to be taken into protective custody before being returned home.

MAKING A DEAL: THE WORLD OF 'UNDERCOVER' PROSTITUTION

If the involvement of organised crime in the traffic in women can be seen at its most brutal in this enforced prostitution of aspiring models abroad, the situation may be little better on home territory. For the thousands of women now working in brothels disguised as massage parlours and escort agencies, the networks which control these money-spinners are just as unlikely to want to let them go. Nevertheless, the swing of the pendulum after the years of strict censorship has given rise in Russia to what has been described, not least in parliamentary documents, as 'pro-prostitution propaganda', inviting young women to contemplate the potential benefits rather than dangers of moving into this sphere ('Materialy k parlamentskim slushaniiam . . .' 1993: 9).

In January 1993 a newspaper report on young women and prostitution declared, 'According to sociologists, in answer to the question, "Which is the most attractive profession?" 60 per cent of Moscow's female school-leavers replied, "prostitution"' ('Besplatnykh zavtrakov . . .' 1993: 7). Though constantly repeated to the point of notoriety, this assertion could scarcely represent the true aspirations of three out of five sixteen-year-old women. It does, however, undoubtedly say something about the doors which they see opening before them. Prostitution, especially for hard currency, is habitually described as 'the only way for women to make a lot of money'. As the social climate in Russia has become ever more oriented towards making money, by whatever means present themselves, becoming a prostitute could be viewed as an entirely rational choice for a young woman to make. The social status of a woman in this situation may, therefore, be regarded quite differently from that of her equivalent in the West: not only is she unlikely to face censure, but, given prevailing conditions, she may also be admired for being smart. Still, this does not mean that every woman personally wants to make such a choice, even if, objectively, she may see it as 'attractive':

> Lots of young women especially go for the easy option. They get themselves a man with money or get involved in prostitution because it's an easy way to get everything you want. I couldn't live like that, living in a gilded cage – and there's the whole question of where the money comes from. I can walk down the street and feel quite calm about myself and my life, and maybe I don't have a lot. But for women like that, they can go around covered in jewellery and they're looking over their shoulders all the time, feeling afraid. I couldn't live like that.

[26]

As this comment suggests, 'prostitution' in Russia at the present time requires a broader definition than simply the largely indiscriminate provision of sexual services for payment. It is clear that a significant group of young women are involved in what might be termed 'undercover' prostitution: a deliberate decision to use their beauty and sexuality to 'buy'

174

for themselves the comforts and lifestyle to which their training and professional work simply does not give them ready access.[1] The deal involves finding a rich lover, or, better still, a husband from the business world, who will amply provide for them in return for the prestige of having a young and beautiful female companion and bedmate. If, at first glance, this looks like the *Pretty Woman* scenario of poor woman meets rich man, the comparison stops there. As the numerous press interviews and features on this phenomenon make clear, the essential fairy-tale element of happily-ever-after is definitely missing. A 1993 feature in the women's magazine *Rabotnitsa*, for example, illustrated one young woman's lack of illusions:

> Of course without much to-do they became intimate.
>
> 'Mummy, Kirill spoils me so, I really shouldn't be ungrateful', she calmly explained her behaviour at home.
>
> 'You might perhaps love him?' asked her mother.
>
> 'Oh Mum, is that really necessary? After all, you said yourself I am a beautiful young woman and I ought to lead a beautiful life.'
>
> (Bogdanova 1993: 29)

The snag in all of this for the women involved is that the men, ultimately, call the shots. Even women who feel that they know exactly what they are doing may find to their dismay that they cannot remain in control. Given that this is so recent a social phenomenon, it is fascinating that the constant risk of being 'traded in for a newer model' has already given rise to an urban myth. Like all good myths, the story is told as having happened to a friend or acquaintance, and goes like this:

> My friend goes out with a successful and wealthy businessman. They were walking along together recently when he suddenly said that they were going to have to stop seeing each other because she simply wasn't attractive enough to impress his associates and clients. He said he was very sorry but he thought he should find someone younger and prettier and more suitable to his needs. She stayed quite calm and said to him, 'Haven't you ever noticed how everyone turns to look at me on the street as we walk by?' To prove the point, she told him to stand on the corner and watch as she walked down the street. Sure enough, every passer-by turned to look at her. What he didn't know was that she was pulling dreadful faces as she walked along, which, not surprisingly, were achieving the desired effect. Returning to him all smiles she said, 'There you are, you just don't realise what a treasure you have in me.'

In the world of myth, the woman involved is able to use her cunning to gain at least a temporary reprieve; in reality, she may not be so lucky. The prostitution element in the deal is underlined by cases where women find themselves treated just like any other asset. This means they can be dumped when they become 'obsolete' or sold off in the event of financial difficulties, ending up in a more overt form of prostitution. This is precisely what had happened to one young woman in a recently reported case:

> She had fallen head over heels in love with a local businessman and he was paying for her keep. She suffered terrible humiliation and beatings. Then he went bankrupt and . . . sold her to his friends together with his dacha. For 5,000 dollars.
>
> (Zinoviev 1993: 8)

Another form of 'undercover' prostitution involves more of a part-time commitment. Explicit personal advertisements make clear the nature of the deal:

> Prosperous man seeks pleasant, liberated girl with good figure, or two sexual partners, for intimate relationship. Financial help guaranteed.
>
> ('Ob"iavleniia' 1992: 8)

Many of the men who place adverts such as these make no secret of the fact that they are married and looking for sexual partners with no strings attached to liven up their business trips. Some want women with their own flats, no doubt to provide trouble-free assignations. All inevitably offer money as the bait.

This kind of deal is not only being made between Russian men and women. Large numbers of advertisements are placed in the Russian press week after week by western men seeking young and accommodating Russian wives. This scenario is not new to the western world. It is simply that Russia's new poverty has opened up an additional market for mail-order brides to add to the well-established traffic from South-East Asia (Lee 1991: 92). In both cases, what the men are looking for is strikingly similar.

American, British and Italian men, mostly over 45, set out their interests and, often, financial status and stipulate above all that they are interested in women between ten and twenty years their junior:

Donald Hepperly, 61/165/79.
Roof layer, evangelist.
Interests: study of birds, butterflies and reptiles.

Preference: 18–48 year old.

('Vyberi menia', 1993: 22)

Ov Slosberg, 45/173/73.
Salesman, divorced.
Pleasant character, romantic, cheerful. Jewish.
Seeks 23–32 year old woman. Attractive,
not overweight, homemaker, who likes to
laugh.

('Svakha' 1993: 15)

These advertisements are profoundly at odds with the content of 'lonely hearts' ads placed by impecunious Russian men. Lacking entirely in words such as 'love' or 'tenderness', the western announcements are particularly jarring when placed alongside the often touchingly sentimental offerings of the 'Sashas' and 'Andreis', who are more likely to write, 'I am tired of being alone. Answer me my one and only if you still believe in love, tenderness and family happiness. Existing children not a problem' ('Svedi nas sud'ba', 1994: 15).

Although the language of romance may well be employed when the westerners finally make their bride-hunting trips to Russia, the economic situation of the women involved makes this ring very hollow. Looking for an illusion of the 'good life', or simply security for themselves and their families, the women inevitably embark on a far from equal partnership.[2] They are, moreover, unlikely to have much idea of what they are letting themselves in for in what will probably be suburban life in a not-very-exciting western town. One American journalist, living and working in Moscow, has described his bride-seeking compatriots and the lives they have to offer in the following stinging terms:

And what do the would-be brides get for their money? . . . plane-loads of overshy or just plain repugnant men. . . . And if they are very, very lucky they can expect to cook and slave and clean and love for life some middle-aged loser in an industrial town in the West.

(Crombie 1992: 31)

There are plenty of reasons why a woman in Russia today might be tempted to enter into any one of these deals. But, in every case, the bottom line is access to something they could not otherwise attain. Larissa Bogdanova, writing in *Rabotnitsa*, made the connection between 'undercover' prostitution and access in the following telling comment on provincial young women with rich Moscow 'sugar daddies':

177

To return to the dead provinces and live as poorly as your parents would be like dying. So there is no choice! There's no knight in shining armour either. You have to pay for your right to live in the capital, to have a good job and a flat with what you have got. With your body. . . . Today thousands of girls are calmly and calculatedly selling themselves. The stupider ones do it just for money, those with more brains and bigger plans do it for a prestigious job and a place to live. In the name of this main aim they say to hell with sentiment.

(Bogdanova 1993: 28)

In this way the connection is firmly and increasingly made that there is a price to be paid by women who want not the luxuries of the *nouveaux riches* but longer-term material security. The idea of a sexual pay-off in return for a job has already been established. It is the repercussions of this which are now beginning to make themselves felt more widely in the developing labour market.

SEXUAL HARASSMENT

While the sensational issues of prostitution and trafficking in women have been hitting the Russian headlines in a big way, any discussion of the problems of sexual harassment in the workplace has been notable only for its absence. On the one hand, this topic seems far too banal to excite much interest from the media, yet, on the other, it is also potentially too hot to handle. Producing shocking revelations about the sex industry is, in a sense, more acceptable: for the vast majority of readers this is something quite separate and distinct from their own everyday lives. Sexual harassment, however, is an issue which may be too close for comfort.

Under the Soviet system, sexual harassment, like all other sexual issues, could not be a matter for public discussion. There was, however, a widespread assumption that sexual favours played an important part in the workplace in gaining promotion, negotiating trips abroad, bonuses and time off. When the women's newspaper, *Delovaia zhenshchina* (*Business Woman*), published a feature in 1993 on sexual harassment in the United States, one exasperated reader wrote to the editors to complain, 'Since you have at last decided to "speak out", then leave the USA in peace with their problems of sexual discrimination and let's talk about our own.' She went on to assert that, while sexual harassment was widespread in the Soviet workplace, a new element had now come into play:

Nothing has changed since then, only the added fear of losing your job. This particularly affects women who are the sole breadwinners for their families. It is these women who are transformed into office prostitutes. Those who refuse any proposition are simply chucked out.

('Ia k vam pishu', 1992: 4)

The silence which had reigned on the issue of harassment at work created a series of problems for women. In the first place, it isolated women from each other: those who were now in relatively influential positions, for example, as a result of the office 'casting couch' might be extremely reluctant to acknowledge its existence. Secondly, this lack of openness made it virtually impossible to assess how serious a threat harassment posed. Finally, while models, for example, might form a coherent group to deal with this issue in a specific area of employment, in a climate of silence harassment across the broad spectrum of women's jobs would remain a far tougher nut to crack.

On the question of acknowledging the existence of sexual harassment, the *Delovaia zhenshchina* reader clearly touched a raw nerve in the offices of the newspaper itself. In an otherwise astonishingly dismissive editorial reply to her letter, one sentence was singled out for particular condemnation: 'I'm totally convinced, that not one businesswoman has got to where she is today, without either paying hefty bribes, or else without having to "frequent", if you'll excuse the expression, her boss' bed.' This statement elicited such a touchy response from the editors that it is tempting to assume that she might have been right.

If this initial attempt to open up debate on the subject was not entirely successful, this only served to emphasise how profound the silence had been, a fact mirrored in the dearth of research on harassment in Russia. One of the few studies to have touched on this issue at all involved a group of fifteen women leaders of political parties, free trade unions, social justice groups and protest movements who were interviewed in 1991–2. All fifteen reported having experienced sexual harassment at the hands of their male bosses (Konstantinova 1992: 114). Others who have attempted to pursue this issue with larger samples, particularly western researchers, have had to tread very carefully to produce any valid results at all.[3]

Our own interviews with Russian women suggest that, whatever the situation in the past, sexual harassment is an important concern at present, especially for younger women seeking work. Some defined what they termed 'sexual aggression' or 'sexual terror' as the main problem facing women entering the labour market:

I've come across this several times when I went for an interview somewhere. Although I would consider myself quite a modest young

179

woman, the first question would still be, do I live alone, with my parents, or . . . you know the type of question. Or else they would ask, do I wear short skirts. I don't think that is what a potential employer should be interested in, but it's a very widespread attitude.

[23]

Those who were already placed in what they considered secure employment did not feel themselves at risk. Similarly, students not yet actively involved in the job market reported that they had not encountered the problem, but expected that they would do as soon as they looked for work. With even a cursory glance at job advertisements in the Russian press it is not difficult to see why. When an employer advertising for an office assistant feels it necessary to add 'No sexual services required', it suggests that the problem is little short of universal (*Priglashaem na rabotu* 1993: 3). Women signing an ordinary employment contract may find that, just like those who agree to modelling work or enter beauty contests, they are faced with the 'hidden extras', of which they have not been made aware:

> Sexual aggression is the main reason why Russian women cannot fulfil their potential. All my friends have met with this when trying to get jobs or once they were working. When a woman has been in her job for say three months and she is just starting to settle in and feel good about herself, suddenly she starts getting all these proposi- tions and she has to leave. It happens all the time, even when your employers have initially promised that it won't.
>
> [23]

Some women suggest that it is in the spheres of trade and commerce that female employees are most at risk, citing as proof the notorious immorality of Russian business practices today. Others say that the new commercial outfits are less riddled with corruption and discrimination than those which have directly inherited from the Soviet state sector. One thing is certain, universal or not, sexual harassment is by no means a rare aspect of Russian women's lives and it is one which may present a very real barrier for women in terms of achievement.

The development of attitudes which treat women primarily as sex objects is unlikely to remain limited to only one aspect of social relation- ships. It is a danger which even very young women are by no means unaware of:

> Attitudes to women are changing from the traditions of the past. Women today are looked upon as some kind of personal possession. Attitudes to women are certainly getting worse and worse, men seem

to think that anything goes. They think they have the right to take whatever they want, by force if needs be.

[28]

These ways of relating to women are producing a new brand of far more overt sexual harassment in public than was permissible in the past. Women may previously have had to suffer unwanted touching in a crushed trolley bus where none of the other passengers could be aware of what was going on, but not leering and jibes in the street, nor overt mauling while passers-by look on but fail to do anything to help. Unfortunately these latter types of behaviour are now becoming all too common. The women we interviewed frequently alluded to their growing concern for their own and their daughters' personal safety, clearly feeling considerable distress at the recent loss of a sense of security on the streets at night. The 'sexual terror' experienced by women in the labour market is part of an overall social climate which is becoming increasingly sexualised, threatening and particularly hostile to women. This is not something which women have had to deal with in the past and learning to confront it now is posing a very specific set of challenges which few groups and organisations are preparing to meet.

The media correspondence which began so inauspiciously with the refutation of the *Delovaia zhenshchina* letter subsequently developed into something more substantial. As a result of further readers' letters on the subject, the editors of the short-lived successor paper, *Novaia zhenshchina*, concluded that sexual harassment was a particularly pressing issue and that women were in great need of support. While the paper was still in existence, they created a support group called 'Women against Sexual Harassment at Work' and invited all concerned to come along to their Moscow office on the first Tuesday in every month (Gaidarenko 1992: 14). Actions such as this were, however, primarily concerned with the support of victims rather than the cessation of the crime. Although women might well feel that they should be protected by law, the fact of the matter remained that, in Russia as in the former USSR, no employer need feel afraid of the law. In this climate it was perhaps inevitable that the muted response to this issue which did emerge should concentrate on how women should respond to an existing evil, rather than on how the evil itself might be removed.

Women's responses to the rapid development of the sex industry and to the issue of sexual harassment in Russia, then, have been both slow and limited. As we have seen, however, there have been occasional isolated attempts at combating some of the worst excesses of sexual exploitation.

The concluding part of this chapter looks at how one Moscow-based organisation has tried a more systematic approach to helping women, especially the young and potentially most vulnerable, to cope with the situation they now face. The Moscow Image Centre deals with all of the issues discussed above, but does so from an angle and within a framework which, to the western eye in particular, is highly unexpected. At first glance, the Image programme for women looks like any other beauty course. There is, however, a great deal more to it than that, as becomes apparent both from the attitudes of its founder and of women who have attended its courses.

THE IMAGE CENTRE – FROM SELF-PRESENTATION TO EMPOWERMENT

The Image Centre was founded in 1989 by the fashion designer, Elena Evseeva. It was set up in response to a demand for the training of fashion models and, at the same time, for the provision of image consultancy to the new breed of politicians emerging through the USSR's first free elections. With moves towards a market economy the demand for both individual and corporate image consultancy has grown. In line with these developments, Elena Evseeva herself has become increasingly concerned to provide advice and information, primarily for women, to enable them to adapt to market conditions. While the Centre attracts its customers through its initial emphasis on appearance, its *raison d'être* in working with women runs far deeper than this and is fundamentally concerned with personal development. The Centre's slogan, 'Our information – your choice', sums up Evseeva's aim of equipping women with the knowledge they need to deal with the changing conditions they are likely to face.

Although the Image Centre has employed a range of teachers and psychologists to work on its various courses, it has been overwhelmingly a one-woman show during all the years of its existence. Elena Evseeva continues to operate as a fashion designer as well as work with the media as a fashion pundit and, to this day, the Image Centre has no permanent home. After a series of problems over premises it now relies on ad hoc arrangements with other institutions, turning necessity into something of a policy. The decision to avoid 'paying a bribe for every fireman', as Evseeva puts it, produces the rather curious impression of a Centre which exists wherever she happens to be. Nevertheless, its reality can be vouched for by the hundreds of businessmen and politicians and the thousands of women who have had contact with it since 1989. Contracts for image consultancy have underpinned the entire venture and kept the show on the road since its inception.

Image consultancy and the funding of the Centre

The Centre's initial contract for image consultancy came from a group of deputies elected to the new Soviet parliament in the 1989 elections. Specialists from drama schools and the Institute of Cinematography advised on speech and movement while psychologists worked with the deputies individually. With the emergence of a women's bloc in the Russian parliament following the elections of December 1993, the Centre has once more been approached to provide this form of image consultancy, this time for some of the emerging women politicians. Similar individual programmes have also been provided for business people and, in particular, heads of former state enterprises now dealing directly with foreign customers and feeling, perhaps, that they lack sufficient polish for the international arena. Evseeva's approach to them is often somewhat unorthodox: 'One businessman told me that he'd realised he didn't look good in a dinner jacket. We made a dinner jacket for him and taught him to dance the mazurka because it helps men's posture' (Evseeva 1993a). In addition to work with individuals, the Centre offers corporate image consultancy, providing anything from an entirely new corporate image to minor changes of style for newer, less prosperous outfits. Increasingly, private firms are now approaching the Centre for help with staff recruitment and training.

Because the image consultancy operates at full commercial rates the Centre is able to subsidise its courses for women. The subsidy may be considerable: in 1993, for example, a course costing 50,000 roubles for 100 hours of tuition was being offered at 3,500 roubles to the women who signed up for it. Elena Evseeva makes no bones about her pricing policies: 'People who come from firms pay a lot, people who walk in off the street pay peanuts' (Evseeva 1993a). This strategy has been extended since the autumn of 1993 with the provision of entirely free sessions for women once a week. This, however, is the third arm of the Image Centre's work; the second has been a further commercial venture, the provision of training for models.

Image, models and the question of sexual exploitation

At the time the Image Centre was first established, Elena Evseeva happened to run into a group of people involved in a Soviet–American venture set up by the USSR Union of Cinematographers. They were impressed by the Centre's programme and placed a contract for the selection and training of 100 fashion models. Although the job description was somewhat misleading – no one was producing enough clothes for so many to model – the intention was, in fact, to provide Russian young women with training to bring them up to the standards expected by western modelling agencies and then to offer them work as extras in films or commercials. Only a tiny minority were expected to make it as full-time professional fashion models.

In the space of five days in 1990, over 1,000 women were interviewed for the 100 places on the course and, from the very beginning, it became apparent that modelling was not the only thing on the agenda. Around a third of the women selected, it transpired, were involved in prostitution and immediately began inviting some of the others to restaurants to meet their pimps. The Image Centre called in the police to talk to the young women, and later their parents, about how recruitment into prostitution took place. In the end, however, the problem was resolved when the course began as none of the prostitutes was prepared to put in an intensive day of classes.

If, as the police maintained, no other action could be taken, it ensured that the issue of prostitution and sexual exploitation immediately became, and indeed has remained, a very live one for Evseeva and her staff, primarily for the danger it presented to women who would otherwise have had little contact with it:

> There are an awful lot of criminal elements hovering around schools like mine. I once asked one of them why he came to a place like this, where young women from respectable families were studying. He told me that the women in their business weren't cultured enough.
>
> (Evseeva 1993a)

As a fashion designer and provider of training for models, Evseeva is in a better position than most to observe the links between modelling and prostitution. Consequently, she has become convinced that sexual harassment in modelling presents a very real threat: 'I'm forever hearing stories about models going along to presentations which don't turn out to be presentations at all. One said to me recently, "you just have absolutely no idea what you're walking into" ' (Evseeva 1993b). As a result, when the Moscow models held their demonstration in August 1993, Evseeva immediately offered her support. Taking the view that 'it's very necessary to try and regulate the business', she has been involved from the beginning in trying to help organise the models' trade union.

By 1993, however, while the Centre's interest in modelling continued, the major thrust of its work had turned decisively towards providing programmes for women with much broader concerns than an entry into the world of fashion.

The Image programme – beauty, fashion and self-preservation

Classes on hair, skin, make-up and clothes are all included in the Image programme, but, behind all of this, there has been an emphasis on personal development from the very beginning. As time has passed, Elena Evseeva has become increasingly forthright in media interviews about the ethos of the Image Centre:

> Look what's going on: there's an endless stream of erotica and pornography washing over us from the covers of glossy magazines, from films, television and theatres and from advertising hoardings. Women are being portrayed as nothing more than objects of sexual desire. At the Image Centre we organise schools and courses and hold competitions because we want to help women to grasp the essence of their charm, to know themselves and to respect in themselves the things that are special, individual, unique to themselves.
>
> (Staroi 1993: 1)

Although couched in the unthreatening language of femininity, the message is unmistakably feminist.

If dealing with sexual exploitation is a major element in the rationale behind the Image Centre, it is certainly not the first thing to attract women onto the courses. The Centre's programme for women was publicised initially through the press and, in particular, through the device of a competition in which women were invited to send in a photograph and describe both their 'ideal woman' and themselves. All the participants – and there were literally thousands in the first competition held in 1992 – would receive relevant information and the best would be invited onto the courses. These, it was promised, would enable young women to make a realistic self-assessment and then provide the kind of polish they needed to find suitable work for themselves in the new private firms.

By the autumn of 1993, Evseeva had switched her recruitment tactics to focus on radio appearances. Radio, she believed, was now having a greater impact than the press: in the first place, in a time of high inflation, it was free and, secondly, it was seen as less politically partisan and more trustworthy than the newspapers. Every Wednesday, therefore, she was hosting a phone-in offering advice on appearance and lifestyle. Women who rang in with questions, on anything from their career to their problems with communication, were often advised to come along to the Image Centre for the free, open-door sessions she was holding on Tuesdays. They could then go on to other courses, for which a fee would be charged, depending on their needs and their financial circumstances.

The full Image programme includes beauty and fashion advice, but goes on to look at health, exercise and communication skills, using fitness sessions and dance as well as role-plays and problem-solving with psychologists. The course also includes sessions on Russian culture and subjects such as the history of costume. It begins with the question of personal appearance because, as Elena Evseeva astutely observes, 'that's what most young women are most hung up about'. Once they have worked through all of that, the theory goes, they are ready to start thinking about problems in communication or health or relationships. Those who are just looking for beauty tips or a make-over, as often happens, are liable to be disappointed. Nevertheless, the emphasis on the course is on the individual: 'we study each individual personality . . . and we give them what they lack'.

The free sessions which ran on Tuesdays through the autumn and winter of 1993–4 covered much of the same ground as the full programme, though inevitably less exhaustively: the sessions were shorter, Evseeva ran them alone and the drop-in nature of the classes did not lend itself to individual work. Nevertheless, as we shall see, even ostensibly standard lectures on personal appearance contained unconventional elements. Over the course of the winter, thirty-eight women attended these classes on a fairly regular basis, although, by the very nature of the sessions, classes were inevitably missed. The women attending fell into three roughly equal groups: fifteen were still at school and between the ages of fourteen and sixteen, eleven were students, either in higher or special secondary education, and twelve were over twenty-two. All the women in this final group had either higher or special secondary education and were engineers, technicians, teachers, librarians and so on, while four were out of work. We interviewed seven of the students and seven of the working or unemployed women after their classes at Image had finished in the spring of 1994.

Most of this group of fourteen had listened to Elena Evseeva's radio programme, although some had heard about the Centre on the grapevine. Their view of Evseeva herself suggested that she was her own best advertisement: women went along to the Centre because they were impressed with the way she responded to questions on the phone-in. As one put it: 'she's such a charming woman, it was a pleasure to go' [30]. Their reasons for going depended largely on their personal situation. For the students, it was primarily a matter of getting information on fashion and make-up and finding a style to suit them. For the unmarried women in their twenties, especially those working in a predominantly female environment, the question of finding a partner was clearly an underlying worry. For the women who were out of work, a need for human contact and some kind of intellectual stimulation might be keenly felt:

> Now, at home, you need some kind of life and emotions, you need to hear something new. So when I found out about the Image Centre I decided I must go to it. . . . I might not have gone to lectures like that only, at the moment, I don't have many people to talk to and I don't know where else there is to go.
>
> [30]

Like so many adult education courses in other countries, the free Image drop-in sessions were evidently answering a social need which might have little to do with the actual content of what was on offer.

Nevertheless, given the nature of the course, it was scarcely a revelation that all the women shared at least a general interest in the question of personal appearance. For the students who would no longer be simply directed into a job on graduation, the question of appearance had taken on a new importance. Although they had not yet experienced the impact of competition, they talked in terms of the need to look businesslike and the importance of first impressions. Some saw the question of appearance as being intrinsically tied up with the need to ensure economic independence and survival: 'These days any woman must be able to fight for herself – it's no good relying on a husband or anything. . . . So women have to look after themselves' [23].

Older women who had already felt the chill winds of insecurity in their jobs and their personal lives had much more to say on the subject:

> I wanted to go on the course because there's so much competition now in every single thing you do. Women have to try hard all the time to look right for where they are and for what they're doing. You have to really think about what you wear so that you'll be respected or, even, so that you'll feel safe, especially if you're coming home late at night. For men it's completely different. You must have seen how our men are completely spoilt. They don't look after themselves. They don't pay the slightest attention to how they look. It's as if they're all saying, 'I'm a man, that's all that matters, take it or leave it.' When you're on the metro, for example, it really hits

you, how the men look such a mess and the women have obviously taken such care and dressed really thoughtfully.

[24]

Coming from an educated woman in a low-paid and no longer secure job in which she had experienced continual discrimination, the bitterness and exasperation behind these observations were very apparent.

Some of the women concerned about the importance of looking good were not interested simply in appropriate styles and make-up but, inevitably, were also worried about weight problems. It is an unpalatable spin-off of Russia's economic reforms that, just as many families are struggling to find the money for a balanced diet, a vast new market for the products of western slimming companies has opened up. When appearance starts to matter more to women looking for work, the current craze for taking 'Herbalife' or following dubious diets is probably inevitable, as are the eating disorders which accompany them. At the same time, sporting facilities and exercise classes are becoming too expensive for many to afford, as one woman who had been considering using slimming products commented: 'You can't do shaping when you earn as little as we do. We haven't got enough to live on even, never mind for things like that. It costs a lot now' [24].[4] It is an area which Elena Evseeva has become increasingly concerned about and which she addresses in her classes:

Women believe that if they simply look good all their other problems will be solved. . . . I try to explain to women that their problems are not really about how much they weigh. If they want to lose weight they must do it sensibly. . . . Many of them are shockingly unfit. I try to teach them a few simple exercises which they can do at home – for free!

(Evseeva 1994)

As a fashion designer, she is in an ideal position to speak authoritatively about the question of size and makes a point of debunking some of the myths which surround the fashion industry.

Perhaps the most useful professional insight she includes in the course is the economic rationale for the perfect model's figure of 36/24/36. Because women feel they have to look like the models in glossy magazines, she explains in her sessions that there is an international standard to which models conform so that designers can produce dresses in one size only for a fashion show anywhere in the world, knowing that they will fit without the expense of sending their own models. Her message, therefore, is that models' figures are an economically determined standard and it is completely unnecessary for anyone else to attempt to look like that. If women are not, therefore, to become slaves to an arbitrary, imposed standard size, neither should they allow themselves to be dictated to by the whims of fashion itself:

> Women can't seem to understand our slogan, 'Our information – your choice'. They don't see that they have a role to play, that they are important. . . . Women don't realise that in terms of the fashion industry they are the consumers and the industry should serve them. They have a right to choose and have an opinion.
>
> (Evseeva 1994)

Coming from someone within the industry, such sentiments, as well as the information which accompanies them, undoubtedly have a particularly strong impact, especially on the younger women who attend the classes.

Much of Evseeva's approach and the content of the sessions is undeniably aimed at women in their teens and early twenties and is directed at reducing their vulnerability and increasing their confidence in themselves. Some of the older women have felt that this leaves them somewhat out in the cold during the sessions, but most saw no need to have separate groups for older and younger women: 'There are some things which have nothing to do with age! A sense of proportion and taste are desirable things at any age' [31]. Even though some of the older women said that much of the content was familiar to them, they were likely to feel that Evseeva's approach, 'as an artist', offered something fresh and those who had missed sessions wanted to go back for more.

The younger women were also eager for more classes, though, as students, they were unlikely to be able to afford an extended course. The fact that the drop-in sessions were free was much appreciated, as 'there's nowhere for women to go for advice if they want new ideas for a hairstyle or make-up. Women have no money to pay for advice' [36]. The chance to get together with others and the professionalism of the sessions were also a source of comment: 'Especially given that they were free, the courses were of a very high standard. Even courses for money are often not that good' [23]. Finally, they expressed appreciation of the sessions on relationships, 'men's psychology', as they put it, and how to deal with harassment: 'it's necessary information for Russian young women. No one else tells them about this' [23].

The fact that there has been so little effective resistance to the sexual exploitation of young women as new commercial firms have sprung up is an issue of some concern to Elena Evseeva. If reliable data on the prevalence of sexual harassment are lacking, she evidently feels that there is enough anecdotal evidence to make it a central issue on her course. The silence of society and the inactivity of women's organisations on what she has come to regard as a major problem is something which she clearly finds exasperating:

> No one is writing or talking about things that are really important now – like the developing sex industry. Girls go out looking for work and they are completely unprotected. We should be forming a committee to offer a place where they could come to talk about what's happened to them, or at least we should be drawing up some kind of blacklist of firms where girls are harassed.
>
> (Evseeva 1993b)

In Evseeva's view, young women are not only unprotected because of the silence which surrounds the harassment itself, but also because of their inability, in the new sexual climate in Russia, to differentiate between liberalisation and exploitation.

Much of Evseeva's concern about this stems from the responses to her 'Ideal Woman' competition in which many of the letter-writers described their ideal as living in the lap of luxury and using their intelligence to keep a rich man happy. Whether this genuinely reflects the aspirations of young Russian women or simply represents a common fantasy is a matter for speculation. All that can be said with confidence is that, when the gulf between the rich and the rest is so visible and so gigantic and the labour market is hostile to women, the attractions of this kind of fantasy are understandable. Equally important in the equation is the fact that the fantasy may appear remarkably accessible. It is the media glamorisation of 'undercover' prostitution which, in Evseeva's view, is so irresponsible, particularly when it is accompanied by total silence on what such a step might mean for the future: 'If someone has invested money in a prostitute in this country, she will never get out of prostitution. No one talks about that' (Evseeva 1993a).

The approach of the Image course is, however, not didactic about what women should or should not do. The aim, as with the rest of the programme, is to allow women to choose for themselves. The course advises women on what to look out for in job interviews and contracts, helps them to understand the implications of going ahead with something which seems suspicious and then, on the basis of all of this, to make a conscious decision. An essential part of this is to have a realistic view of their own skills and experience:

> We tell them – look, if you're offered a high salary and you can't

type or do shorthand or whatever, then they're expecting something more from you. You don't get lots of money just for having a pretty face. You've got to know how much you are worth.

(Evseeva 1993b)

Perhaps the most useful aspect of this part of the programme is the fact that it is being presented to young women who are not yet entering the labour market. When the subject is not discussed anywhere else it at least allows some young women to know what to expect before they find themselves walking straight into situations they cannot control. The importance of being forewarned was keenly felt by some who had already experienced the pitfalls of the new job market, as one of the Centre's older customers remarked: 'If you're looking for something yourself, you have to know the rules of the game and decide whether you want to play'[26].

For the Image Centre, then, the issue of remaining in control is the key to its entire programme. As Evseeva expresses this, the aim is 'for women to see themselves as individuals and to rely on their own judgement of themselves and of what they want' (Evseeva 1994). Even on the very short drop-in course, this ethos could evidently be felt, especially where women had attended regularly. Several of the women we interviewed, for example, felt that they already knew a lot of the fashion and beauty information, yet still thought the course was excellent for how it made them feel about themselves. The younger women, in particular, felt that the sessions had made them more self-confident and were very receptive to Evseeva's underlying message of self-reliance: 'She sort of gave us a sense of hope. She made us feel that we were really women and that we had a right to have our say, that our opinions were important and that we could do things too'[28].

Among the chaotic range of organisations and agencies springing up all over Russia there may well be others of which we are unaware that attempt to tackle the issue of sexual exploitation and to provide support for young women entering the job market. Indeed, in view of the Image Centre's limited resources, one would hope that it is not on its own. What distinguishes the work of the Image Centre, however, and makes it particularly effective, is its accessibility, its non-dogmatic approach and its emphasis on information as the key to control. Moreover, the fact that its founder operates from within an industry which has become increasingly associated with sleaze, makes what it has to say especially authoritative. Nevertheless, the Image Centre remains just one small Moscow-based agency offering a service to a relatively restricted number of women each year. Given the apparent scale of the problem, the achievements of an agency such as this, like the other voluntary organisations we have considered in this book, will inevitably be little more than a drop in the ocean. The success of Image, like that of Missiya and Guildia, would need to be repeated on a massive scale across the country to make significant inroads into the problems women currently face. In present conditions, the question is whether existing organisations can survive, rather than whether new ones can develop.

IN CONCLUSION:
TRANSITION'S VICTIMS
OR HEROINES OF
SURVIVAL?

When summing up the impact of transition on women in Russia, the losses they have incurred are so very visible that it is often hard to avoid characterising women as simply the victims of economic reform. Yet this would be to ignore two facts: some women have already made gains as a result of the move to the market and many women, even while suffering the knocks of this process of change, are displaying levels of ingenuity, tenacity and adaptability which sit uneasily with the notion of 'victim'. It is, however, undeniable that women have borne a disproportionate share of the economic fallout of transition and that the attitudes towards women which have developed in the new Russian labour market indicate that this will not be swiftly overcome.

The loss of security of employment with the ending of the planned economy does, of course, affect both men and women. Yet it is clear that men have been favoured both in retaining existing employment and in being offered the new opportunities which have arisen in commercial firms. In addition, their prominence in public life and state and Party organisations in the former USSR has ensured that men have had significantly wider access to networks and spheres of influence which have smoothed their path into the new world of the entrepreneur. It is this political dominance, moreover, which ensures their continued control of current policies which may act directly to the detriment of women. For the women who have been hit by the first waves of redundancies in post-Soviet Russia, alternatives have not been ready and waiting. Finding their skills and experience unwanted in the new economic order, many, especially those over thirty-five, have been reduced to accepting manual jobs or stitching together a whole patchwork of activities to provide subsistence. In the absence of realistic benefit levels, women who are obliged to get by through a combination of street trading, domestic services and self-sufficiency simply drop out of statistics altogether and, to all intents and purposes, disappear from the workforce.

It should be borne in mind, however, that the highly educated women who have formed the focus of this study are merely the tip of an extremely large iceberg: redundancies and lay-offs which began with white-collar jobs are increasingly affecting industrial workers at all levels. Given the predominance of the giant factory and the one-horse town in the former USSR, it is difficult to feel much enthusiasm for the employment prospects of millions of women as major industries begin to collapse. In the light of recent evidence of the scale of hidden unemployment, it is apparent that a substantial minority of the workforce is now being effectively pushed into the informal sector. Lacking alternative opportunities, increasing numbers of women are engaging in a range of survival strategies, not through the attractions of a 'culture of enterprise' but through the unavoidable demands of economic restructuring.

In addition to the loss of secure employment, women have simultaneously lost the network of social services, however inadequate they might have seemed, which they relied on under the Soviet system. Most significant among these, in terms of women's employability, was readily accessible child care. While it may be argued that far better quality child care can ultimately be provided by a market system this does not necessarily resolve the question of access, on grounds of both availability and cost, as so many western women are only too well aware. The loss of subsidised workplace nurseries goes hand in hand with cut-backs in the employment of women with children, effectively removing the costs from employers and placing them back within individual families. When wages are being effectively driven down, this becomes a further factor removing women from employment and returning them to the invisibility of the domestic sphere.

Hand in hand with the economic rationale for such a development has come the renewed and increasingly mainstream ideological force of Russian nationalism which would see women consigned to a peripheral role in the regeneration of the Russian nation. While many commentators have viewed the crude emphasis placed on women as wives and mothers by a substantial body of political opinion as simply a neat way of emptying the job centres, some have seen it as a logical development of the preoccupations of the Soviet state. The manipulation of women implicit in the nationalist 'back to the home' mantra does, they would argue, have rather more in common with long-dead slogans such as 'women – to the tractors!' than most mainstream politicians employing nationalist language would care to admit. If the substance is very different, the form of such exhortations is remarkably similar, neither being in the least concerned with women's own interests (Voronina 1994).

The paternalism and patronising tone of Soviet social policy has also been carried forward into the new Russian state without a trace of self-consciousness, as some writers were observing in the very first months after independence. Galina Semenova, vice-president of Women and Development, for example, drew the parallel in a hard-hitting article which appeared in September 1992:

> How can we fail to notice that even in the very latest document about the market, the draft Programme on extending economic reform, women only get a mention in the sub-section on 'demographic policy' bound up with the issue of the well-being of the family. It immediately reminds you of the traditional list of the socially weak – 'invalids, veterans and women' – which used to appear in decrees on benefits in the Brezhnev era.

As Semenova remarked, actions such as this were fundamentally at odds with the new rhetoric of the free society, individual rights and personal interests and did nothing but reinforce the impression to the world at large that 'the world's newest democracy is a men's club' (Semenova 1992: 1). Certainly, the powerlessness of women implicit both in such policies and in the attitudes which produced them was an issue about which many of the women we interviewed were acutely sensitive. As one, with heavy irony, summed up her feelings on the matter:

> If you're going to write about women in this country now, what you should write is this: that the cleverest woman today is the one who pretends she hasn't got any brains. That way she gets men to do what she wants for her. That's how you get to be really successful.
>
> [26]

It would, however, be a mistake to conclude that nationalism and all it produces is an exclusively male phenomenon in which women play no part. While the nationalist agenda, as defined by its chief male protagonists, would prefer to see women in a passive, submissive, primarily domestic role – and there are undoubtedly Russian women who would themselves subscribe to such views – it can be argued that there is an alternative approach to nationalism in which women see a very different role for themselves. Though few would go so far as former vice-president, Alexander Rutskoi, in declaring the 'survival of the motherland' to be the purpose of the women's movement, there is a sense in which women may well see their actions as part of the rebirth of Russia (Buehrer 1992: 9). At its most overt, this can be observed in the actions of businesswomen and their organisations sponsoring the development of Russian culture, both high art and traditional crafts, or in their concern that too many men in business simply squander money on themselves and fail to invest for the future of their communities. It is a message which was also explicitly spelled out in the electoral platform of 'Russia's Women' prior to the December 1993 elections (Pilkington 1995).

This view evidently strikes a chord far beyond the worlds of business and politics. The sense that it is women, rather than men, who are serious both about building for the future and conserving what was good from the past was a theme which repeatedly made itself felt in our interviews with women using voluntary agencies. Sometimes this would be expressed in openly nationalist terms, as in the comment of an eighteen-year-old student that 'It's in women that I see the rebirth of Russia, both morally and spiritually' [28]. Yet nowhere was this linked to notions of passivity or of women providing the stable moral and physical background against which men would be free to act for the nation's good. Rather, women related this theme to social and political action and a need for women to move centre stage. Paradoxically, one might argue that it is the standard prescriptions of Russian nationalism with their wilful disregard for the talents and education of a generation of women which run directly counter to the national interest. Meanwhile, women who are disturbed by the impact of change on their society see a need for women as a whole to be not peripheral but central to the processes that will determine the future well-being of their communities: a point clearly made by the 'Russia's Women' bloc, that women in politics will somehow be 'different' and more worthy of trust.

It would, perhaps, be easy to characterise women's views of their own potential and, especially, their oft-repeated descriptions of the general hopelessness of men as no more than gut prejudice or an anti-male rhetoric employed as the sole weapon of the powerless. Yet there is evidence that, in some quarters at least, such protestations are being taken increasingly seriously. Women are already becoming more prominent in established commercial firms, especially in banking, where their professional and managerial skills and their commitment are beginning to be valued (Skliar 1994b: 17). By the same token, there is some evidence that foreign firms employing Russians may prefer women as managers because of their greater reliability and organisational skills (Bruno 1995). In October 1994, with the dismissal of Viktor Gerashchenko as head of the Central Bank following the catastrophic slide of the rouble, Russia unexpectedly found itself with a woman, Tatyana Paramonova, in the role of the country's top banker. As *The Economist's* Moscow correspondent pointed out, this might have unlooked-for benefits for the country as 'her sex precludes her from the herring-and-vodka sessions at which so many government spending decisions are taken' ('Over to Tatyana' 1994). It might, therefore, not be too wide of the mark to suggest that, even in the short term, some women may be able to benefit significantly from the market's demand for an efficient and highly motivated workforce and that this may mark the beginning of a shift in social attitudes.[1]

Whether this will genuinely change the climate for women in Russia or whether women such as these will continue to be regarded as isolated individuals remains to be seen. As things stand, given the dominant ethos in the country as a whole, the majority of women continue to face very real psychological and physical barriers in the labour market which are unlikely to be overcome rapidly by a dawning appreciation of the potential benefits of employing women. Yet even those who have gained nothing from the process of change and, indeed, may have lost work they valued highly and seen their standard of living plummet, cannot easily be seen as simply the passive victims of economic reform. The most striking element in interviewing women in this situation is just how active they are. Whether in their endless schemes for ensuring their family's survival, the sheer physical burden they shoulder in market gardening or trading, or the determination they display in considering their future, there is a marked desire to remain in control. It may well be that the women in our interviews, as users of voluntary agencies, had already set themselves apart as individuals who were keen to do something about their situation. In this respect they may be untypical of the mass of women who face similar problems. Nevertheless, their stories are interesting, less for what they have to say about their achievements in the new conditions which, on any measure of success, are not dramatic, but rather for the attitudes they display. Typical or not, it is evident that it is not at all difficult to find Russian women who, however unpromising their circumstances, will simply not allow themselves to be defeated by them.

In the same way, the organisations examined in the course of this study were remarkable examples of what could be achieved in extremely trying circumstances. The founders of all three had employed considerable ingenuity both in setting up their organisation and in keeping it going despite the economic and organisational problems they faced. In all three, their major strength – the vision and drive of these individuals – was, at the same time, potentially their greatest weakness. Where small outfits such as these were receiving neither support nor funding either from government or from larger organisations, their future survival depended not only on constantly negotiating economic hurdles but also on the continued commitment, energy and goodwill of one or two people. Given the scale of the responsibility they had willingly shouldered, it remained a matter for conjecture how long any of them would be able to go on before running out of steam. In the light of the problems they had encountered, it was by no means certain that anyone else would be ready and willing to step into their shoes. Valuable organisations providing much-needed services for women were, therefore, in a position of constant precariousness with no guarantee that their long-term survival would ever be ensured. As time passes, the question of who will support those who support others becomes increasingly pressing.

This intrinsic vulnerability on the part of organisations which are, in any event, operating in a hostile environment is unlikely to be resolved without the development of forms of partnership between state and voluntary bodies. In an area such as this, western practice and, indeed, direct involvement may be particularly useful. At present, there is a great deal of criticism in Russia of western practices in the process of transition. Quite apart from Russian sensitivity to any whiff of post-Cold War triumphalism, there is the purely practical issue of where the money is going. Criticism that western assistance means little more than 'jobs for the boys', whether the boys concerned are highly paid western consultants or erstwhile communists in their new guise as zealous free marketeers, is increasingly common (Cheporov 1994). Western agencies are criticised for not taking a long hard look behind the glossy brochures churned out by the former Party elites in their search for western hand-outs, or for failing to ask sufficient questions about what will actually work in Russian circumstances. Above all, being expected to be grateful for the parts of the assistance gravy train that actually leave the West clearly sticks in the gullet (Cheporov 1994).

The assumption of western cultural superiority implicit in the very language of western programmes of assistance, 'know-how' being a prime example, may not only be unwelcome but also inappropriate. Western agencies may well be able to offer what they regard as exemplary models of good practice, but it cannot be assumed that these can simply be transferred root and branch into the Russian environment. As funding policies are currently formulated, the emphasis is on the importation of western skills and methods through locating Russian partners who will adopt them wholesale into their own organisations. Yet this approach fails to acknowledge that Russian agencies may themselves have good ideas and innovative approaches which, moreover, may be more effective within the Russian cultural setting.

Receiving western assistance, such as it is, is likely, therefore, to mean accepting western models and approaches which have been developed in societies with very different traditions. As a process, it smacks of colonialism in a way which plays directly into the hands of Russian nationalists and feeds growing anti-western sentiment in a people whose hopes have been so bitterly disappointed.[2] Much of the success of the voluntary sector in the West has stemmed from its ability to stay tuned to local needs and to provide flexible services for which there is proven demand. Support of grass-roots initiatives which work in Russia, either directly with finance or with the practical involvement of relevant western agencies, might similarly suggest itself as a better way forward than to proceed from the breathtaking assumption that Russia after communism is simply a blank page on which to write.[3]

From the point of view of western non-governmental organisations interested in developing links with Russian partners, the issue of cultural difference is an important one to bear in mind. Feminist organisations, in particular, may experience some difficulty with both the actions and language employed by women's organisations in Russia. For the reasons set out in Chapter one, Russian women are unlikely to embrace the attitudes and terminology which would be viewed as 'politically correct' by many western feminists. Lacking the ideological baggage, they are not inclined to flinch from taking pragmatic steps which might cause some anxiety to feminist organisations in the West. As we have seen, this is apt to involve them in unorthodox schemes such as developing homeworking, promoting Avon Cosmetics and running beauty courses, all of which have proved their effectiveness in circumstances which are scarcely imaginable to most women in the West. Perhaps the central issue in all of this for western governmental and non-governmental agencies alike is that the West too has something to learn in this process: that this is a highly developed culture whose traditions are not inferior but different.

The transformation of the situation in which Russian women currently find themselves will not be either simple or quick. It will require at the very least economic stabilisation, major changes in social policy and the development and enforcement of effective anti-discrimination legislation. None of this, it is abundantly clear, is likely to happen overnight and, indeed, the situation seems likely to get worse before it gets better. Certainly, the development of links between voluntary bodies is scarcely enough to wave a magic wand upon the lives of millions of women affected by economic change. Yet, if nothing else, it may help a little to alleviate the situation as it stands. Russian women have already had far more experience than most of waiting for 'jam tomorrow'. What many are most concerned with now are practical steps, however small, which would make at least some difference in the here and now; not the big issues of parliamentary legislation but the small beginnings of networks and support groups to offer immediate help and advice. Yet in the wake of the Soviet era with its expectation that the state would provide, taking steps such as these is not necessarily a simple matter, as Elena Evseeva observed:

> What we need is something more practical . . . organising jumble sales or cheap second-hand children's clothes sales. Neither of these would be difficult to organise but nobody does it. . . . Charities think their role is just to beg money from the government or the West.
>
> (Evseeva 1994)

It is indicative of the power of the Soviet legacy that when such simple initiatives do take place they may even rate a mention in the national press (Levina 1994c: 11). Perhaps at these very basic grass-roots levels the involvement of western voluntary organisations might be at its most effective, transferring fund-raising experience and knowledge of self-help initiatives which can then be adapted by groups in a society where until so recently virtually any form of autonomous action was proscribed. Offering ideas which can be developed to suit local needs, rather than ready-made programmes which offer little room for manœuvre, may not be much, but at least it has the advantage of a certain humility. In the light of the very palpable achievements of Russia's unsung heroines in the exceptionally difficult climate of today, this might be by far the most appropriate and effective posture to adopt.

APPENDIX: BACKGROUND TO THE CASE-STUDIES

The studies of the three voluntary organisations which illustrate this book were carried out between May 1993 and April 1994. The founders and organisers of Missiya, Guildia and Image gave multiple interviews throughout this year, provided us with large quantities of documents relating to the activities of their organisations and gave us access to their customers so that further interviews could be organised. Guildia also facilitated the link-up with Dubna Employment Centre which arranged meetings for us with women who had attended Guildia's seminar.

Semi-structured interviews were carried out with thirty-six women who had used the services of these agencies and who are identified by number only in Table 3 and in the text. Eight women were interviewed from Missiya, fourteen from Guildia and fourteen from Image. The women from Missiya and Guildia were first interviewed in the summer of 1993 and half of them were interviewed again in the spring of 1994. The fourteen women from Image were a random sample of the thirty-eight women who had regularly attended the winter drop-in sessions and filled in our questionnaires. They were then interviewed in spring 1994.

The thirty-six participants fell into three roughly equal age-groups: ten were under twenty-five, eleven were aged between twenty-five and thirty-five, ten were aged between thirty-five and forty-five, and a further five women were over forty-five. They were a uniformly well-educated group: seven were studying in higher education, five had specialised secondary education and the remainder all had higher education. Of these twenty-four graduates, thirteen were engineers, while all but one of the rest were either economists or in other scientific and technical fields.

All twenty-nine of the women who had completed their education had in some way seen their employment affected by the transition. Only two had not been touched directly by cut-backs or lay-offs and still saw themselves as being in reasonably secure employment. These women were,

Table 3 Interviewees' details

Interviewees	Age				Agency	Education	Profession
	under 25	25 −35	35 −45	Over 45			
1		★			Missiya	HE	biologist
2			★		Missiya	HE	economist
3			★		Missiya	HE	computer programmer
4		★			Missiya	HE	engineer
5				★	Missiya	HE	engineer
6				★	Missiya	HE	statistician
7			★		Missiya	HE	chemist
8				★	Missiya	HE	economist
9			★		Guildia	HE	doctor
10			★		Guildia	HE	economist
11			★		Guildia	SpecSec	dancer
12	★				Guildia	HE	economist
13		★			Guildia	HE	engineer
14		★			Guildia	SpecSec	technician
15	★				Guildia	HE	engineer
16		★			Guildia	HE	engineer
17		★			Guildia	HE	economist
18		★			Guildia	HE	engineer
19			★		Guildia	HE	engineer
20		★			Guildia	HE	engineer
21				★	Guildia	HE	engineer
22			★		Guildia	HE	engineer
23	★				Image	student	mathematics
24		★			Image	SpecSec	librarian
25		★			Image	SpecSec	librarian
26		★			Image	HE	musician
27	★				Image	SpecSec	nurse
28	★				Image	student	languages
29	★				Image	student	languages
30			★		Image	HE	engineer
31			★		Image	HE	engineer
32				★	Image	HE	engineer
33	★				Image	student	economics
34	★				Image	student	accountancy
35	★				Image	student	fashion design
36	★				Image	student	fashion design

however, now in atrociously badly paid jobs. Of the rest, two were expecting imminent redundancy and actively looking for other work and all the others had already suffered either redundancy or prolonged administrative leave which had forced them to seek alternative employment. At the time of the first interview, sixteen were unemployed, though only ten were officially registered.

Finally, a word is needed about the process of interviewing in the Russian situation. Describing the interviews as 'semi-structured' scarcely does justice to the way in which many of these interviews evolved. Russia has still a remarkably communal society and a language which lacks a word to cover adequately the concept of privacy. As a result, many of the concerns which have been voiced by western feminists about the potentially exploitative nature of interviewing women appear in a somewhat different light in the Russian context. The problem of living space and travelling distance is one which makes itself felt very keenly in a city like Moscow. Women were therefore invited to choose a place to meet on the basis of what seemed most convenient and congenial to themselves: some chose their own homes, a small minority came to us, while others preferred their workplace or even a public space such as a museum or a cafe. In many cases, this meant that interviews were continually interrupted by children, relatives, colleagues, background music and observations about passers-by.

The interviews were clearly seen to be very informal both by the women themselves and those around them: people chipped in with their own observations, asked often entirely unrelated questions and generally got on with the business of their own lives while the interview was proceeding. Some of the women interviewed, especially the students and the women who were out of work, clearly saw a meeting with a western researcher as a chance for some entertainment and had secretly arranged to invite their friends along in the middle. This then would explain the copious quantities of refreshments set out in advance and the mysterious telephone calls ('Is she there? What's she like?') which peppered the interview. For many of these women, it was evident that, despite their educational background and life in Russia's capital city, meeting a foreigner was still a great novelty. As a result, while expressing interest in the research project and keen to talk about their concerns, there was, for many, a desire to participate which went well beyond any notion of 'contributing to research'.

Many women made it very clear that they viewed the prime object of the exercise as doing something out of the ordinary and gaining some first-hand information about the West in the process, in this way very consciously turning the interview into a two-way process. As a result, the interviews often felt highly anarchic but extremely enjoyable, ending after a couple of hours with regrets that we had to go 'so soon' and demands that we keep in touch. Although, at the end of the process, the interpretation and use of what had been said would inevitably bring us back to the issue of the power of the researcher, the utter lack of awe – and, indeed, almost the disrespect – which these women expressed for the interviewing process makes Russia a particularly interesting place for feminist researchers to work.

NOTES

INTRODUCTION: NO MORE HEROINES?

1　There have been numerous important memoirs written by women about their experiences of life in some of the darkest periods in Soviet history, some of the most famous being the works by writers such as Nadezhda Mandelshtam (1971) and Evgeniia Ginzburg (1967). A far more recent development, with the relaxation of censorship, has been the growing interest in oral history which has prompted the collection of accounts by women which, otherwise, would almost certainly never have been recorded. One of the first of these was Svetlana Alekseevich's fine collection of women's Second World War reminiscences, *U voiny ne zhenskoe litso* (1988). Current work in this field includes accounts which are all the more moving for their ordinariness, such as the recent work by Marina Malysheva of the Centre for Gender Studies (Malysheva 1995).

2　These points were made by participants at a series of OECD conferences in the early 1990s, as well as by researchers in the ILO (Wapenhans 1991; Holzmann 1991; Standing 1991; Fischer 1993). Moreover, researchers at the World Bank itself had drawn parallels between developing countries' experiences of structural adjustment and the probable impact of transition in Eastern Europe, concluding that measures would be needed to alleviate the social impact of job losses and the simultaneous cut-back of subsidies on food, housing and services (World Bank 1990). For further discussion of the costs of economic restructuring in developing countries, see Cornia *et al.* (1987).

3　Over the last two decades the question of the gendering of the labour market has received considerable attention, to which it would be impossible to do justice here. Two relatively recent works which provide a useful introduction both to the theoretical issues involved and the significant body of work which has developed are Redclift and Sinclair (1991) and Rees (1992).

4　Economists writing on restructuring have usually ignored the issue of gender. Even when discussing social costs, studies have focused on 'the household' or used the pronoun 'he' to describe the unemployed, despite the fact that women are in a clear majority in this category. See, for example, Winiecki (1993) and Aslund (1992).

5　See, for example, the range of areas earmarked for immediate attention in the 'policy action matrix' set out in the World Bank report on women in Russia (Fong 1993: 30–1).

6　The spelling of the names of the three agencies is that which they themselves use in English-language documentation. Otherwise, the Library of Congress transliteration system has been used throughout, except where different spellings are in common use in the West, for example, Yeltsin, rather than Eltsin.

1 THE LEGACY OF PERESTROIKA

1　Throughout the 1970s and 1980s, numerous Soviet sociological surveys documented the inequality of men and women within the home. Women were found to spend more than double the time spent by men looking after home and family. It was estimated that the time women spent on housework and child care was not significantly less than their total working time in production.

2　For more detailed discussion of this issue see Attwood (1990).

3　The *Domostroi* was a guide setting down rules on domestic affairs first published with the imprimatur of the Russian Orthodox Church in the sixteenth century.

2 WOMEN AND UNEMPLOYMENT

1　The most exhaustive analysis of occupational segregation and the resulting impact on wage levels in the Soviet labour force can be found in McAuley (1981). For a detailed discussion and analysis of women's position in the Soviet industrial workforce and the beginnings of a process of excluding women from their role in production see Shapiro (1992).

2　The draft law produced an outcry among women's groups and organisations, especially in the light of the fact that, in a reversal of glasnost traditions, it had been prepared with little if any consultation. The law failed to pass its second reading in spring 1993 and, having been postponed until the autumn, subsequently disappeared when the parliament was dissolved in September 1993. Hilary Pilkington points out:

> It would be comforting to associate the failure to pass the bill at its second reading in Spring 1993 with the intensive campaign mounted by opponents of the bill after its first reading. It is certainly the case that at least the thirty-five-hour week clause would have been removed as a result of the campaign against it. However, the reality is that the bill above all fell victim to the instabilities of the Russian political scene of 1993.
>
> (Pilkington 1995: 165)

3　Mr Melikian's comment was published in the western press, but although an account of this meeting with the press was reported in *Izvestiia* (9 February 1993), it gave no mention of this extract. The author, Khudiakova, whose articles often bring attention to the unequal lot of women and criticise government policy, focused instead on hidden unemployment and the falling standard of living in general.

4　This situation is reversed in the countryside where young women under the age of thirty make up 72 per cent of the rural unemployed. However, the predicament of Russian agriculture and the deepening crisis in rural areas is a topic which requires more profound investigation and analysis than can be incorporated in the scope of this book and so we shall focus mainly on the unemployment of urban women.

5 The Russian preferred translation of *umstvennyi trud*, literally mental or intellectual work, is white–collar professions; that is, not routine, but creative work with an intellectual end-product, usually requiring higher education.

3 LIVING STANDARDS: THE NOT SO SMOOTH TRANSITION TO THE MARKET

1 The Shatalin 500-day plan was originally devised in response to an initiative by Mikhail Gorbachev, who called in August 1989 for an expert group of specialists and scholars to draw up a programme for the transition to a market economy on a Union-wide scale. The group headed by Stanislav Sergeyevich Shatalin produced a radical fast-track programme for transition within a period of 500 days. Although it was not in fact endorsed by the USSR government, this programme was independently approved by the Russian Supreme Soviet on 11 September 1990.

4 TACKLING UNEMPLOYMENT: THE STATE'S RESPONSE TO A CHANGING LABOUR MARKET

1 The Soviet Union, with its policy of full employment, had a system known as *raspredelenie*, by which new graduates were assigned a job on graduation for the first three years of their career. This was used by the state as a means of ensuring specialist staff were available in rural areas and small provincial towns and, in this respect, was unpopular with students who wanted to remain in the major cities. When the system began to collapse, graduates were given 'free diplomas' (*svobodnye diplomy*) which placed them under no obligations regarding their career but, similarly, left them with the task of finding a job.

2 The informal sector here is taken to include homeworking, unofficial small-scale businesses and self-employment, trading and subsistence farming, where the work is characterised by a lack of legal regulation of pay and conditions.

7 SURVIVAL STRATEGIES

1 Both these images appeared within a month of each other in *The Independent* early in 1994. The library in Moscow had opened up a hall where women who could no longer afford to feed their pets could look for someone to adopt them. The photograph from the St Petersburg shop showed an elderly woman on a pension of 35,000 roubles a month selling her hair for which she could expect to receive between 40,000 and 100,000 roubles a kilo (*The Independent* 18 January 1994: 9, 14 February 1994: 9).

8 SEXUAL EXPLOITATION AND THE NEW LABOUR MARKET

1   Wendy Lee (1991), in her study of prostitution and sex tourism in South-East Asia, uses this term to cover legal marriage and polygyny, basing this on Lindsey's definition in which 'a woman contracts to sell her sexual and other services to an individual man in exchange for economic security and/or protection from other men' (Lindsey 1979: 4). This definition, however, is particularly appropriate to the Russian situation described here. Lee's discussion of the position in South-East Asia provides several interesting points of comparison with the present Russian situation, particularly on the issue of mail-order brides for western men (Lee 1991).

2   The question of the unequal partnership between Russian women and western men in the operation of the new marriage bureaux has been particularly well portrayed by the Yorkshire Television documentary, *Russian Love Connection*, which was shown in the *Network First* series on 8 November 1994.

3   Anastasia Posadskaia, director of the Moscow Centre for Gender Studies, has described the cultural problems western researchers have encountered in trying to deal with the issue of sexual harassment in Russia. Importing American concepts and language and using questionnaires in such a sensitive area are likely to produce unreliable results (Posadskaia 1994: 198). One western study which illustrates these problems was published in 1993 (Kauppinen-Toropainen 1993).

4   'Shaping' (*sheiping* in Russian, the word is borrowed straight from English) is a fitness craze which first hit the USSR in a big way in 1991. Developed initially by three male sports trainers in Leningrad, the central idea of shaping is appealingly simple: first you decide what kind of body you would like to have, for example, Madonna, Jane Fonda, Melanie Griffiths, and then you are assigned a personal fitness programme to help you get there. Thousands of women who still look like none of the above have flocked to centres offering shaping since its invention.

IN CONCLUSION: TRANSITION'S VICTIMS OR HEROINES OF SURVIVAL?

1   In a recent interview with prominent women in banking and business, for example, some drew a direct link between their new-found financial independence and changed attitudes towards men. As one remarked, 'I want to see a man first and foremost as a friend, not as a breadwinner' (Skliar 1994b: 17).

2   Pronounced changes in public attitudes towards the West, from the fantasy view of western lifestyles of the early days of transition (Klimenkova 1994) to a growing view of western exploitation and hostility had become a source of some comment by late 1994. For example, Georgi Arbatov, director of the prestigious USA and Canada Institute, made the following observation in discussing potentially worsening relations between Russia and the West: 'In 1991 after the coup, I never heard anti-American or anti-western statements. But now anti-American and anti-western feelings have spread. One can notice them in parliament and in everyday life one can feel the disappointment'

(*Guardian* 17 November 1994: 13). Perhaps the most graphic illustration of this was provided by the overwhelming vote in the Duma in late October 1994 in favour of compulsory Aids testing for all foreigners visiting Russia.

3 This point is increasingly being made by Russian and East European specialists involved with grass-roots movements. At the ESRC seminar on Women and Gender Relations in Russia, the former Soviet Union and Eastern Europe held on 15 March 1995, for example, Tat'iana Zabelina and Zoia Khotkina from Moscow and Kriszta Szalai from Budapest all stressed the need for cultural sensitivity in importing western experience of community initiatives. They praised the approach of Canadian and German institutions in particular for providing inputs which allow Russian and East European partners to play a leading role in decision-making. In Britain, Charity Know How was established in November 1991 with a similar aim, yet it is unclear how far this ethos permeates the approach of all the bodies which it funds. One good example of co-operation, however, has involved the UK housing charity SHAC. In their report to Charity Know How they state: 'Our offer was to partner a new organization, providing technical assistance and moral support but we felt that the nature of homelessness in Russia demanded a local response and not stock western solutions' (Charity Know How 1994: 20).

BIBLIOGRAPHY

Aleksievich, S. (1988) *U voiny ne zhenskoe litso*, Moscow: Sovetskii pisatel'.

Allen, S. and Truman, C. (1993) *Women in Business: Perspectives on Women Entrepreneurs*, London: Routledge.

Allen, S. and Wolkovitz, C. (1987) *Homeworking – Myths and Realities*, London: Macmillan.

Almazov, B. and Iushkevichus, V. (1993) 'Kartochnyi "Domik schast'ia" sem'iu ne ustroit', *Rossiiskaia gazeta* 25 February: 2.

Altynova, A. (1993) 'Malyi biznes – delo zhenskoe', *Ploshchad' mira* 22 June: 3.

Androsenko, A. (1993) 'Zhit' do zarplaty bylo ne na chto', *Rabochaia tribuna* 7 September: 1–2.

Aristova, M. (1992) 'Novaia zhenshchina za okeanom', *Novaia zhenshchina* 1: 7.

Arkhitektor, E. (1994) 'V karmane – pusto, na stole – gusto', *Argumenty i fakty* 12: 8.

Aslund, A. (1992) *The Post-Soviet Economy: Soviet and Western Perspectives*, London: Pinter.

Attwood, L. (1990) *The New Soviet Man and Woman*, Basingstoke: Macmillan.

Babak, E. (1992) 'Zhenshchina i rynok', *Ekonomika i zhizn'* 22: 24.

Babukh, L. (1992) 'Riskovat' nado gramotno', *Delovaia zhenshchina* 18: 7.

Baklanova, E. (1993) 'Khoziaika odnazhdy na rynok poshla', *Rabotnitsa* 8: 2–3.

'Bank dannykh' (1992) *Novaia zhenshchina* 1: 5.

Barr, N. (1992) 'Income transfers and the social safety net in Russia', *World Bank Studies of Economies in Transition 4*, Washington DC: The World Bank.

Baryshev, V. (1988) 'O chem signaliat oranzhevye zhilety?', *Rabotnitsa* 7: 16–18.

Baskakova, M. (1993) Interview with S. Bridger, 10 August.

Beliaev, Iu. (1992) 'Ochered' za nadezhdoi', *Sovetskaia Rossiia* 24 September: 2.

'"Besplatnykh zavtrakov ne byvaet"' (1993) *Argumenty i fakty* 1: 7.

Bialecki, I. and Heyns, B. (1993) 'Educational attainment, the status of women and the private school movement in Poland', in V. Moghadam (ed.) *Democratic Reform and the Position of Women in Transitional Economies*, Oxford: Clarendon Press.

Bogdanova, L. (1993) '"Uzh zamuzh . . ." ili novoe pokolenie vybiraet?', *Rabotnitsa* 6: 28–9.

Boikova, T. (1994) 'Pomoshch' bezrabotnym', *Delovoi mir* 24 March: 2.

Bragina, E. (1992) 'Zabytaia zhenshchina u vrat rynka', *Delovaia zhenshchina* 18: 6.

Bruno, M. (1995) 'The second love of worker bees: gender, employment and social change in Moscow', in S. Bridger (ed.) *Women in Post-Communist Russia*, Bradford: Interface. Bradford Studies in Language, Culture and Society, 1.

Buehrer, J. (1992) 'Women demand a role in reforms', *Moscow Times* 18 September: 9.

Bunich, P. (1990) 'Kto privyk za pobedu borot'sia, s nami vmeste puskai . . .', *Rabotnitsa* 12: 12–13.

Centre for Gender Studies (1993) *From Problems to Strategy. Second Independent Women's Forum, Dubna, Russia 1992*, Moscow: Centre for Gender Studies.

Chapman, J.G. (1991) 'Recent and prospective trends in Soviet wage determination', in G. Standing (ed.) *In Search of Flexibility: The New Soviet Labour Market*, Geneva: ILO.

Charity Know How (1994) *Annual Report 1993–1994*, London: Charity Know How.

Cheporov, E. (1994) 'Komu pomogaet Amerika? Rossii ili sebe, liubimoi?', *Literaturnaia gazeta* 9 March.

Cherepakhova, E. (1987) 'Opiat' subbota bez mamy', *Rabotnitsa* 11: 15–17.

'Chto my umeem, kogda dumaem, chto nichego ne umeem' (1991) *Krest'ianka* 5: 2–5.

'Chto-to zakhotelos' krasoty' (1993) *Moskovskii komsomolets* 29 August: 1.

Cornia, G., Jolly, R. and Stewart, F. (1987) *Adjustment with a Human Face. A UNICEF Study*, Oxford: Clarendon Press.

Crombie, R. (1992) 'Fifty bucks a pop', *Moscow Magazine* February–March: 31.

Deliagin, M. (1994) 'Bezrabotitsa v Rossii ugrozhaiushche rastet', *Finansovye izvestiia* 12: 1.

Driakhlov, N., Litvinova, I. and Pavlova, V. (1987) 'Otsenki muzhchinami i zhenshchinami uslovii truda: sblizhenie ili differentsiatsiia?', *Sotsiologicheskie issledovaniia* 4: 113.

Dudukina, I. (1988) 'Domokhoziaika na rabote', *Rabotnitsa* 10: 9.

Ebzeeva, S. (1993) Interview with K. Pinnick, 7 June.

Egides, A. (1986) 'Lider nachinaet i . . . proigryvaet', *Literaturnaia gazeta* 1 October: 13.

Elenikova, E. (1987) 'Byt' pokhozhei na sebia . . .', *Krest'ianka* 11: 36–7.

Engert, S. (ed.) (1993) 'Frauenanstiftung', *ZHIF* 1: 6.

Ershova, L. (1987) 'Zavisimost' ot liubvi', *Rabotnitsa* 12: 32.

Evseeva, E. (1993a) Interview with K. Pinnick, 9 June.

——(1993b) Interview with S. Bridger, 26 August.

——(1994) Interview with S. Bridger and R. Kay, 30 March.

Fedorova, N. (1993) 'Chtob ne propast' poodinochke', *Rabotnitsa* 3: 2.

Fedotova, M. (1990) 'Trudnoe proshchanie s kazarmennym kollektivizmom', *Sel'skaia nov'* 12: 31.

Fischer, G. (1993) 'Social protection', in G. Fischer and G. Standing (eds) *Structural Change in Central and Eastern Europe: Labour Market and Social Policy Implications*, Paris: Organisation for Economic Co-operation and Development.

Fong, M. (1993) *The Role of Women in Rebuilding the Russian Economy*, Washington DC: The World Bank.

Gaidarenko, N. (1992) 'Ne boites' skazat' "net!"', *Novaia zhenshchina* 1: 14.

Gavriushenko, L. (1988) 'Pust' budet zhenshchina schastlivoi!', *Rabotnitsa* 9: 10–12.

Ginzburg, E. (1967) *Into the Whirlwind*, London: Collins/Harvill Press.

Glinka, T. (1993) 'Zametki dlia potomkov', *Vechernyi klub* 17 August: 3.

Gontmakher, E. (1993) 'Ne do zhiru byt' by zhivu . . .', *Argumenty i fakty* 33: 4.

Gorbachev, M. (1988) *Perestroika*, London: Fontana.

Gorbunova, N., Maidanskaia, N. and Nenasheva, O. (1992) 'Zhenskii biznes: utopia? real'nost", *Delovaia zhenshchina* 17: 8–9.

Gordon, L. (1994) 'Perezhit' "smutnoe vremia"', *Moskovskie novosti* 14: 8.

Graff, P. and Gracheva, A. (1994) 'Workers picket in Moscow', *Moscow Tribune* 26 March: 1, 5.

Gruzdeva, E. (1993) Interview with S. Bridger, 18 August.

Guseinov, E. (1988) 'Odin konkurs i dva vospominaniia', *Nedelia* 21: 14–15.

Hearst, D. (1994) 'Trouble looms in red Manchester', *Guardian* 25 July: 7.

Holzmann, R. (1991) 'Safety nets in transition economies: concepts, recent developments, recommendations', in P. Marer and S. Zecchini (eds) *The Transition to a Market Economy: Special Issues*, Paris: Organisation for Economic Co-operation and Development.

Hubner, S., Maier, F. and Rudolph, H. (1993) 'Women's employment in Central and Eastern Europe: status and prospects', in G. Fischer and G. Standing (eds) *Structural Change in Central and Eastern Europe: Labour Market and Social Policy Implications*, Paris: Organisation for Economic Co-operation and Development.

Iakusheva, G. (1990) 'Zhenshchina v epokhu zastoia i posle', *Rabotnitsa* 8: 16–17.

'Ia k vam pishu' (1992) *Delovaia zhenshchina* 16: 4.

Ivanova, T. (1989) 'Roditel'skii den"', *Rabotnitsa* 6: 31.

Kaidash, S. (1988) 'On the "women's problem"', *Moscow News* 33: 13.

'Kak vybrat' nevestu?' (1992) *Argumenty i fakty* 16–17: 1.

Kanaev, G. (1991) 'The future role of trade unions', in G. Standing (ed.) *In Search of Flexibility: The New Soviet Labour Market*, Geneva: ILO.

Kariakina, I. (1991) 'Okh, idu na rynok!', *Rabotnitsa* 9: 22–3.

Kas'ianikova, A. (1993) 'Filosofiia katastrof', *Moskovskii komsomolets* 28 August: 1.

Kauppinen-Toropainen, K. (1993) 'Comparative study of women's work satisfaction and work commitment: research findings from Estonia, Moscow and Scandinavia', in V. Moghadam (ed.) *Democratic Reform and the Position of Women in Transitional Economies*, Oxford: Clarendon Press.

Kharchev, A. (ed.) (1982) *Sem'ia i obshchestvo*, Moscow.

Khar'kov, O. (1993) '"Menia pytaiutsia sdelat' zhivotnym"', *Argumenty i fakty* 5: 8.

Khotkina, Z. (1987) 'Problemy zaniatosti zhenshchin v usloviiakh realizatsii kursa na uskorenie sotsial'no-ekonomicheskogo razvitiia strany', in E. Klopov, E. Gruzdeva and E. Chertikhina (eds) *Trud i vneproizvodstvennaia zhiznedeiatel'nost' zhenshchin–rabotnits*, Moscow.

——(1993) *Kak organizovat' domashnii biznes? 100 idei dlia initsiativnykh i predpriim-chivykh zhenshchin*, Moscow: Finvest.

——(1994) 'Women in the labour market: yesterday, today and tomorrow', in A. Posadskaya (ed.) *Women in Russia: A New Era in Russian Feminism*, London: Verso.

Khripkova, A. and Kolesov, D. (1981) *Devochka – podrostok – devushka*, Moscow.

Khudiakova, T. (1993a) 'Ofitsial'naia bezrabotitsa – 1 protsent, real'naia – okolo 10', *Izvestiia* 16 September: 2.

——(1993b) 'Reforma sotsial'noi sistemy nachinaetsia: uvelicheny pensii i posobiia detiam', *Izvestiia* 16 December: 2.

Kilesso, N. (1992) 'Ego dochen'ki', *Moskovskii komsomolets* 23 September: 4.

Kinsman, F. (1987) *The Telecommuters*, Chichester: Wiley.

Kleiman, T. (1993) 'Alla Shvartz: "Esli sebia ne slomat' – ne vyzhit' "', *Sudarushka* 29: 8–9.

Klimenkova, T. (1994) 'What does our new democracy offer society?', in A. Posadskaya (ed.) *Women in Russia: A New Era in Russian Feminism*, London: Verso.

Klopov, E., Gruzdeva, E. and Chertikhina, E. (eds) (1987) *Trud i vneproizvodstvennaia zhiznedeiatel'nost' zhenshchin-rabotnits*, Moscow.

Kobzeva, E. (1992) 'Sotsial'naia zashchishchennost' i zaniatost' zhenshchin v usloviiakh monopromyshlennogo goroda', in Z. Khotkina (ed.) *Zhenshchiny i sotsial'naia politika*, Moscow: Institut sotsial'no-ekonomicheskikh problem narodonaseleniia RAN.

Kolchin, S. (1994) 'Bol'she vsego dorozhaet samoe neobkhodimoe', *Argumenty i fakty* 12: 8.

Kolesnikov, A. (1993) 'Vnimanie, snimaiu!', *Moskovskie novosti* 36: 10.

Kononova, L. (1992) 'Muzhchiny i zhenshchiny ravny, no nekotorye ravny bolee?', *Delovaia zhenshchina* 20: 6.

Konstantinova, V. (1992) 'Zhenshchiny i problemy politicheskogo liderstva', in Z. Khotkina (ed.) *Zhenshchiny i sotsial'naia politika*, Moscow: Institut sotsial'no-ekonomicheskikh problem narodonaseleniia RAN.

Korchagina, I. (1992) 'Ne khodite, damy, v biznes', *Novaia zhenshchina* 1: 6.

Korina, N. (1987) 'O traktore i o sebe', *Krest'ianka* 8: 14–18.

Kostakov, V. (1991) 'Labour surplus and labour shortage in the USSR', in G. Standing (ed.) *In Search of Flexibility: The New Soviet Labour Market*, Geneva: ILO.

Kostygova, T. (1991) 'Reshaites' – ne raskaetes"', *Krest'ianka* 8: 10–11.

Kotliar, E. and Turchaninova, S. (1975) *Zaniatost' zhenshchin v proizvodstve*, Moscow.

Krylova, Z. (1992) 'Shkola semeinogo biznesa', *Rabotnitsa* 5–6: 10–11.

Kuznetsov, A. (1994) 'Economic reforms in Russia: enterprise behaviour as an impediment to change', *Europe–Asia Studies* 46 (6): 955–70.

Kuznetsova, L. (1988) 'Val i Valentina', *Rabotnitsa* 9: 23.

——(1990) 'Razgovor pered zerkalom?', *Rabotnitsa* 3: 14.

Laputina, O. (1991) 'Zhenshchina v "pirozhkovyi" period', *Rabotnitsa* 2: 12–13

Lee, W. (1991) 'Prostitution and tourism in South-East Asia', in N. Redclift and M. Sinclair (eds) *Working Women: International Perspectives on Labour and Gender Ideology*, London: Routledge.

Legostanev, I. (1993) 'Krasota tela ne dlia griaznogo dela', *Moskovskii komsomolets* 18 August: 2.

Levina, A. (1994a) '. . . My – evropeiskie slova i aziatskie postupki', *Rabotnitsa* 1: 10–11, 16.

—— (1994b) 'Oni iz "Biznes–Inkubator"', *Rabotnitsa* 2: 10–11.

—— (1994c) 'Profil' bednosti', *Rabotnitsa* 6: 10–11.

Lindsey, K. (1979) 'Madonna or whore?', *ISIS International Bulletin* 13: 4–5.

Luce, E. (1994) 'ILO alleges free-marketeers are concealing Russia's jobs crisis', *Guardian* 1 November: 16.

Luk'ianchenko, P. (1993a) 'O griadushchem obmene deneg i "sekretnykh" kursakh', *Argumenty i fakty* 12: 4.

——(1993b) 'Spad proizvodstva: net khuda bez dobra', *Argumenty i fakty* 13: 1.

Luk'ianenko, T. (1993a) Interview with K. Pinnick, 8 June.

——(1993b) Press conference at Central Artists' House, Moscow, 3 September.

Lukina, V. and Nekhoroshkov, S. (1982) *Dinamika sotsial'noi struktury naseleniia SSSR*, Moscow.

McAuley, A. (1981) *Women's Work and Wages in the Soviet Union*, London: Allen & Unwin.

Malysheva, M. (1991) 'The politics of gender in Russia', in M. Allison and A. White (eds) *Women's Voice in Literature and Society*, Bradford Occasional Papers No. 11, Bradford: Department of Modern Languages, University of Bradford.

——(1995) 'The social experiences of a country woman in Soviet Russia', in *Yearbook of Oral History 1995*, Oxford: Clarendon Press.

Mandelshtam, N. (1971) *Hope against Hope*, London: Collins/Harvill Press.

Martin, S. (1993) 'The women have their work cut out for them', *Irish Times* 15 February: 7.

Mashika, T. (1989) *Zaniatost' zhenshchin i materinstvo*, Moscow: Mysl'.

'Materialy k parlamentskim slushaniiam "O likvidatsii vsekh form diskriminatsii v otnoshenii zhenshchin"' (1993) Moscow: unpublished parliamentary document.

Mekhontsev, V. (1988) '"Zhenshchiny mogut vse!"', *Rabotnitsa* 1: 12–13.

Meliia, M. (1993) 'Kak stat' delovym chelovekom', *Argumenty i fakty* 13: 4.

Meliksetova, E. (1994) 'Poimesh' sebia – naidesh' rabotu', *Argumenty i fakty* 12: 12.

Menitskaia, N. (1989) 'Ne khochu byt' bezrabotnoi!', *Rabotnitsa* 7: 10–12.

Mezentseva, Y. (1994a) 'Equal opportunities or protectionist measures? The choice facing women', in A. Posadskaia (ed.) *Women in Russia: a New Era in Feminism*, London: Verso.

——(1994b) 'What does the future hold? Some thoughts on the prospects for women's employment', in A. Posadskaya (ed.) *Women in Russia: A New Era in Russian Feminism*, London: Verso.

Minasian, L. (1988) 'Kar'era ili dom?', *Sobesednik* 10: 10.

Musaeva, T. (1990a) 'Klub delovykh zhenshchin', *Rabotnitsa* 8: 11–13.

——(1990b) 'Klub delovykh zhenshchin', *Rabotnitsa* 10: 12–13.

Narodnoe khoziaistvo v SSSR v 1984g. (1985) Moscow: Finansy i Statistika.

Narodnoe khoziaistvo v SSSR v 1988g. (1989) Moscow: Finansy i Statistika.

Nasha sovremennitsa (1989) Moscow: Znanie.

Nechaev, E. (1993) 'Po kakomu vedomstvu lekarstvennyi golod Rossii', *Rabochaya tribuna* 9 June: 3.

Nemova, L. (1993) 'Khotia bezrabotitsa nevelika, obol'shchat'sia ne stoit', *Finansovye izvestiia* 8 December: 2.

Nevel'skii, V. (1993) 'Ia ne protiv rynka lekarstv, no rynka – kul'turnogo', *Izvestiia* 3 September: 5.

Novikova, T. (1993) 'Broshu vse, pereedu v derevniu', *Rossiskaia gazeta* 3 August: 8.

'Ob"iavleniia' (1992) *Chastnaia zhizn'* 5: 8.

Oleinik, L. (1993) 'Chto polozheno odinokoi materi', *Izvestiia* 15 December: 7.

Os'minina, N. (1990) 'Rossiia – svet moi, bol', nadezhda', *Rabotnitsa* 8: 2–4.

——(1993) 'Rossiia – muzhskogo roda?', *Rabotnitsa* 5: 10–11.

'Osnovy zakonodatel'stva o trude Rossiiskoi Federatsii' (1993) *Rabochaia tribuna* 11 June: 3–7.

'Ot podpor'ia do spasen'ia' (1992) *Krest'ianka* 2: 16.

'Over to Tatyana' (1994) *The Economist* 22 October: 119.

Pilkington, H. (1995) 'Can "Russia's Women" save the nation? Survival politics and gender discourse in post-Soviet Russia', in S. Bridger (ed.) *Women in Post-Communist Russia*, Bradford: Interface. Bradford Studies in Language, Culture and Society No. 1.

Pokrovski, V. (1991) 'USSR', in P. Marer and S. Zecchini (eds) *The Transition to a Market Economy: The Broad Issues*, Paris: Organisation for Economic Co-operation and Development.

Polenina, S. (ed.) (1990) *Trud, sem'ia, byt sovetskoi zhenshchiny*, Moscow: Iiuridicheskaia literatura.

Polovezhets, G. (1994) 'Discussing inflation and unemployment', *Business World Weekly* 12: 8.

Posadskaya, A. (1994) 'Self-portrait of a Russian feminist', in A. Posadskaia (ed.) *Women in Russia: A New Era in Feminism*, London: Verso.

'Postanovlenie Verkhovnogo Soveta SSSR. O neotlozhnykh merakh po ulushcheniiu polozheniia zhenshchin, okhrane materinstva i detstva, ukrepleniiu sem'i' (1990) *Pravda* 14 April: 1–2.

'Poverty of numbers' (1993) *The Economist* 10 July: 34.

'Predlozheniia uchastnikov parlamentskikh slushanii: O vypolnenii v Rossii mezhdunarodnoi Konventsii o likvidatsii vsekh form diskriminatsii v otnoshenii zhenshchin, priniatoi General'noi Assamblei OON 18 dekabria 1979 goda' (1993) Moscow: unpublished parliamentary document.

Priglashaem na rabotu (1993) 43: 3.

Priglashaem na rabotu (1994) 9: 2.

'Prodolzhaem operatsiiu "Stupeni masterstva"' (1987) *Rabotnitsa* 12: 20–1.

Proshina, L. (1992) 'Umeet li liubit' delovaia zhenshchina', *Kuranty* 4 July: 7.

'Rabyni pod krasnym fonarem' (1993) *Nedelia* 32: 3.

Razumnova, I. (1993) Interview with K. Pinnick, 4 June.

—— (1994) Interview with the authors, 24 March.

Redaktsionnaia kollegiia (1988) 'XIX Vsesoiuznaia Konferentsia KPSS: Vystuplenie tovarishcha Pukhovoi V. V.', *Pravda* 2 July: 11.

Redclift, N. and Sinclair, M. (1991) *Working Women: International Perspectives on Labour and Gender Ideology*, London: Routledge.

Redkollegiia zhurnala *Rabotnitsa* (1989) 'Vnimaniiu Soveta ministrov SSSR – tri voprosa, otveta na kotorye zhdut chitateli zhurnala "Rabotnitsa"', *Rabotnitsa* 3: 10–11.

Rees, T. (1992) *Women and the Labour Market*, London: Routledge.

Reklamnoe prilozhenie (1993) 35: 6.

RFE/RL (1994) *Daily Report no: 224*, 29 November.

Ronina, G. (1987) 'Obida traktoristkoi Kovalevoi', *Sel'skaia Nov'* 8: 8–11.

'Rossiiskaia Federatsiia Doklad o vypolnenii v Rossiskoi Federatsii Konventsii o likvidatsii vsekh form diskriminatsii v otnoshenii zhenshchin. Chetvertyi periodicheskii doklad, (1993) Moscow: unpublished parliamentary document.

Rzhanitsina, L. (ed.) (1993) *Rabotaiushchie zhenshchiny v usloviiakh perekhoda Rossii k rynku*, Moscow: Institut ekonomiki RAN.

Sachs, J. (1994) 'The bank that foreclosed on Russia', *The Independent* 26 January.

Sargin, A. (1993) '"Ia liubila draznit' muzhchin"', *Argumenty i fakty* 5: 8.

Savel'eva, I. (1993) Interview with K. Pinnick, 8 June.

Savin, M. (1993) 'Economic situation vexes Russian entrepreneurs', *Delovoi mir* 27 August: 6.

Sazonov, V. (1991) 'Chto dumaiut muzhchiny o sem'e i zhenshchine?', *Rabotnitsa* 1: 4.

Sel'skaia zhizn' (1994) 23 January: 3.

'Semeinyi klimat: vchera i segodnia' (1988) *Sobesednik* 10: 10.

Semenova, G. (1992) 'Zhenshchiny i rynok: vyzhivat' – ne vyzhidat'', *Rynok* 16 September: 1.

Semkiv, T. (1993) 'Palochki vy moi schetnye, otdam za rubli! Poniali, chto pochem?', *Moskovskii komsomolets* 26 August: 2.

Sergeeva, L. (1993) 'Madam, sadites' za iglu!', *Chastnaia zhizn'* 14: 4.

Seward, D. (1993) 'Russian mothers face headaches as school starts', *Moscow Tribune* 1 September: 8.

Shapiro, J. (1992) 'The industrial labour force', in M. Buckley (ed.) *Perestroika and Soviet Women*, Cambridge: Cambridge University Press.

'Shkol'nitsy . . . v kupal'nike?' (1989) *Sobesednik* 2: 4.

Shuliat'eva, N. (1992) '"U zhenshchin drugoi sklad uma" – schitaet Prezident Soiuza malykh predpriiatii Rossii', *Novaia zhenshchina* 1: 4.

Shuvalova, E. (1993) 'Schast'e v sem'e – mir v strane', *Rabochaia tribuna* 10 April: 1.

Sivkova, V. (1993) 'Po karmanu li bolezn'?', *Argumenty i fakty* 15: 5.

——(1994) 'Eshche odin pereraschet pensii', *Argumenty i fakty* 13: 5.

Skliar, I. (1988) '707–i: imenem detstva', *Rabotnitsa* 6: 2, 4–5.

—— (1989) '"Ne nado zhdat' milostei ot . . . muzhchin!"', *Rabotnitsa* 3: 22–3.

—— (1990) '"500 dnei" . . . do luchshei zhizni', *Rabotnitsa* 8: 5.

—— (1994a) 'Na nikh upovaem', *Rabotnitsa* 2: 18–19.

—— (1994b) 'Zhenshchiny pri den'gakh', *Rabotnitsa* 3: 16–17.

Sorokina, E. (1992) 'U rynka zhenskoe litso', *Moskovskii komsomolets* 22 July: 4.

Standing, G. (ed.) (1991) *In Search of Flexibility: The New Soviet Labour Market*, Geneva: ILO.

——(1993) 'Labour market policies for economic restructuring', in G. Fischer and G. Standing (eds) *Structural Change in Eastern Europe: Labour Market and Social Policy Implications*, Paris: Organisation for Economic Co-operation and Development.

Staroi, V. (1993) 'Zhdite siurprizov', *Klubok* 1: 1.

'Stop-Kadr' (1989) *Rabotnitsa* 7: 8.

'Svakha' (1993) *Sudarushka* 31: 15.

'Svedi nas sud'ba" (1994) *Sem'ia* 10: 15.

Telen', L. (1988) 'Kakaia zhe ona, zhenskaia dolia?', *Sotsialisticheskaia industriia* 22 January: 2.

Tereshchenko, N. (1989) 'With milk and honey', *Moscow News* 11: 10.

Tokareva, E. (1987) 'Eto printsipial'noe odinochestvo', *Sel'skaia molodezh'* 9: 8–12, 53.

Tolokina, E. (1989) 'Tak skol'ko dolzhna rabotat' zhenshchina?', *Rabotnitsa* 9: 2–5.

Valiuzhenich, G. (1994) 'Zarplatu vygodnee vydavat' . . . chainikami', *Argumenty i fakty* 14: 5.

Vasilets, E. (1988) 'Imeiu pravo znat' . . . o svoikh l'gotakh', *Rabotnitsa* 1: 20.

Vasil'eva, L. (1987) 'Eshche raz o zhenskoi dushe', *Pravda* 17 October: 3.

Vasil'kova, E. (1993) 'Bezhit pensiia za infliatsiei', *Rabochaia tribuna* 8 September: 1, 3.

Vestnik statistiki (1991) 2: 39–40.

Vetokhin, Y. (1993) Interview with S. Bridger and K. Pinnick, 31 August.

Virkunen, T. (1991) 'Klub delovykh zhenshchin', *Rabotnitsa* 6: 16–17.

Vladimirova, D. (1987) 'Fabrika vodvore', *Rabotnitsa* 10: 14.

Volkova, O. (1993) 'Tselluloidnyi mir', *Moskovskii komsomolets* 20 August: 4.

Voronina, O. (1988) 'Na dva shaga pozadi muzhchiny?', *Sotsialisticheskaia industriia* 18 June: 4.

——(1994) 'The mythology of women's emancipation in the USSR as the foundation for a policy of discrimination', in A. Posadskaya (ed.) *Women in Russia: A New Era in Russian Feminism*, London: Verso.

Vovchenko, O. (1992) '"Zhenskii" put' v rynok', *Delovoi mir* 10 June: 1.

'Vsesoiuznaia konferentsiia zhenshchin. Doklad V. V. Tereshkovoi' (1987) *Izvestiia* 1 February: 3.

'Vyberi menia!' (1993) *Sem'ia* 32: 22.

'Vy bez raboty i reshili stat' predprinimatelem' (1993) *Izvestiia* 8 December: 7.

'Vyplaty rabotnikam, nakhodiashchimsia v vynuzhdennykh neoplachivaemykh otpuskakh' (1993) *Izvestiia* 1 December: 7.

Walker, M. (1986) 'The party men who looked west and saw the warning', *Guardian* 22 July: 19.

Wapenhans, W. (1991) 'The World Bank', in P. Marer and S. Zecchini (eds) *The Transition to a Market Economy: The Broad Issues*, Paris: Organisation for Economic Co-operation and Development.

Winiecki, J. (1993) *Post-Soviet Type Economies in Transition*, Aldershot: Avebury Press.

World Bank (1990) *World Bank Development Report 1990*, Oxford: Oxford University Press.

Zakharova, N., Posadskaia, A. and Rimashevskaia, N. (1989) 'Kak my reshaem zhenskii vopros?', *Kommunist* 4: 56–65.

'Zdras'te: avgustovskie strasti – mordasti' (1993) *Vechernaia Moskva* 17 August: 1.

'Zhenshchina ishchet sebia' (1988) *Pravda* 19 February: 5.

Zhenshchiny i deti v SSSR (1985) Moscow: Finansy i Statistika.

Zhenshchiny v SSSR (1990) Moscow: Finansy i Statistika.

Zhuravleva, M. (1993) Interview with S. Bridger and K. Pinnick, 31 August.

Zinoviev, A. (1993) 'Veshch', ia veshch'! Nakonets-to slovo dlia menia naideno! . . .', *Rossiiskaia gazeta* 10 August: 8.

Zybtsev, V. (1987) 'Ob ispol'zovanii zhenskogo truda v metallurgicheskoi promyshlennosti', *Sotsiologicheskie issledovaniia* 4: 110.

INDEX